History Under Control:

Studies in the Book of Revelation

Harold T. Bryson

History Under Control:

Studies in the Book of Revelation

Harold T. Bryson

Mossy Creek Press

Copyright © 2011 by Harold T. Bryson

ISBN:	Softcover	978-936912-23-0

All rights reserved. No part of this book may be reproduced or transmitted in any form or by any means, electronic or mechanical, including photocopying, recording, or by any information storage and retrieval system, without permission in writing from the publisher.

This book was printed in the United States of America.

The profits from the sale of this book go to support the students of Carson Newman College.

To order additional copies of this book, contact:

Mossy Creek Press
1-423-475-7308
www.mossycreekpress.com

Dedication

to

my wife

Jane Lockett Bryson

and to
our grandchildren

Harris Bryson
Joshua Bryson
Nathan Hethcox
Lauren Hethcox
Elizabeth Morrison

Contents

Introduction   11

1. A Book That Happened in History   21
   Background

2. The Presence of Christ in History   46
   Revelation 1:1–20

3. The Church during History, Part 1   65
   Revelation 2:1–17

4. The Church during History, Part 2   84
   Revelation 2:18–3:22

5. The Controller of History   103
   Revelation 4:1–11

6. The Redeemer of History   117
   Revelation 5:1–14

7. The Pageantry of Suffering throughout History   129
   Revelation 6:1–8:1

8. A Pause in the Suffering for Comfort   144
   Revelation 7:1–17

9. The Attempts for Attention during History   156
   Revelation 8:2–9:21; 11:5–9

10. The Faithful Sharing of God's Word   178
    Revelation 10:1–11:14

11. The Evil Intruder into History **196**
   Revelation 12:1–17

12. The Historical Manifestations of Evil **213**
   Revelation 13:1–18

13. An Interlude about the End of History **230**
   Revelation 14:1–15:4

14. The Judgment of God Both during and Beyond History **245**
   Revelation 15:5–16:21

15. An Example of God's Judgment during History **264**
   Revelation 17:1–19:10

16. The Images about the End of History **292**
   Revelation 19:1–21:8

17. The Scenes of Life beyond History **316**
   Revelation 21:9–22:5

Epilogue **335**
   Revelation 22:6–21

Selected Bibliography **345**

Introduction

The book of Revelation is the strangest book in the New Testament. It opens with an unusual vision of a person who has hair white as snow, eyes as a flame of fire, feet like burnished bronze; and from his mouth comes a sharp, two-edged sword. The narrative continues with One seated on a throne who is described with precious jewels. He is surrounded by twenty-four elders and four living creatures. In the throne area a Lamb appears and looks as if he has been killed. But the Lamb is alive, and he takes a scroll from the right hand of the One on the throne.

Action in Revelation intensifies with seals opening, trumpets sounding, and bowls pouring. Strange creatures appear: a beast with the qualities of a leopard, bear, and a lion; a woman clothed with the sun, the moon under her feet, and a crown of twelve stars on her head; an enormous red dragon with seven heads, ten horns, and ten crowns on his head; an army of locusts with human-like faces and tails that sting like scorpions; and a rider riding a white horse and wearing a robe dipped in blood. Readers of Revelation encounter frequent use of numbers such as seven seals, seven trumpets, seven bowls, ten horns, and ten crowns. They wonder about a beast numbered 666, a reign of a thousand years, and the appearance of 144,000 people surrounding the One on the throne. The book of Revelation closes with the appearance of a celestial city with streets of gold and gates of pearl.

Though Revelation is a strange book, it is intended to be an understandable book. Do you think God would have given a message to John that the seven churches of Asia could not understand? The reason Revelation seems so different to modern readers is because of its unusual language. The kind of writing is called apocalyptic literature. First-century readers knew about Jewish apocalypses and the messages they conveyed. The writer of Revelation adopted the figurative and symbolic language of apocalyptic literature to communicate God's message to seven churches. Revelation was understandable to its first-century readers. It can be understood by any reader who takes the time to learn the book's life situation and its unique, apocalyptic style.

Under God's inspiration John writes to believers in an alien, hostile environment. These readers desperately needed the message of Revelation. They suffered persecution from the Roman authorities. It was a time of chaos, uncertainty, and fear. The future seemed extremely dark and painfully hopeless. God instructed John to lift the veil so the readers could look beyond the visible. The central truth John wants to communicate is that the world and all its events are under the control of God.

Before studying Revelation in detail, we need to gain an overall perspective of the book and to see how the writer developed the theme of God being in control of history. For the overview, a visual aid may be helpful. Numbers in the following visual help the reader understand the path of reasoning. The long horizontal line (*1-5*) represents the course of history from its beginning to its end.

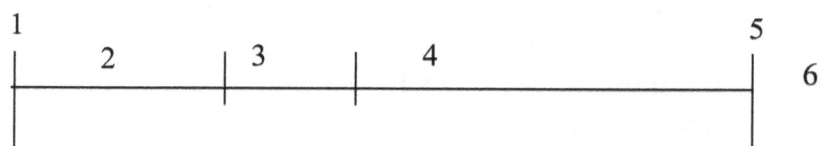

1. Number 1 represents the beginning of history. "In the beginning God created the heavens and the earth" (Gen. 1:1). The Bible affirms that God began history. John communicates that God begins and ends history with the designation that God is the Alpha (the first letter of the Greek alphabet) and God is the Omega (the last letter of the Greek alphabet).

2. Number 2 represents the time from the beginning of creation to the birth Jesus. It would cover the period reported by the Old Testament. John believes and respects the Hebrew Scripture, for he has 278 allusions to the Old Testament.

3. The two vertical lines with the number three in the

middle represent the three decades of Jesus' birth, life, ministry, death, resurrection, and ascension. John alludes numerous times in Revelation to events in Jesus' earthly life. He also describes Jesus' divine character and power.

4. Number 4 symbolizes the time from Jesus' ascension to his final return. No one can measure the length of that line because only God knows when Christ will return. John wrote about the principles of history in his time, which he deemed applicable to any time.

5. Number 5 indicates the final return of Christ. The event is mentioned throughout Revelation.

6. Number 6 appears without a line because it represents eternity. It symbolizes life beyond earthly existence.

Revelation opens with the assertion that Christ is the source of the message as well as the subject of its contents. Chapter 1 has information about the author and the readers. John concludes the chapter with an introductory vision of the exalted, incomparable Christ (1:12–20).

John continues in chapters 2 and 3 with messages to seven churches in Asia. These churches characterize all churches throughout human history. They represent God's character and fulfill Christ's ministry to the world.

Beginning in Revelation 4 and continuing through chapter 19, John reports of characteristics existing in history from his time to the end of time. In Revelation 4, John relates his vision of God on the throne. Readers get the message that God, not worldly rulers or evil powers, controls history. God reigns now, and he will reign forever. The vision in chapter 5 depicts the Lamb taking a scroll from the One on the throne and breaking its seals. The Lamb symbolizes the fact that only Christ is worthy to open the seals and direct the course of history.

John then reports visions of seven seals, seven trumpets, three enemies, and seven bowls (6:1–19:5). Each vision has a distinctive characteristic which exists in history, and each vision closes with God's victorious conclusion of history. The seals portray the pageantry of suffering during earthly existence, and they depict the ultimate end of suffering with history's termination. The trumpets symbolize God's continuous attempt to get people's attention. Ultimately God sounds his last trumpet for attention, and time will end.

After the seals and the trumpets, John gives a vision of the three enemies of God: a dragon, a beast from the sea, and a beast from the earth (chapters 12–13). These three figures symbolize Satan and his allies' opposition to God. This condition of conflict continues until Christ comes and annihilates evil.

The vision of the seven bowls depicts God's judgment upon those who oppose him from the time of the first-century evil rulers to the final evil earthly rulers (chapters 15–16). John sees God's judgment happening in history, at the end of history, and beyond history. He gives a parenthesis of a particular picture of God's judgment on Rome in 17:1–19:5. The bowls, like the seals and trumpets, cover the same time span, from the first advent to the second advent of Christ. Evil meets its Armageddon at the end of time.

The preceding visions have portrayed events happening both during and at the end of history. The main focus has been on situations existing from the time of Christ's first coming to his final coming. Beginning in 19:6 and continuing through 20:15, John focuses primarily on the end of time. John portrays in symbolic language the coming of Christ to destroy the enemies of God. In chapter 19 John reports Christ's destruction of the beast from the sea and the beast from the earth. With dramatic symbols John describes the ultimate destruction of Satan in 20:1–15.

A beautiful scene of the new heaven and the new earth follows the long struggle portrayed in Revelation. John gives scenes of God's people's lives beyond history. In 21:1–22:5 John depicts a life of intimacy with God, a life of utmost relationship with people, a complete wellness, and a life free from self-centeredness. John closes Revelation with an epilogue in 22:6–21 to attest that all he had written is trustworthy.

John addresses the message to the "seven churches of Asia." We have no reason to doubt that the first readers comprehended what John wrote. They knew the apocalyptic style. They understood the messages behind the visions and symbols. The book's message meant more to them than the manner in which it was written. Its message came across with encouragement, warning, comfort, challenge, and hope. When future readers beyond the first century place Revelation in its original life situation and understand apocalyptic literature, the same message comes through as it did for the Asian believers.

Because of its symbolic and figurative language, Revelation is a debated book. The prominent disagreements seem not to be about truth but about time. Most interpreters believe truths about the return of Christ, Armageddon, the millennium, the tribulation, the final judgment, and the two destinies beyond death. But interpreters debate about when some of these events occur.

Excessive emphases seem to be placed both on past time and on future time. Some think that all the events in Revelation took place in the past. They relate everything to the church living under the threat of the Roman Empire. They associate the picture of judgment as the overthrow of that Empire. They think the major prophecies of Revelation took place with the fall of Rome.

Others think that most of the events in Revelation will take place in the future. Though some of these thinkers may recognize a historical background on the first century, as is the case of the seven churches, they insist that everything beyond Revelation 3 is in the future.

Maybe the problem in Revelation can be solved not by excessive emphasis on the past or the future but by including three time zones—the past, the present, and the future. Readers of Revelation need to consider what happened in the first century to cause the book to be written. It came as a tract for the time during Roman persecution of Christians. Readers need also to consider how the principles present in Revelation relate to every age. Human nature has not changed. Evil has not ceased to oppose God. Finally readers need to be aware of what is yet to come in the future: a future return of Christ, a future judgment, and a future destiny. The truths John discloses apply to life in any age.

Since Revelation is timeless, it is a relevant book. It related to people's needs in the latter part of the first century, and it relates to those same needs today. What Revelation *said*, it continues to *say*. What it *meant* is what it *means* today. Understanding how relevant Revelation is involves comprehending how relevant it was.

First-century believers in Asia asked significant questions: "How do believers survive in an evil, hostile world?" These believers suffered many forms of opposition from the pagan world: ridicule, slander, seizure of property, beatings, and even death. John writes God's words of comfort, encouragement, and hope to these persecuted people. Being a believer in Caesar's world involved trouble, but it could be managed. Modern readers of Revelation can see Christ's promise of presence in hard times, and they can have strength to cope. They also read hope beyond the tough times.

First-century believers also asked: "Why all this suffering? How long will it last?" These original readers of Revelation faced persecution from the Roman authorities. John writes that suffering is an inevitable part of life. It appears in many forms: mental, physical, and emotional. John assures the readers repeatedly of God's presence during suffering and the promise of ultimate deliverance from suffering. Marva J. Dawn writes, "The Revelation teaches us that God always gives victory eventually, but that the meanwhile entails suffering."[1]

Without a doubt these Asian Christians looked at life about them with all of its evil and asked the colloquial question, "What is this world coming to?" They heard that there was no plan for history. It was one day following another in regular monotony. John wrote to tell the readers that time is moving toward an end. Each day moves the world to a climax with the final return of Christ. Meanwhile, believers find life meaningful by abiding in Christ and doing his work.

Church was relatively new to these first-century believers. They must have asked, "How can we be the church in an environment of secular atheism, intellectual agnosticism, and religious pluralism?" John writes to seven churches challenging every believer to be a brighter light for God and urging every corporate community of believers to be a "heavenly colony on earth" ruled by the authority of Christ.

Death was a familiar scene to these first readers. They saw friends and family members die. They saw some martyred because of their commitment to Christ. As they faced death, they must have asked, "What happens when we die?" John gives a picture of the believer's life with existence in a new heaven and a new earth. There is no greater answer to death than Christ's defeat of it and his gift of life after death for his followers.

Revelation does not need to be neglected or ignored in today's churches. Bruce M. Metzger made a realistic assessment when he wrote that "for most church members, the book of

---

[1] Marva J. Dawn, *Joy in Our Weakness: A Gift of Hope from the Book of Revelation* (Grand Rapids: William B. Eerdmans Publishing Company, 2002), 13.

Revelation is a closed book."² Instead Revelation needs to be read privately, preached in pulpit, and studied academically.

For over fifty years I have had an interest in this appealing book of Revelation. Early in my life I read the book and became frightened over its contents. In my first year in seminary, Ray Summers came to my home church, and my parents hosted him for a meal. He learned about my being a student in the seminary. He responded by sending me his book on Revelation entitled *Worthy Is the Lamb: An Interpretation of Revelation.* This book introduced me to Revelation's historical background, apocalyptic language, and various interpretative approaches used to unveil its meaning. Revelation began to make sense, and it became a relevant book in my life.

Interest in Revelation continued after reading Summers' book. I enrolled in a graduate course in seminary taught by Ray Frank Robbins. He was a noted New Testament scholar and author of a stimulating work entitled *The Revelation of Jesus Christ.* He helped me read Revelation in its original language. He also introduced me to classical commentaries written by John W. Bowman, R. H. Charles, Edward A. McDowell, G. B. Caird, Donald Richardson, Leon Morris, James Moffatt, T. F. Torrance, and many others.

After completing my formal education, I have continued to read books on Revelation. I have read books with various viewpoints from many such authors as J. Dwight Pentecont, Hal Lindsey, and J. F. Walvoord. I also read books by George Beasley-Murray, George Eldon Ladd, and John Newport. More recent commentaries by Bruce M. Metzger, Eugene H. Peterson, M. Eugene Boring, Simon J. Kistemaker, Craig R. Koester, G. K.

---

[2] Bruce M. Metzger, *Breaking the Code: Understanding the Book of Revelation* (Nashville: Abingdon Press, 1999), 9.

Beale, Mitchell G. Reddish, Joseph L. Trafton, Robert Mounce, and Grant S. Osborne have continued to attract my attention.

In reading these commentaries, I found myself agreeing with some and disagreeing with others. I refused to keep my reading within one perspective. I needed to hear what others have to say; to respect their opinions; and to challenge, confirm, or change my interpretation. My primary help did not come from the commentaries, however. It came from reading, rereading, and rereading Revelation in my favorite translation and in many other translations and paraphrases.

My association with Revelation has become more than academic study and widespread reading. It has involved using Revelation in teaching and preaching. Hundreds of students at Mississippi College in Clinton, Mississippi, enrolled in my class on Revelation. They engaged in creative dialogue with me. They challenged me to practice honest scholarship, logical clarity, and communication competency. Probably the primary motivation for writing this book came from student requests that I write what I taught.

Numerous churches have listened to my sermons and my teaching lectures. The church members have been intrigued with the original life situation of Revelation and its apocalyptic genre. I could not talk to laypersons solely about the academic "then" of Revelation. I had to build a bridge from the ancient past to the present day. These laypersons also urged me to write my thoughts about Revelation.

I could not begin to thank the numerous persons who made this book a reality. Students motivated me to crystallize my thoughts. Church members helped me apply Revelation to life today. Scholars from my theological perspective caused me to think and to form what I believe. Professors in my education pilgrimage helped me think critically and form my beliefs based on the life situation and literary uniqueness of Revelation.

My wife Jane deserves special gratitude. She listened attentively to every word I wrote. She heard my lectures and sermons on Revelation. She had dialogues with me frequently, expressing how Revelation relates to her life.

Let me suggest that you make this volume secondary and a translation of Revelation primary. Read Revelation many, many times. It will take about an hour and a half for the average reader to read it once. The special blessing of Revelation comes when the words are read, heard, and obeyed. "Blessed is the one who reads aloud the words of the prophecy, and blessed are those who hear, and who keep what is written in it; for the time is near" (Rev. 1:3).

I express my appreciation to Amy Aycock, graduate of Carson-Newman College and current student at Duke Divinity School, for typing the manuscript. Thanks also to Judi Hayes for her repeated readings of the manuscript. She has helped me with my confidence for writing and with tutorial help in expressing ideas and arranging content. Her gentle encouragement has helped me move this writing to completion.

All biblical references, except otherwise noted, come from the *English Standard Version*.

Chapter 1
A Book That Happened in History

Background

WHERE DOES A STUDY of Revelation begin? One might think the study begins in chapter 1 verse 1. But serious students of Revelation begin with the background of the book. Historical conditions caused the writing of Revelation. It did not just happen or appear. Christians living in Asia Minor in the latter part of the first century AD faced a crisis from the Roman authorities. God then inspired a man named John to encourage these first-century believers to stand firm despite the threat of adversity and martyrdom. To understand Revelation, we need to take the time to learn as much as possible about the book's historical situation. When we learn about such issues as the identity of the author, the intended audience, and the probable date, Revelation becomes understandable. We shall then be more able to enter sympathetically into the mind and heart of the author and his readers. Edward A. McDowell wrote, "Perhaps no other book of the Bible has suffered more from being wrenched from its historical context than Revelation."[1]

A background study of Revelation must also include the book's unique literary style. It abounds in symbolic language,

---

[1] Edward A. McDowell, *The Meaning and Message of the Book of Revelation* (Nashville: Broadman Press, 1951), 1.

which appears unique to the modern readers. Symbolic language, however, is one of the chief characteristics of apocalyptic literature, of which Revelation is an outstanding example. Such literature enjoyed wide popularity in both Jewish and Christian circles from 200 BC to AD 100. Learning the nature of apocalyptic literature will help us understand the message behind the symbols.

Every verse in Revelation needs to be studied in light of its historical background and its unique literary style. Maybe a personal analogy could illustrate the importance of historical context. Ringling Brothers and Barnum & Bailey Circus came to my hometown each year. Growing up, my parents took me to that circus. Performances occurred under the "Big Top" (the large tent). I noticed that other tents and trailers existed by the big tent. Those places advertised appealing attractions such as the world's strongest man, the two-headed calf, the world's shortest woman, and others. My curiosity prompted me to ask my parents to see these shows. They told me: "These attractions are not part of the circus. They are sideshows. The circus, son, takes place under the 'Big Top.'"

Oddly enough, I have applied that parental line to my study of Scripture. "The circus, son, takes place under the 'Big Top.'" Every word in Revelation needs to be studied under the "Big Top" of the book's historical situation. Taking texts outside the background could cause sideshows. Actually, sideshows often appear with appealing titles such as "Reading the Signs of the End of the Word," "Roadmaps of Future Events," "Identifying the Antichrist," "The End of the World Is Near." Staying under the "Big Top" will prevent making Revelation a sideshow. Instead it will be a grand production displaying the meaning of the message both for its original readers and for its modern readers.

Background study of Revelation helps us see how it relates to our times. The book was written in a time of crisis to help first-century Christians deal with problems caused by that crisis. If we take the time to learn the nature of the crisis, the book speaks to us and to our time. We are able to see behind the strange symbols and the unfamiliar imagery the truths that had vital meaning to the first readers. We discover elements prevalent in their world which exist in our world today. Our adventures into background study enable us to see that the message spoken by the Holy Spirit in a specific historical situation can be applied to our day. What the message meant is what it continues to mean. No biblical passage can ever mean what it never meant.

This chapter will construct the "Big Top" under which the texts in Revelation have meaning. It will be a covering for every text, word, phrase, image, concept, vision, and number to be interpreted. As we proceed through the chapters and verses of Revelation, we shall always be aware of the book's life situation and literary uniqueness. Our main question throughout the study will be, "What did the text mean to the original readers?"

The Historical Circumstances

Before engaging in the skills of a biblical interpreter, we need to engage in the craft of a historian. The historian enters into the experiences of past generations to bring a story to life. As historians, we shall study data about the author, the date, the readers, and the message of Revelation. Studying the information will help form the narrative about the occasion and the purpose of writing Revelation.

Author

Scholars through the years have concluded that John wrote not only Revelation but also the Gospel and the three Johannine letters. In recent years this conclusion has received many objections. The objections originated in the stylistic differences among the proposed Johannine writings, lack of adequate identification of John in Revelation, and later writings suggesting another author.

Naming the author of a Bible book involves looking at both internal and external evidence. The internal evidence, or the evidence within the book itself, is minimal. The author claims to be John (1:1, 4, 9; 22:8), a brother, a servant, and a witness of Jesus Christ who had been exiled to Patmos. He gives no more information about himself. Since he wrote with such little identification and seemed to exercise a certain authority, scholars have assumed that he was a well-known Christian leader in Asia. Many take this internal evidence to identify John, the apostle and son of Zebedee, as the author of Revelation.

External evidence involves other notable writers' comments on the authorship of a Bible book after it was written. Much external evidence strongly favors John, the apostle, as the author. Justin Martyr wrote before AD 166 that John the apostle had prophesied by means of a revelation. Justin had lived in Ephesus in AD 135 and probably had a close acquaintance with Revelation. Irenaeus, a student of Polycarp, wrote in about AD 185 that the apocalypse had been written by "John, the disciple of the Lord" (*Against Heresies*, 130). Clement of Alexandria in about AD 215 wrote of the apostle John's exile on Patmos. Tertullian in AD 200 agreed with Justin and Irenaeus on John the apostle (*Against Marcion*, III.14).[2]

Dissident voices about John the apostle being the author of Revelation sounded in the third century. These critics claimed that the internal evidence did identify the author as John, but nowhere did he claim to have been an apostle. Dionysius of Alexandria was probably the first to reject apostolic authorship of Revelation. He did so because of the great differences in the Johannine writings. Early in his writings (AD 265) he conjectured that John Mark wrote Revelation, but he dropped that idea. He mentioned other

---

[2] Morris Ashcraft, "Revelation" in *The Broadman Bible Commentary* (Nashville: Broadman Press, 1972), 246–47.

men named John and referred to two tombs of John in Ephesus. Eusebius, writing in his work *Ecclesiastical History* in the early part of the fourth century, identified one of these Johns as "the elder John." He says that it was probably this elder John who wrote the Apocalypse bearing the name John.[3]

A possibility has been proposed that the author of Revelation was neither the apostle nor the elder John but another John who was well known to the churches of Asia. Whoever he might have been, he could have been strongly influenced by John the apostle. He could have been an heir of the thinking and spirit of the son of Zebedee.

Though the author may not be known specifically, some general information can be discerned about him. He is an unidentified John living in Asia Minor in the closing years of the first century. The authority with which he wrote indicates that he was well known to the churches in Asia Minor. He also possessed an intimate knowledge of the churches. He made extensive use of the Hebrew Bible and awkwardly expressed many Hebrew or Aramaic idioms in the book. This would suggest that he was a Jewish Christian, likely originally from Palestine. This author ran into trouble because of his leadership in the churches and as a result was exiled to the island of Patmos where he received a revelation from God. The specific identity of the human author bears little relevance for understanding Revelation. Further references in the work will simply refer to the author as John.

Date

Scholars have proposed either an early date or a late date for the composition of Revelation. Early dating is in the mid-sixties, during the reign of the Roman emperor Nero (AD 54–68). Late dating is in the mid-nineties during the reign of the Roman

---

[3] Ibid., 247.

emperor Domitian (AD 81-96). Advocates for early and late dating gather evidence from both internal and external sources. In other words they cite evidences within the book of Revelation as well as the opinions of other writers from the first few centuries.

Advocates of the early date during Nero use internal evidences to support their position. Some hold that Revelation 11 indicates that the temple at Jerusalem was still standing. It was destroyed in AD 70, and these supporters think the book had to be written before AD 70.

Another passage assumes the early date. "This calls for wisdom: let the one who has understanding calculate the number of the beast, for it is the number of a man, and his number is 666" (13:18 RSV). Numerous writers ascribe the number to Nero. They think that the number 666 is a cryptograph for *Neron Kaisar* (Greek) reduced to *Nron Ksr* (Hebrew) reduced to the numbers 50, 200, 6, 50, 100, 60, and 200, which add up to 666. Those who hold this interpretation appear to be in the minority.[4]

A related passage that intimates a time reference is found in Revelation 17:10-11. "They are also seven kings, five of whom have fallen, one is, the other has not yet come, and when he does come he must remain only a little while. As for the beast that was and is not, it is an eighth but it belongs to the seven, and it goes to destruction." Some creative alignment of Roman rulers identifies Nero as the sixth ruler. A variety of other methods have been employed for identifying these kings; therefore, one cannot say dogmatically that the six refers to Nero.

External evidences do not possess a great case for the early date. Few writers in the early church hold to the theory that Revelation was written during the reign of Nero.

The most generally accepted date of Revelation is during the

---

[4]Ray Summers, *Worthy is the Lamb: An interpretation of Revelation* (Nashville: Broadman Press, 1951, 80.

reign of Domitian. This is the traditional date going back to the writing of the book. The external evidence is on the side of this date. Irenaeus, writing in *Against the Heresies* between AD 181 and 189, says the book was written at the end of the reign of Domitian. Eusebius, writing in his work *Ecclesiastical History* in the fourth century, says that Revelation was written during Domitian's time. This same position was held by Clement of Alexandria and Jerome.

The persecution of the Christians reflected in Revelation fits the period of Domitian. Under Nero the Christians were persecuted in Rome, but there is no evidence that the persecution extended into the provinces. The persecution instituted under Domitian came at the latter part of his reign. We, therefore, date Revelation AD 95-96.

The persecution instigated by Domitian seems to be in regard to emperor worship. Julius Caesar had been worshiped as a god during his lifetime, and temples in honor of Augustine were erected in some of the provinces. Emperor Caligula demanded that his statue be worshipped. Nero persecuted the Christians, but it was because he wanted someone to blame for the great fire in Rome, not because he claimed to be divine. Most agree that the significant advance in emperor worship took place during the reign of Domitian (AD 81-96). Domitian regarded himself as a god, and he demanded worship from his subjects. In light of emperor worship in the province of Asia, dating Revelation in the last part of Domitian's reign seems to be plausible.

Another reason for accepting the time of the book's writing as during Domitian's reign is the use by the author of the myth of Nero's resurrection. A legend arose after Nero's death to the effect that he would come from Parthia leading an army and would reestablish himself as the head of the Roman Empire. Of course, the author of Revelation did not believe the myth, but it seems fairly certain he used it as an illustration of the evil reign of

Domitian.⁵

Still another reason for accepting the late date is the state of the churches as reflected in the seven letters (chapters 2–3). Some of the churches did not exist prior to the sixties. These churches mentioned in Revelation had existed long enough for heresies to enter and for the loss of first enthusiasm. We conclude that both the internal and the external evidences favor the writing of Revelation during the reign of Domitian. Dating the book at this time will help with insights about the original readers and the occasion and purpose of the book as well.

Readers

John makes clear the recipients of Revelation. The text of Revelation indicates that the book is addressed to "the seven churches that are in Asia . . . to Ephesus and to Smyrna and to Pergamum and to Thyatira and to Sardis and to Philadelphia and to Laodicea" (1:4, 11). All of the churches were located in western Asia Minor. Today this area is part of Turkey. These churches were located in cities serving as important centers of culture, commerce, and agriculture. The province of Asia Minor was under the rule of the Romans.

The original readers in the churches of Asia had more than a geographical address. They lived in a social, political, cultural, and multireligious environment. The seven churches clearly existed in a hostile environment which came primarily from two directions—the Jewish world and the Roman world. The Jews had turned against the Christians. Relations between the Jews and Christians deteriorated in the last couple of decades of the first century. The Romans gave the Jews a special privilege which allowed them freedom from worshiping the Roman gods and participating in the Greco-Roman cults. Christianity was

---

⁵ McDowell, 304.

considered a part of Judaism by the Romans until the Jewish War in AD 66–70.⁶

The Jews worked hard to separate themselves from the Christians. They tried to get the Romans to recognize their separateness and to disallow Christians' exemption from worshiping the Roman gods. Jewish people brought charges against the Christians before the Romans, however, causing the Jews to become a distinct threat to the churches. John notes the Jewish synagogues in 2:9 and 3:9 and associates them as the "synagogue of Satan." The Jews slandered the Christians and became instigators of their persecution.

The churches also faced a hostile environment from the Roman world. They felt a large amount of social and economic pressure to participate in Roman life. Numerous trade guilds existed in most of these seven cities, and Christians felt pressure to participate in their idolatrous feasts. When Christians refused to participate, hostility was directed to them. Believers had to cope with strains caused by a secular environment.

The Christians also faced possible persecution from the Roman world. The demand for believers to worship the emperor was the occasion of the persecution. If Christians refused to worship the emperor, they would suffer persecution. If they complied with the Roman demand, they would be unfaithful to Christ.

Internal evidence supports the existence of persecution when Revelation was written. John wrote from exile (1:9), and Antipas died a martyr's death in Pergamum. John warns those in Smyrna of suffering to come (2:10). He also warns those in Philadelphia of an hour of trial coming to the whole world (3:10). John sees in a vision under the heavenly altar those who have been

---

⁶Grant R. Osborne, *Revelation* (Grand Rapids: Baker Academic, 2002. 11

slain for the word (6:9). John describes the harlot Rome drunk with the blood of the martyrs (17:6).

The external evidence for persecution of believers in non-Christian sources is more difficult to find. Tacitus and Suetonius write of Nero's persecution in AD 64. Suetonius relates that Domitian was a devotee of the gods and built temples to them bearing his name. Numerous Christian writings allude to Domitian's persecution of Christians. Tertullian and Lactantius wrote of Domitian's persecution being like that of Nero. Michael Grant in *The World of Rome* concludes that by the time of Domitian the identity of Christians was more defined and that "Domitian persecuted them for refusal to accept his divinity."[7]

Rome had a tolerant attitude toward other religions because of the polytheistic nature of their own. Conquered peoples were allowed to worship their gods or goddesses as long as they did not violate Roman laws. The practices of emperor worship developed slowly in the Roman Empire. Early in Roman history, Julius Caesar claimed that he was divine and placed his statue in the temples with the gods. Augustine (31 BC-AD 14) accepted the title of *Sebastos* ("worthy of worship") and promoted emperor worship in the province. Domitian (AD 81-96) demanded such worship, and Revelation is dated in his reign. Emperor worship took place in the provinces more than in Rome itself. The distance of the provinces from Rome prompted homage to Rome.[8]

Roman provinces were ruled by proconsuls. They administered Roman justice, guaranteed order, and collected taxes. Religious matters were also under the control of these rulers. The proconsuls delegated most religious matters to priests who were in

---

[7]Michael Grant, *The World of Rome* (New York: The New American Library, 1960), 212

[8]Ashcraft, "Revelation," 248.

charge of religious temples. These priests helped to enforce emperor worship in the provinces.

In John's day Rome demanded that all subjects in the provinces address Caesar as "lord." To most residents this was nothing more than an oath of allegiance to the country. But Christians viewed the confession of Caesar as "lord" as a violation of their commitment to Jesus Christ as Lord. John writes Revelation to urge believers to remain faithful to Christ.

In addition to the pressure from the Jews and the Romans, the churches of Asia had internal problems. Some evidence in Revelation 2–3 suggests that commitment to Christ was threatened. The church at Ephesus had lost its first love (2:4). The church at Sardis was dead despite its reputation of being alive (3:1). The church at Laodicea was lukewarm (3:15–17). Doctrinal errors crept into the church and caused problems with both theology and morality. In the churches of Laodicea and Sardis, many believers had become complacent because of their material prosperity.

The church also suffered internally from many problems caused by the Roman pressures. Some in the churches saw no problem in confessing, "Caesar is lord," along with the Christian confession, "Jesus is Lord." Many who suffered for their faithfulness to Christ looked with disdain on those who compromised this commitment. Believers also disliked fellow believers' participation in the idolatrous and immoral practices of the trade guilds.

The churches of Asia needed a word from God. God chose to reveal a message to John to meet the needs of these churches. The churches needed comfort for those suffering from seizure of property, imprisonment, and death of their loved ones and friends. Believers living in a pagan world system yearned to hear about the presence of God with them and about God's absolute sovereignty. The churches also needed to be challenged not to compromise with secular culture or to be seduced by false teachers. Looking at the picture of the original readers of Revelation causes us to conclude that the churches needed a word from God.

The Literary Uniqueness

Casual reading of Revelation prompts the question, What kind of writing is the book of Revelation? The work contains many strange visions, horrendous creatures, confusing numbers, and natural calamities. Readers recognize immediately that Revelation does not resemble the writings of other New Testament books. To a great extent the apparent strangeness of the book is due to its literary uniqueness. Understanding the literary qualities of Revelation will help us grasp the message in the way John wanted to it to be understood.

In the first five verses of the prologue, John employs three different categories of composition in referring to his work. The first word he writes is the term "revelation" (*apokalypsis*). This description of the book has given the name of the whole class of writings with which it is most closely related, namely "apocalyptic literature." In 1:3 John speaks of revelation as a "prophecy," and he proceeds in 1:4 with the form of a letter, namely the designation of author, writer, and greeting. John's book takes its literary uniqueness from its combination in a unique manner of all three of these forms.[9] Richard Bauchham summarizes the literary uniqueness, "Revelation seems to be an apocalyptic prophecy in the form of a circular letter to seven churches in the province of Asia."[10]

---

[9] G. R. Beasley-Murray, *The Book of Revelation* (Greenwood, SC: The Attic Press, 1974), 12.

[10] Richard Bauchham, *The Theology of the Book of Revelation* (Cambridge: Cambridge University Press, 1993), 2.

Prophecy

John identifies his work as a "prophecy" in five places (1:3; 22:7, 10, 18, 19). Revelation's beginning resembles the introduction in some Old Testament prophetic books (cf. Rev. 1:1–3; Jer. 1:1–2; Amos 1:1). The word *prophecy* means different things to different people. We should not allow *prophecy* solely to mean "prediction." The word does allow for prediction, but basically the word points to divine origin. Revelation is a book from God. John calls readers to hear it as well as obey it. He does not wish to stimulate people's interest in the future but to influence their actions in the present.[11]

John uses the word *prophecy* in the context of the prophetic ministry. Three couplets of words help us understand the nature of biblical prophecy: revelation and proclamation, interpretation and prediction, and hearing and obeying. The first couplet is revelation and proclamation. Israel believed that God revealed his message to chosen individuals. Deuteronomy 18:18 refers to God's giving a message to Moses and his proclamation of God's message to the people. "And I will put my words in his mouth, and he shall speak to them all that I command him." When God revealed the message to Moses, he expected the word to be proclaimed to Israel.

The book of Revelation fits into the Hebrew concept of revelation and proclamation. The opening word, *revelation*, indicates the uncovering of something hidden. John claims the visions in the book come ultimately from God. After John received the revelation, God commissioned him to write the message to the churches in Asia.[12]

The second couplet of words inherent in biblical prophecy is interpretation and prediction. Before God's revelation is

---

[11] Leon Morris, *The Revelation of St. John: An Introduction and Commentary* (London: Tyndale Press, 1969), 46–47.

[12] Mitchell G. Reddish, *Revelation* (Macon: Smyth and Helwys, 2001), 3–4.

communicated, it needs to be understood. The grace gift of prophecy is the gift of understanding the will of God and the direction of the Holy Spirit and then being gifted to interpret that message to others. The prophets assisted people in discerning the will of God.

God's message not only included interpretation of life situations, but it also included prediction of the future. For example, Jeremiah interpreted the spiritual condition of Judah, but he also predicted the fall of Judah in the future. The Old Testament prophets were primarily concerned with current events, but they realized the future arose out of the present. When prediction appeared in the prophet's message, it was not just to forecast the future but to interpret God's message and how that message affected the future.

John in Revelation interprets history between Christ's first coming and his final coming, but he also has elements of predictions in his work. He tells the readers about Christ's future return, the extinction of evil, and a new existence for believers beyond the grave. The book of Revelation thus fits the feature of biblical prophecy as interpretation and prediction.

The third couplet of words which describe biblical prophecy is hearing and obeying. Some of the Old Testament prophets spoke to life situations; their message was not intended merely for cognitive understanding. Their messages were intended to comfort, challenge, censor, complement, and call to change. The Hebrew prophets frequently used the expression, "Hear this word!" The Hebrew word for *hear* also means "to obey." Although there are two words in the couplet, there is only one concept, namely a hearing which leads to obeying.

John pronounces a blessing on those who read Revelation, hear its message, and keep what is written (1:3). If John primarily wanted to dispense information about the future, he would have pronounced a blessing on those who know and give information about the future. To understand Revelation as a prophecy, therefore, means to interpret it in light of the features of the Old Testament prophets.

Apocalypse

John chose the apocalyptic genre as the dominant literary style of Revelation. This type of literature was popular in Palestine from 200 BC to 100 AD. Books belonging to this type of literature have been called "tracts for hard times" because they were written mainly in times of distress to give encouragement to oppressed and persecuted people. These writings are called "apocalyptic literature." The word *apocalyptic* comes from the Greek word *apokalypsis* in Revelation 1:1. The verb form of the word means "to unveil." Revelation is a unique apocalypse in that it is an unveiling of what God has made known.

The language and imagery of Revelation are strange to many modern readers. But John and most of his readers would have recognized this kind of language. In the Bible and in several streams of Judaism, apocalyptic writings existed. Daniel was the great apocalypse that set the pattern for most of the apocalyptic writings that followed. Other Old Testament passages belong to the apocalyptic style, notably Isaiah 13-14; Ezekiel 28-39; and Zechariah 9-14. John was strongly influenced by the symbols used by these Old Testament writers.

Outside the Old Testament, numerous apocalypses circulated among the Jews. The most notable of these noncanonical works include *Enoch* (200 BC), *The Assumption of Moses* (first century), *Second Enoch* (early part of the first century), *The Book of Baruch* (AD 70), and *The Testament of the Twelve Patriarchs* (second century BC). When John selected the apocalyptic genre for Revelation, he was moving in an atmosphere thoroughly familiar to many Christians of his time.

Identifying the characteristics of apocalyptic literature is difficult. Revelation resembles many of the Jewish apocalypses, but it also differs from them in many ways such as substance and form. Modern students of Revelation would benefit greatly by examining the characteristics of apocalyptic literature as it touches Revelation.

Seven qualities of apocalyptic literature will now be examined. First, apocalyptic writings disclose otherworldly matters. John J. Collins gives a classic description of apocalyptic literature: "Apocalypse entails the revelatory communication of heavenly secrets by an otherworldly being to a seer who presents the vision in a narrative framework; the visions guide readers into a transcendent reality that takes precedence over the current situation and encourages readers to persevere in their trusts. The visions reverse normal experiences by making the heavenly mysteries the real world and depicting the present crisis as a temporary, illusory situation."[13] In Revelation, the exalted Christ, angels, and an elder function as otherworldly mediators. The apocalypses unveil information about the otherworldly region and the events of the final days.

Second, apocalypses have a historical significance. While apocalypses deal with otherworldly matters, they originate from earthly key situations and address the needs of people in those situations. There are some critical historical situations with which the apocalypse has been connected. These situations could have been social, political, or theological. Apocalypses have often been called "crisis literature." The writer of Revelation used the writing style of an apocalypse to give hope and comfort to people frightened and confused during the persecution of Domitian.

Third, apocalyptic literature communicates truth through visions. Revelation abounds with visions. The visions vary from scenes in heaven to scenes on earth. Michael Wilcox, in his work

---

[13] John J. Collins, "Introduction: Toward the Morphology of a Genre" in *Apocalypse: The Morphology of a Genre*, Semeca 14 (1979), 9.

The Message of Revelation, interprets Revelation along the line of visions. He identifies eight visions prefaced by the words "I saw," "was seen," "I looked," and "I will show you" (1:4–3:22; 4:4–8:1; 8:2–11:18; 11:19–15:4; 15:5–16:21; 17:1–19:10; 19:11–21:8; 21:9–22:19). John presented truth by means of vision.

Fourth, apocalyptic literature communicates the vision in the form of symbols. The prophet saw images which were to be interpreted and understood. The intention was not to fix the thought upon the symbol but upon the truth the symbol represented. These symbols in Revelation were intended for the mind of a poet not the brush of a painter. When we think of the truths these symbols represent, the vision becomes vivid, instructive, and real.

The writer of Revelation uses many symbols from the Old Testament. Such images as the tree of life, the temple, Mount Zion, the Holy City, Babylon, the ark of the covenant, and many others made the message of Revelation plain to those acquainted with the Old Testament. Natural objects and phenomena lent color to the visions. The writer used the sky, the sun, earthquakes, thunder, lightning, stars, rivers, mountains, and trees to convey his message.

Numbers form an important feature in the symbolism of the book. Only a few are used: 2, 3, 3 ½, 4, 6, 7, 10, 12, and their multiples and squares and cubes. Two is the minimum number needed to give a legitimate witness. Three can imply divine representation. Four can stand for the world or created order. Six carries a sinister sense or implication of evil. Three and one-half represents something cut off or limited. This often appears in Revelation as 3 ½ years of persecution, 42 months, or 1,260 days, all of which are approximately the same length of time. The number seven represents the complete number. The multiplication of three by four yields twelve, the number used to represent God's people. The number ten represents human completeness.

Multiples of ten are a symbolic way to indicate many. One

thousand seems to depict the numerous years between Christ's ascension and his return. Twelve thousand is a foundational large religious number, and 144,000 is the supreme religious number that represents the complete people of God.[14]

The writers of apocalypses sometimes included animal symbolism. They used animals known to them and often created new animals by combining parts of existing animals. The writer of Revelation used the lion, the bear, the tiger, the goat, the ox, and the eagle to communicate truth. John, like other apocalyptic writers, also used colors. He used white as a symbol of triumph, red the color for conflict, black the color for famine, greenish-gray the color for death, and purple the color for royalty.

Fifth, apocalyptic writings have a dramatic element. The writers wanted to make truth as vivid and forceful as possible. In Revelation, John made dramatic impressions on the readers with such things as a darkened sun, a bloody moon, and falling stars. He depicted a dragon knocking a third of the stars from the sky. He told of death riding on a horse and hailstones weighing one hundred pounds. All of these are exaggerated symbols used for dramatic effect.

Sixth, apocalyptic writing concentrates on the close of the age and the dramatic inauguration of the age to come.[15] The apocalyptist thinks of two worlds, two kingdoms set against each other. He does not anticipate any slow evolution of the bad into the good. He sees transformation on the other side of history. He thinks of a day of winding up the powers of darkness and liberating the powers of light. The apocalyptist looks beyond the crises in life to heaven.

---

[14] Gerald Borchert, "Revelation" in *New Living Translation Study Bible* (Carol Stream, IL: Tyndale House, 2008), 2173.

[15] Robert H. Mounce, *The Book of Revelation* (Grand Rapids: William B. Eerdmans, 1977), 23.

Seventh, the writers of apocalyptic literature provide an alternate way of understanding the world. Their readers suffered from "cognitive dissonance," which means their preconceived notions about the world and reality did not match the life situations they experienced. The intended readers of Revelation lived under the persecution of Domitian. Their theological understanding of the world was that God was supreme, not Rome. Their personal experience was just the opposite. Domitian seemed to be the supreme power as he persecuted those who were faithful to Christ. Apocalyptic writers assured readers that God was ultimately in control of history and the universe, in spite of current appearances. God would eventually intervene to defeat evil and to vindicate the righteous.[16]

Revelation shares certain characteristics common to the apocalyptic genre. Yet Revelation differs widely from other apocalyptic writings. It is supreme among all apocalyptic productions and therefore rightly belongs in the genre of apocalyptic.

This brief survey of the characteristics of apocalyptic literature helps us see the unique literary quality of Revelation. This Christian apocalypse unveils God's message. This message can only be understood when the symbols and figurative language of apocalyptic are related to the background of the book. Its meaning for the first readers is its meaning today.

Letter

John writes his apocalyptic prophecy in the form of a letter. Charles H. Talbert says, "In Revelation one finds

---

[16]Reddish, Revelation, 4–5.

prophetic/apocalyptic visions with an epistolary framework."[17] Ancient letters had certain standard elements. The opening of an ancient letter identified the author, named the intended recipient, and extended a greeting. These conventional components appear in the beginning of Revelation. The author names the sender as John and the churches in Ephesus, Smyrna, Pergamum, Thyatira, Sardis, Philadelphia, and Laodicea as the recipients. He greets these churches with grace and peace. Ancient letters often had benedictions. At the conclusion Revelation reads, "The grace of the Lord Jesus be with all. Amen" (22:21).

Letters served as vehicles for communicating God's messages to congregations and to individuals. Paul expected his letter to be read in congregations (cf. 1 Thess. 5:27; Col. 4:16), and Revelation also was to be read aloud. The situations and needs of the churches in Asia were in John's mind. He wrote to comfort them and to give them hope as they faced their numerous crises. Interpreting Revelation involves the same techniques of interpreting Paul's letters. The interpreter needs to see what the author sent to the original recipients in their circumstance and then apply that truth.

The Interpretive Approaches

No one should be surprised that Revelation, with its apocalyptic symbols and visions, has been interpreted in many different ways. We assume that its original readers understood the book's main message without too much difficulty. As the years passed, however, people became less familiar with apocalyptic writings. Consequently, numerous interpretive approaches of Revelation have emerged. Four major types of interpretation have

---

[17] Charles H. Talbert, *The Apocalypse: A Reading of the Revelation of John* (Louisville: Westminster Press, 1994), 4.

been developed in the history of the church. The differing interpretations are all variations and combinations of these four basic approaches.

Preterist

The word *preterist* comes from a Latin word which means "relating to the past." Those who interpret Revelation from this approach think that the author is writing in symbolic form about situations that have gone on during his lifetime. Such an interpreter thinks all the nationalistic references in the book have to do with Rome. He believes John refers to Rome by his figures of the dragon and the beasts from the sea on earth. He sees a cryptographic account of Rome's rise to power and her fall.

The preterist approach has merit for making Revelation exceedingly meaningful for its original readers. And it has demerit of making it less meaningful for all subsequent readers. Numerous variants of this approach are espoused by modern scholars.[18] W. K. Kummel wrote, "The Apocalypse is a book of its time, written out of its time and for its time, not for the distant generations of the future or even of the end-time."[19] Revelation has a message for our day in the same way Galatians has a message for believers. Though not written to us specifically since we are neither Galatians nor members of the seven churches in Asia, the ancient letters still have a message for us. We understand their message to us only by first understanding their message to their original audience.

Few would disagree that the preterist approach is the proper beginning place to interpret Revelation. It emphasizes the book's historical origin. Many advocates of this approach find no message in the book except one for John's day. They do not see an

---

[18] Morris, *The Revelation of St. John*, 16.

[19] Quoted in Morris, *The Revelation of St. John*, 17.

application to life today. The preterist approach also has problems with the future in the latter chapters (chapters 19–21).

Historicist

Those who adopt the historicist approach claim that Revelation is an inspired forecast of Roman history. They think visions in Revelation refer to the development of the papacy, the Reformation, the Napoleonic wars, the rise of Hitler and the Soviet Union, and the like. Advocates of this view tend to develop schemes of history and calendars which date the end.

Perhaps the profit of the approach is that it makes Revelation meaningful to the present generation. It also strengthens faith to see the whole of history under God's control. But the original readers would not have benefitted from a book that predicts later periods. It is also interesting that a book forecasting human history ignores the entire world outside Western Europe. The interpreters of the historicist view do not agree with one another, and as time progresses, they have to change their predictions. Constant revisions are made as the end stubbornly refuses to materialize.

Futurist

The futurist approach interprets Revelation primarily as a prophecy of future events. The futurists have taken two forms which we may call the classical premillennial view and the dispensational premillennial view.

Dispensationalists see the seven churches (chapters 2–3) as seven periods of church history, the last of which will be a period of decline and apostasy (Laodicea). They believe the church age (from Christ's ascension to the rapture) is a parenthesis in God's plan. They also think that beginning in Revelation 4:1 is the rapture of the church, and all subsequent chapters in Revelation belong to a period known as the great tribulation. It is a period when the Antichrist will all but destroy God's people. Dispensationalists also believe Israel to be God's people. Israel will be restored to Jerusalem, and the temple will be rebuilt. At the end of the great tribulation, dispensationalists speak of Christ's returning in judgment. This will be followed by a thousand-year reign of Christ on earth with his followers. After the thousand years dispensationalists think there will be a judgment, and afterwards eternal destinies begin.

Classical premillennialists differ from dispensationalists at several points. They do not distinguish sharply between Israel and the church. They also see no reason to interpret the seven letters as seven stages of church history. Both views agree that the primary purpose of Revelation is to describe the consummation of God's redemptive purpose and the end of the age.[20]

Idealist

This approach argues that the symbols do not relate to historical events but rather to timeless truths. They feel that Revelation sets forth the ageless struggle between the kingdom of evil and the kingdom of God. Symbols are understood to refer to forces or tendencies and may be fulfilled over and over as these forces or tendencies are repeated in history.

The principles in Revelation are ageless and belong to all days. John writes of the great principles which are always at work in the world. The principle which controlled the history of John's time controls the history of all times, and the things symbolized are just as applicable to any day as they were to John's day. The idealist approach has certain strengths. It emphasizes the symbolic nature of Revelation, and it stresses the book's relevance for all times. Its primary weakness seems to be the absence of historical

---

[20]George Eldon Ladd, *A Commentary on the Revelation of St. John* (Grand Rapids: William B. Eerdmans, 1971), 463.

connections. Advocates of the view fail to connect Revelation in any way with history, which the text does in several instances.

Eclectic

Many students of Revelation in the last few decades prefer to combine more than one of the approaches mentioned above. The historicist view seems to have limited value, but the other three can be combined to capture how John probably intended the book to be understood. This volume allows the preterist, idealist, and futurist approaches to interact in such a way that the strengths are maximized and the weaknesses minimized.[21]

With the preterist view the interpreter recognizes that often the particular figures used in Revelation come from the days in which it was composed, the days of the Roman oppression of believers in the latter part of the first century. With the idealist view the interpreter recognizes that situations similar to those in the first century will likely reoccur. With the futurist view the interpreter sees that much of the hope of the writer is yet to be fulfilled.

The eclectic approach recognizes that Revelation is not just a description of the first century, nor is it merely a sketch of the final generation. It is a God-inspired ancient document that portrays life then as well as here and now. Its first-century context is a transparency through which we can see our own world, which might already be in its final phase. The eclectic approach considers seriously the apocalyptic nature of Revelation. It perceives it as speaking to our day through the symbolic codes and offering a special blessing to those who hear and live its message.[1]

The "Big Top" has been constructed. The sections of historical background, literary uniqueness, and interpretive

---

[21] Osborne, *Revelation*, 21.

approaches have been put together to form a covering for the texts. Each chapter and verse of Revelation will be interpreted in light of the covering. Seeing the texts under the "Big Top" of background will lend to understanding what the texts meant to the original readers and what they mean to us today.

Chapter 2
The Presence of Christ in History

Revelation 1:1–20

THE BOOK OF REVELATION opens in chapter 1 with a strong emphasis on Jesus Christ. His name appears frequently in the chapter in both noun and pronoun forms. John gives several titles for Jesus Christ that describe his character and his work. In the opening eight verses, John alludes to every event in the saving career of Jesus. He refers to the Lord's earthly ministry, his sacrificial death, his victorious resurrection, his supreme exaltation, his saving work, and his final, visible return.[1] John closes the chapter by telling about his vision of the exalted Christ. When the original readers read or heard Revelation read, they got the message that the book centered on Jesus Christ.

The writer of Revelation and the other New Testament writers never restricted Jesus to their decades in history. The New Testament writers reported his birth in Bethlehem, his boyhood in Nazareth, and his public ministry throughout Palestine. They included his miracles and teachings. They wrote of his death,

---

[1] John R.W. Stott, *The Incomparable Christ* (Downers Grove: InterVarsity Press, 2001), 174.

burial, and resurrection. In the writing of these historical events, however, they went deeper than Jesus' earthly ministry. They wrote of his existence before Bethlehem and his existence after his death and resurrection. The writer of Revelation speaks of Jesus as the one who was, who is, and who is to come (cf. 1:8). He alludes in Revelation to Jesus not only as the historical Jesus but also as the eternal Christ.

John begins Revelation with the witness of Christ's continual presence in the world. Over six decades have passed between Jesus' ascension and the writing of Revelation. John wants the readers to know that Christ is alive and present with his people from the time of his ascension until his final return. Time and circumstances have not diminished Christ's presence with his people. He is not an absentee landlord. On the contrary, he is in the midst of his churches, walking with them in hard times. He continues to speak to them with words of comfort, criticism, and challenge. In 1:13 John reports about his vision of the Christ who is present with his people: "And in the midst of the lampstands one like a son of man." Revelation 1, as well as the other twenty-one chapters, stresses the historical Jesus, but the chapters also give witness to the contemporary Christ, the one who is always present with his people.

According to John, Jesus is not dead, absent, hidden, or silent. He is with his people, supporting them during hard times. John opens chapter 1 with a preface which relates that his message is about Christ (1:1-3). He continues with a salutation that contains the name of the author, the readers, and a word of greeting (1:4-8). John identifies with his readers by telling of their kindred experiences in Christ (1:9-11). John concludes the chapter by telling his vision of the exalted Christ. The book is "the revelation of Jesus Christ" (Rev. 1:1).

The Preface
1:1-3

Prefaces prepare readers for the message of a literary work. John lets his readers know at the outset that his message to them came originally from God. John proceeds to give insights into how he got that message and what the content of the message is. He relates to the readers a vision of the exalted Christ. John closes the preface by pronouncing a blessing on those who hear and heed the message he wrote.

The Source of the Message
John first wants his readers to know where he got the message. He lets them know that it did not originate by human invention or imagination. It came as a divine disclosure from God. "The revelation of Jesus Christ, which God gave him to show to his servants the things that must soon take place. He made it known by sending his angel to his servant John" (1:1). The Greek word *apokalypsis*, translated "revelation," means an unveiling or disclosure. It refers to supernatural truths unknown to human beings and incapable of being discovered by them.

Grammatically, the expression "the revelation of Jesus Christ" can be read in two ways. It can be translated as an objective genitive, which would render a reading, "the revelation *about* Jesus Christ." It can also be read as a subjective genitive, which would render the translation as "the revelation *from* Jesus Christ." Actually, John received a revelation from Jesus Christ, who is both the source and content of the revelation. John wants the readers to understand that the same Jesus Christ who became incarnate, revealed himself in human flesh, died on the cross, and rose again is the one who mediates the vision of this book.[2]

---

[2]Osborne, "Revelation," 52.

John describes a four-stage process by which the revelation came to the churches. God first gave the revelation to Jesus. Then Jesus gave it to the angels. The angels communicated the message to John. Finally, John wrote the message to the churches. The process underscores the source of the book of Revelation. Furthermore, the verb *gave* indicates the initiative of God. The message was God's idea, and he graciously shared it with his servants.

John writes that the events which constitute the revelation "must soon take place." The expression "soon" (*en tachi*) is not defined. The same expression appears in 22:6, and a similar one occurs in 2:16; 3:11; 22:7, 12, 20. It has been interpreted to mean "soon" or "certain." More than likely the expression communicates the idea of imminence. The early church believed that when Christ ascended and the Holy Spirit came on his followers, the last days had actually begun (cf. Acts 2:16f). The language of impending happenings draws the readers into a sense of expectation and responsibility, a sense which is to characterize every generation of Christians. In salvation history the events in the book have already started happening and await the final consummation.

The Means of the Message

Oddly enough John lets the readers hear a few things about the process of God's revelation. The medium of the message is described with two expressions—"to show" and "made it known." The verb "show" indicates the idea of visions. The verb "made it known" has a special insight, for it is the verb cognate of the word *sign*. It communicates the idea of making the revelation known by means of symbols. This is particularly appropriate in light of the predominant symbolism of the book.

The process of receiving the message by signs is conferred by John's comment about his reception of the revelation. He bore witness to "all that he saw." The verb "saw" is particularly appropriate in a book where there are so many visions. From the beginning the readers of Revelation are alerted to the fact that the message came from God, and it was communicated by means of signs or visions. That was the way God gave it, and that is the way John writes it. This should alert all readers to interpret Revelation with great theological truths presented in signs or symbols.

The Content of the Message
John's primary responsibility as the "servant of Christ" is to testify to two things: "the word of God" and "the testimony of Jesus Christ." John "bore witness to the word of God and to the testimony of Jesus Christ, even to all that he saw" (1:2). The content of the message is not human speculation, but it is the word of God and the testimony of Jesus. The "word of God" and "testimony of Jesus" form a formula for gospel truth and faithful Christian witness to it. The "word of God" is used in Scripture both for prophetic utterance and for the apostolic message.

The content of the message is further described as "the testimony of Christ." This phrase occurs six times in Revelation (1:2, 9; 12:17; 19:10 (twice) and 20:4). In all but one reference it is used in the same context as "word of God." Because the message has a divine origin, the content of the book can be described as God's word and Jesus' testimony.

The Impact of the Message
God intends for the message of Revelation to be more than information. He wants the message to impact lives. "Blessed is the one who reads aloud the words of the prophecy, and blessed are those who hear, and who keep what is written in it, for the time is near" (1:3). This is the first of seven beatitudes in Revelation (14:13; 16:15; 19:9; 20:6; 22:7, 14). The first blessing goes to those who read the Revelation. First-century churches followed the pattern of the synagogue by reading Scripture.

The next blessing John pronounces is on those who listen to the reading. The hearer is defined by two expressions: "those who hear" and "who keep what is written." Hearing and keeping appear together frequently in both the Old and New Testaments. In fact the Hebrew verb for "hear" also means to "obey." John does not wish to stimulate people's interest but to influence their actions. The fact that the readers were to obey the words of the prophecy indicates that the work was considered pastoral not mere prediction.

John closes the preface with a sense of urgency to hear and obey God's message. "For the time is near." To the early church the Lord's coming was always near, and this is the appropriate attitude for every Christian generation. The nearness of Christ's return calls believers to live responsibly. John's focus is not just on last things but on ethics. The fact that Christians think that the time is near calls for faithfulness to the church.

The Salutation
1:4–8

Beginning in 1:4 Revelation resembles the opening of a letter. The book concludes like a letter in 22:21 with a benediction. The initial mention of the author, reader, and greeting is standard in letters of this period. Revelation in 1:4–8 is reminiscent of the letters of both Paul and Peter. The author takes the revelation he has received and puts it in the form of a letter, which he now sends to those for whom the message is intended.

The Postal Information
John gives some information for the readers about the author, reader, and greeting. "John to the seven churches that are in Asia: Grace to you and peace" (1:4). The author identifies himself as John (cf. 1:4; 1:9; 22:8). He does not describe himself any further. He was

likely so well known in Asia that he needed no further identification.

The Revelation is addressed to "the seven churches of Asia." It is not clear why Revelation was addressed to these seven specific churches. There were other churches in Asia (Troas, Colossae, and others). These seven churches were set in major cities in the provinces and are addressed in the geographical order in which a courier would have delivered the letters. John probably chose to address these particular churches but intended them to represent all the other churches.

The greeting, "grace and peace," is typical in most New Testament letters. The greeting is more than formality. It contains great theological truth. The word "grace" is that unearned, undeserved, freely given favor of God expressed in Jesus Christ which results in authentic peace. The word "peace" is not a state exempt from struggle or war. It is an inward calm confidence born of rightness with God. It enables believers to cope courageously with the hardships of life.

John details the source from which this grace and peace come. "From him who is and who was and who is to come, and from the seven spirits who are before his throne, and from Jesus Christ the faithful witness, the firstborn of the dead, and the ruler of kings on earth" (1:4-5). The origin of grace and peace is threefold: God, the seven spirits, and Jesus Christ. The first source clearly refers to God, the eternal Father: "him who is and who was and who is to come." The expression is based on the self-revealed name of God in Exodus 3:14 as "I am." John reminds his readers that God is eternally existent, without beginning or end. God is self-existent. God's eternal power as seen in the past and promised in the future still works in the present.

The second source of this grace and peace is "from the seven spirits who are before his throne." Some think the spirits are angels surrounding the throne of God. John likely refers here to the Holy

Spirit. The number "seven" symbolizes fullness; therefore this would be a reference to the fullness of the Holy Spirit's work. Also, coming between the references to God and to Jesus Christ seems to communicate a reference to the Holy Spirit.

The third source of grace and peace comes "from Jesus Christ the faithful witness, the firstborn of the dead, and the ruler of kings on earth." As with God in 1:4, three descriptive titles are used to identify Jesus. The first title, "faithful witness," points to Jesus who was faithful to the Father's will, even if it meant his death. Jesus is the model for the believer who must stand against evil and idolatry even when it may cost one's life.

Jesus' title, "the firstborn of the dead," has two primary emphases. The first emphasis comes from the firstborn as the next head of the Jewish family, who controlled the inheritance. As firstborn Jesus is the sovereign one over life and death. Christ has defeated death, and he controls it. The second emphasis stresses Jesus' resurrection. This depicts what Christ has done to make the believer's resurrection possible.

John also describes Jesus with the title "the ruler of kings on earth." The same Christ who is sovereign over life and death stands above the rulers of the earth. The "kings" represent the enemies of Christ. The caesars are the earthly rulers, but Jesus is "King of kings and Lord of lords" (19:16). Only Christ, not Caesar, is worthy of worship.

The Praise to Jesus
John's description of Jesus with the three titles leads to a doxology directed to Jesus. "To him who loves us and has freed us from our sins by his blood and made us a kingdom, priests to his God and Father, to him be glory and dominion for ever and ever. Amen" (1:5-6). There is no question about the object of praise because John begins with "to him," which is a reference to Christ. This doxology praises Jesus for three activities: loving us, freeing us from

our sins, and making us a kingdom of priests.

First, Christ loves us. The tense is present: "to him that loves us." Christ's love is a permanent, abiding fact. Second, Christ freed us from our sins. The tense changed from present ("loves") to the aorist, which relates to the past redemptive work of Christ on the cross. "By his blood" refers to Christ's giving his life for our sins. Christ's giving his life points to the unambiguous evidence that he loves us. In Greek there is only one letter's difference in the spelling of *loosed* and *washed*. The word *loosed* is better attested in the manuscripts. Christ has loosed or set us free from the bondage of sin.

The third action of Christ's work that is worthy of praise is his inclusion of us in his royal and priestly office—"made us a kingdom, priests to his God and Father." The terms "kingdom" and "priests" echo the thought of Exodus 19:5-6, where God told Israel that they would be a kingdom of priests and a holy nation. The early church understood itself to be the new Israel. Corporately, the church is a group of people in whom Christ rules, and individually believers are priests who serve God and mediate between God and the human race. As priests, the people of God have both direct access to God and the responsibility of serving him.

John closes the praise to Jesus with a crescendo of words. "To him be glory and dominion for ever and ever. Amen." John delights in the Lord, and he brings this out in his doxology. This doxology is addressed "to him," which is a reference to Jesus Christ. By using the word "glory," John alludes to Christ's character. It celebrates the worth and works of Christ in defeating evil powers and effecting salvation. When John used the word "dominion," he thinks of Christ's sovereignty. His power transcends temporal leaders and guarantees the future for God's people.

The doxology concludes with "Amen." It carries with it the

Old Testament idea of "so be it." It authenticates and guarantees the efficacy of the worship of Christ.

Two Comforting Assurances

John's readers had doubt and uncertainty about their God and about their future. John writes to give the readers two gigantic assurances. "Behold, he is coming with the clouds, and every eye will see him, even those who pierced him, and all the tribes of the earth will wail on account of him" (1:7). John first assures his readers of the certainty of Christ's final return. Verse 7 fuses Daniel 7:13 with Zechariah 12:10. John adapts these two prophetic verses to describe the impending coming of Christ. The event is so imminent and certain that John can say, "Look! He is coming." John uses a present tense to describe Christ's coming. His coming includes his incarnation (past), his Spirit to build up the church (present), and his final coming to consummate earthly history (future). The phrase "with the clouds" symbolizes mystery and glory. The cloud in Hebrew thought was associated with divine presence (Exod. 13:21). John therefore assures the believers that Christ's coming is certain, and it will be personal.

Christ's coming has universal significance. "Every eye will see him." This is John's way of saying that Christ's return will not be a remote event in Palestine but will be an event observed by everyone. John gives a parenthetical clause "every one who pierced him." John uses those responsible for placing Christ on the cross, but it should be expanded to include all who treat Christ cruelly. At Christ's coming all the tribes of the earth will mourn for him. This mourning comes as a result of Christ's judgment upon the unbelievers.

Christ's return will be both joyful and sad. It will be a joy for the believers. It will mean a time of vindication and glorification for them. For the unbelievers, however, it will be a sad day. They will mourn because of the judgment coming upon them.

John voices his excitement over Christ's return with "Even so. Amen" (1:7). John combines the Greek and Hebrew forms of affirmation. It expresses vigorous approval of Christ's coming.

Second, John assures the readers of Christ's sovereign lordship over history. "'I am the Alpha and the Omega,' says the Lord God, 'who is and who was and who is to come, the Almighty'" (1:8). Readers find comfort in hearing the direct voice of God. Only here and in 21:5-9 does God himself speak. God identifies himself in three ways. First, he affirms that he is "the Alpha and the Omega." God is the sovereign Lord who began history and will end history. He is also sovereign over all that takes place from history's beginning until its end.

God also reveals himself as the "The Lord God, who is and who was and who is to come." The language portrays the timelessness of God. It is the equivalent of saying that God has always existed and will always exist.

Third, God describes himself as "the Almighty." This title for God appears only ten times in the New Testament, and nine of the occurrences are in Revelation (1:8; 4:8; 11:7; 15:3; 16:7, 11; 19:6, 15; 21:22). The title stresses God's sovereign power over all earthly forces. God reveals his eternity and his power to show that he has superiority over the Roman emperors' limitations of life and power.

The Setting
1:9-11

The writer resumes from verse 4 the epistolary form of his address to the churches. He provides information about himself and his relationship to the readers. John also tells of his private experience "in the Spirit" (v. 11) which caused him to write the book.

The Common Experiences of Writer and Reader

To set the stage for his "in the Spirit" experience, John identifies himself and his relationship with the readers. "I, John, your brother and partner in the tribulation and the kingdom and the patient endurance that are in Jesus, was on the island called Patmos on account of the word of God and the testimony of" (1:9). John identifies himself first by name and then by his relationship with the readers. The opening, "I John," frames the book. His name has already appeared twice in chapter 1 (1:1, 4). The only identification of this John thus far is in Revelation 1:1 where he calls himself a "servant." The writer was apparently well known to the Christians in Asia Minor.

John next identifies himself with his readers by calling himself "your brother," in the sense of his being a fellow Christian. John and his readers had a vital union with Christ. They were "in Christ." Because of this relationship of being fellow believers, they share in three common experiences: tribulation, kingdom, and patient endurance. The word "partner" comes from the concept of *koinonia* emphasized throughout the New Testament. It carries with it the idea of community togetherness and mutual participation in the family of Christ.

The first area the believers share is in "tribulation." The word "tribulation" refers to a time of distress though the cause of the distress is not inherent in the word. It can refer to sickness, persecution, or any kind of hardship. John joins "kingdom" and "patient endurance" with "tribulation." The three in some sense belong together. The term "kingdom" refers to the emerging rule of God that began with Christ and continues with his followers. The reign of Christ will be fully actualized when he returns. "Patient endurance" means faithfulness to God's rule in trying circumstances. John and his readers share a relationship with Christ, meaning that they endure the trying circumstances.

John's situation as he shared in their affliction is next

described. He was "on the island called Patmos." This was an island in the Aegean Sea located thirty miles southwest of Miletus. It was about ten miles long and six miles wide. The Romans used the island as a prison. John states the reason he was on Patmos was because of "the word of God and the testimony of Jesus." More than likely John was banished to Patmos as a punishment for his Christian faith. Apparently the Roman authorities interpreted John's preaching as seditious and removed him from the mainland to inhibit the growth of Christianity. John, like his readers, suffered because of commitment to Christ.

The Private Experience of the Writer
John turns from his mutual experiences with the readers to his private experience with the Lord. "I was in the Spirit on the Lord's day, and I heard behind me a loud voice like a trumpet saying, 'Write what you see in a book and send it to the seven churches, to Ephesus and to Smyrna and to Pergamum and to Thyatira and to Sardis and to Philadelphia and to Laodicea" (1:10-11). The phrase "in the Spirit" occurs four times in Revelation (1:10; 4:2; 17:3; 21:10). Joseph L. Trafton organizes the book around these four references.[3] The phrase "in the Spirit" means to be caught up in an ecstatic experience. Such visions or trances were often experienced by Old Testament prophets. The expression means to be in a kind of ecstasy in which a person is lifted beyond the human level to the spiritual level. John became open to God's truth, and he was ready to see visions.

John's ecstatic experience involved both hearing and seeing. He heard a voice, and he saw a vision. The voice commanded him to write in a book what he was about to see. John turned to see the source of the voice, and he was given his first vision, that of the

---

[3]Joseph L. Trafton, *Reading Revelation: A Literary and Theological Commentary* (Macon: Smyth and Helwys, 2005), 25.

exalted Christ. All of John's experiences of hearing and seeing underscore for the reader the authority of John's book as truly a revelation from God.

John hears the voice and sees the vision "on the Lord's day." The presence of the possessive "Lord's" suggests that the day referred to Christ's resurrection on the first day of the week, or Sunday. As early as the middle of the first century, Christians attached special significance to the first day of the week (cf. Acts 20:6-7; 1 Cor. 16:1-3).

The voice commands John to send his book to "the seven churches" which are named. William Ramsay thinks that the seven cities named by John were chosen because they were distribution centers for the seven postal districts of Asia Minor.[4] The entire scroll was to be read at each church. The number seven, signifying completeness, is probably intended to include the entire Christian communities in Asia, which to the author were synonymous with the entire church. The letters were written to real churches in the first century, and their messages from the Lord relate to any church at any time or place.

The Vision
1:12-20

John turns to see from whom the voice came. "Then I turned to see the voice that was speaking to me, and on turning I saw seven golden lampstands, and in the midst of the lampstands one like a son of man" (1:12-13). John first sees "seven golden lampstands." In the holy place of the Jewish temple stood a single candelabrum bearing seven lamps (Exod. 25:36ff). From Revelation 1:20 we learn that the lampstand symbolizes the seven churches to

---

[4]William A. Ramsay, *The Letters to the Seven Churches of Asia*, (Grand Rapids: Baker Book House, 1904), 191.

whom the letters are addressed. The purpose of the church is to bear the light of God's character in a darkened world.[5]

John sees "one like a son of man" in the middle of the lampstands. John wants his readers to know that Christ is not an absentee landlord. He offers his presence to believers as they live life on earth. This image begins a series of images depicting Christ's presence with the church. He is "in the midst of the lampstands" (1:13); "in his right hand he held seven stars" (1:16); and finally, Christ "walks among the seven golden lampstands" (2:1). All three images depict Christ's being involved in the lives of his people.

The "seven golden lampstands" serve only as the framework. Much more important is the person standing among them. He is called "one like a son of man." This expression comes from Daniel 7:13. It designates Jesus as the heavenly king and points out that while he is like a man, he is not merely a man. He is the eternal Christ. The one who speaks to John is none other than the exalted Christ.

The Vision of Christ

John begins to describe the vision he saw of Christ. John was surprised by Christ's clothing. "I saw . . . one like a son of man, clothed with a long robe and a golden sash round his chest" (1:12–13). It could have been garments worn by a priest, a king, or a judge. John sees Jesus as an exalted, dignified figure.

Next John describes various parts of Christ's body—head, eyes, feet, and voice. "The hairs of his head were white, like white wool, like snow" (1:14). Daniel describes the Ancient of Days with hair "like pure wool" and raiment "white as snow" (Dan. 7:9). Christ shares eternal existence with the Father. In this vision Christ is pictured in his eternal wisdom and in the respect due him. In the ancient world, white hair indicated both dignity and the wisdom

---

[5] Mounce, The Book of Revelation, 77.

attained from years of experience.

John observes the unusual eyes of the exalted Christ. "His eyes were like a flame of fire" (1:14*b*). This seems to symbolize Christ's searching omniscience. It expresses the penetrating insight of the one who is sovereign. He sees the conditions of the churches and the world.

Below the long robe, John sees the feet of Christ. "His feet were like burnished bronze, refined in a furnace" (1:15). The shining, bronze-like feet symbolize strength and stability. He has the ability to walk among the churches and help.

John describes the voice of Christ. "His voice was like the roar of many waters" (1:15). This could be a picture of a great waterfall or a white-water cascade of endless pounding of the shore of Patmos by the waves of the Aegean Sea. The images communicate awesomeness or majesty. The voice of Christ is strong and majestic.

John sees stars in the right hand of the exalted Christ. "In his right hand he held seven stars" (1:16). The right hand in the Jewish world symbolized power and authority. The seven stars are identified in 1:20 as the angels of the seven churches addressed in chapters 2 and 3. This image symbolizes Christ's sovereign control over the churches as well as his protection.

John sees a sword coming from the mouth of Christ. "From his mouth came a sharp, two-edged sword" (1:16). The sword is the Word of God. The only weapon of warfare Christ uses is his word. That word is sharper than any two-edged sword. It pictures the penetrating power of divine truth. This is a figurative representation of the double nature of God's Word: salvation and judgment. The message of God is either salvation or judgment, depending on the decision of the hearer.

John concludes his description of the vision of Christ with a word about his countenance. "His face was like the sun shining in full strength" (1:16). The sun represents the utmost brilliance a person can conceive. It symbolizes a revelation of the glorious deity of Christ.

In verses 12-16, John has used various figures to communicate truths about Christ to his readers. He did not intend for the readers to see literal pictures, but he wants them to see gigantic truths about Christ. The purpose of the pictures was to exhibit by a series of symbols the authority and majesty of Christ. Nothing could help the churches who struggled with evil more than a vision of the exalted Christ in their midst.

The Writer's Response
The vision of the exalted Christ overwhelmed John. "When I saw him, I fell at his feet as though dead" (1:17). Encountering the living Christ is a humbling experience creating awe and wonder.

Christ responds to John's humility. He gives a comforting word and a comfortable touch. "But he laid his right hand on me, saying, 'Fear not, I am the first and the last, and the living one. I died, and behold I am alive forevermore, and I have the keys of Death and Hades'" (1:17-18). The Christ who inspired awe brought comfort. He placed his right hand on John and said, "Do not be afraid." How could John not be afraid? Not only did the vision cause him to fear but also his situation in exile. What did the future hold for him and for the Christian communities in Asia? Christ's words to John helped him not to fear. First, Christ shares the eternity of God. The title "I am the first and the last" is identical with God's claim in 1:8 as the Alpha and the Omega. It is another application of divine titles to Christ.[6]

Second, Christ calls himself the living one. Christ's earthly existence resulted in death. His dead body was resurrected and transformed. He is alive forever and ever, never to die again. Because of his resurrection victory, Christ has authority over death

---

[6]Leon Morris, *The Revelation of St. John*, 55.

and Hades. Death has lost its terror because of Christ's eternity and Christ's earthly victory over death.

The risen Christ repeats and expands John's commission. "Write therefore the things that you have seen, those that are and those that are to take place after this" (1:19). The glorified Christ instructs John to write three things: (1) "the things that you have seen," the present vision and probably the vision to follow; (2) "those that are" may mean both what currently is (condition of the churches) and what eternally is; and (3) "those that are to take place after this" could refer to what will take place after Christ's ascension and after his return. The relationship between the present and future underlies the entire book of Revelation. It recognizes that most of the visions belong in the past and the present as well as the future.

The first vision concludes with an explanation of the seven stars and the seven golden candlesticks. "As for the mystery of the seven stars that you saw in my right hand, and the seven golden lampstands, the seven stars are the angels of the seven churches, and the seven lampstands are the seven churches" (1:20). The word "mystery" means what Christ makes known that human beings could not have worked out for themselves. The stars, he says, symbolize the messengers of the church. The lampstands represent the churches themselves.

John has set the stage for the rest of the book. He has recounted the circumstances surrounding his commission to write to the seven churches of Asia. He has presented a powerful picture of the One who commissioned him, namely Jesus. John introduces the readers to Jesus Christ: Jesus as God, Jesus as Redeemer through his death and resurrection, Jesus present with the church throughout history, and the final coming of Jesus.[7] Indeed, John's work is "the revelation of Jesus Christ." He was present in John's

---

[7] Trafton, *Reading Revelation*, 30–31.

day, and *he is present with his people* until history ends.

Chapter 3
The Church during History, Part 1
Revelation 2:1-17

Ephesus, Smyrna, Pergamum

THE FIRST CHAPTER OF REVELATION has set the tone for the rest of the book. The writer has introduced himself and the circumstances under which he received the Revelation. He has spoken of seven churches who were to be the recipients of his writing. He has introduced the exalted Christ in an inaugural vision. In the beginning of each letter to the church, Christ identifies himself by means of a descriptive phrase taken from the vision as appropriate for the specific church. Chapters 2 and 3 form a distinct section in the Revelation. These two chapters remind us that this book is not just a prophecy or an apocalypse, but it is a letter sent to the seven churches. John writes to strengthen, encourage, challenge, criticize, and console these churches as they faced the evils of the Roman world. Do not lose sight as you read Revelation that it was first intended for the seven churches of Asia.

These seven churches existed in the latter part of the first century in Asia Minor. They were God's light in the midst of the great centers of secular culture, heathen worship, and rampant immorality. Other churches exited in Asia, but John selected these seven churches to be representative of the church throughout history. The church, or the people of God, represents God's character to the world and ministers to the needs of people. Paul appropriately called the church "the body of Christ." Christ lives in his people to empower and to direct them to do his work. Christ is present in his church on the earth. He walks (lives) in her midst, seeing, knowing, and judging with eyes of infallible insight and with piercing words of commendation, criticism, or comfort. There is no room for discouragement when the church faces hard times. Christ is present with his people, and he promises his power, his wisdom, his guidance, and his loving discipline. He guarantees the church of her ultimate triumph. So chapters 2 and 3 of Revelation tell us about Christ present and directing the church during the long, troublesome course of history.

The author followed a fairly uniform pattern in the position of the letters. Each letter has six distinct sections: address, identification of Christ, commendation, reprimand, exhortation, and promise. The address has an identical form in every letter with the exception of the different city. Each identification begins with the same phrase: "the words of." The commendation and the reprimand contain a word about Christ's knowledge of the church. The form for commendation does not appear in two letters, namely Sardis and Laodicea. Also, the form for reprimand does not appear in the churches of Smyrna and Philadelphia. They received no criticism. Each exhortation closes with a call to repentance and a word of warning and/or encouragement. Also, each exhortation closes with a plea: "he who has an ear, let him hear what the Spirit says to the churches." Each letter to the seven churches closes with a promise based on "the one who conquers."

William M. Ramsay, in his classic book *The Letters to the Seven Churches of Asia*, helps us understand why only seven churches were selected. He thinks those seven were representative of all the churches in the province of Asia and maybe the empire. It is not faulty interpretation to think these churches are representative of churches today.

According to Ramsay, the churches were chosen and listed because of a postal route. The assumption is that John sent Revelation from Patmos, and that letter bearer would first stop at Ephesus and from Ephesus would pass on to the other cities in the order in which they appear in Revelation. Each one of the cities would have an influence on people living in an approximate hundred-mile radius. Furthermore, Ramsay says that each one of the letters is addressed to a particular church, but each church was to read the other six messages to the church as well as the rest of Revelation.[1]

"Seven" represents the perfect, or complete, number. It seems legitimate to regard the seven individual churches of the province of Asia as together representing the universal church. Studying the compliments, complaints, counsels, and comfort given to these churches will help God's people throughout history to be more effective churches. Each letter ends with "hear what the Spirit says to the churches." Contemporary churches could ask: "How does this message fit our church? How can we improve our strengths and correct our weaknesses?"

Ephesus
2:1–7

The church in Ephesus was an appropriate recipient for the first message. Ephesus, in the first century, was the capital and foremost city of the Roman province of Asia. It was the most populated city in the province. Maybe Revelation arrived first in Ephesus because it was closer to the island of Patmos. It was the first postal stop in travel from the Aegean Sea to Asia.

The church at Ephesus was founded in AD 52 by the apostle

---

[1] William H. Ramsay, *The Letters to the Seven Churches* (London: Hodder and Stoughton, 1904).

Paul at the beginning of his ministry in the city. When Revelation was written, the church had been in existence for over forty years. Paul made the city his headquarters for some three years. According to tradition the apostle John made his home in Ephesus in his latter days. The church at Ephesus influenced the formation and life of other churches in Asia. It was known as the mother church of the region.

Address. The letter begins with an address to the church. "To the angel of the church in Ephesus write" (2:1). Each one of the seven letters is addressed to the angel of each respective church. Various opinions exist about the identity of the angel. The Greek word *angelos* was used as a supernatural being or an earthly messenger. Suggested identification of the term "angel" include angels or supernatural beings in heaven who represent the church, the heavenly or supernatural characteristic of the church, or the earthly pastor of the local church.[2] The angel is so identified with the church that the qualities and actions of the church are referred to as his own. Ray Frank Robbins said, "The angel seems to be the bishop or pastor of the church, but he may be the celestial counterpart of the earthly organism."[3]

John writes to the church in Ephesus. The city where the church was located was on the Aegean Sea at the mouth of the Cayster River. Three important trade routes converged at this seaport, producing one of the greatest shopping facilities in the ancient world. It was the third largest city in the empire with a population between a quarter and a half million people.

Ephesus was a city of political importance. She had the title "Supreme Metropolis of Asia." Though not the capital of the

---

[2]Beasley-Murray, *The Book of Revelation*, 69–76.

[3]Ray Frank Robbins, *The Revelation of Jesus Christ* (Nashville: Broadman, 1975), 53.

province—an honor reserved for Pergamum—Ephesus was the residence of the Roman proconsul.

Ephesus was a culturally sophisticated city with one of the greatest theaters of the known world. Another cultural part of Ephesus was the magnificent temple of Diana. The city was also the center of the Pan-Ionian Games. These games were held in the month of May, and crowds flocked to see them. The Greek name for "May" was *Artemesion*, the month sacred to Artemis, which is the Greek name for Diana.

Ephesus was a city of great religious importance. It was best known for its temple to the fertility goddess Artemis (Roman Diana). The temple was outside the city, and it had thousands of priests and priestesses, most of whom were devoted to sacred prostitution. Ephesus was also home to sacred temples devoted to some of the Roman emperors. The imperial cult thrived in the city.

According to Acts 19:19-20 we learn that people in Ephesus showed great interest in magic and sorcery. There was also a significant Jewish population.

Against the backdrop of a busy seaport, a sizable population, a sophisticated culture, pagan temple worship, and the practice of magic, the church in Ephesus existed. For God's people in Ephesus to learn what being church really meant was important.

Identification of Christ. John begins by identifying the action of the risen Christ. This description of Christ was mentioned earlier in 1:13 and 20. "The words of him who holds the seven stars in his right hand, who walks among the seven golden lampstands" (2:1). These stars represent another level of symbolism being added to the angels, for Revelation 1:20 clearly says, "The seven stars are the angels of the seven churches." However we interpret the angels—pastors, manifestations of the church's spiritual life, or supernatural beings—John assures the readers that they are held securely in the hand of God's sovereignty, the right hand.

Notice the two participles used in this identification of

Christ—"holds" and "walks." The word "hold" means to get a firm grip. This special action of Christ indicates his absolute power and sovereign protection over the churches. He holds the messengers of the churches in his right hand, the hand of power. The word "walks" communicates the presence of Christ with his people and the awareness of their activities. Christ is present in his church.

Commendation. In verses 2-3, the risen Christ cites three commendable qualities about the church in Ephesus. "I know your works, your toil and your patient endurance, and how you cannot bear with those who are evil, but have tested those who call themselves apostles and are not, and found them to be false. I know you are enduring patiently and bearing up for my name's sake, and you have not grown weary" (2:2-3). These praises did not arise out of human information but from divine insight. The word "know" appears three times in Christ's commendation of the church. The verb is used in all seven letters. It means intimate acquaintance with the church. Everything in the church, good or bad, is known perfectly by Christ.

Christ first compliments the church for its exceptional energy—"works, toil, patient endurance." The word "works" describes the business, employment, or that with which anyone is occupied. Two nouns, "toil" and "patient endurance" stand in opposition to "works." The word "toil" means labor to the point of exhaustion. "Patient endurance" comes from two Greek words meaning "to abide under." This suggests the steadfastness that bears up under the burdens of service or suffering.

Christ also knows the incredible intolerance of the church for evildoers. "You cannot bear with those who are evil, but have tested those who call themselves apostles and are not." "Those who are evil" probably was a descriptive of false teachers. It could refer to moral or spiritual evil. The church tested those who claimed to be apostles. Perhaps the test involved belief about Christ. Apparently the evildoers acted like wandering teachers going from house to house calling themselves apostles. These Ephesian believers found this work to be false. Ephesus came to be known as a church that would not tolerate false teachers.

Christ gives a third commendation to the church: the patient perseverance of the church in tough circumstances. "You are enduring patiently and bearing up for my name's sake, and you have not grown weary." The Lord returns to the church's patient endurance in trying circumstances. These believers had endured "for my name's sake." This means they had stood up for Christ numerous times in the midst of persecution and against the false teachers.

Reprimand. The complimentary note changes abruptly—"but" (*alla*) in verse 4. "But I have this against you, that you have abandoned the love you had at first" (2:4). The church at Ephesus had abundant energy and doctrinal orthodoxy, but it lacked one thing. That lack undid all the good the other virtues might have done. They lacked Christian love.

The expression about the love the believers had at first included both love of God and love for other human beings. A cooling of personal love for God inevitably results in the loss of meaningful relationships within the community of Christ. Jesus had made clear that "by this all people will know that you are my disciples, if you have love for one another" (John 13:35). Brotherly love was the distinctive characteristic of Christian discipleship. In the Ephesian church hatred of heresy and excessive involvement in Christian ministry allowed the first enthusiasm for Christ and one another fade.[4] Their early love had grown cold and had been replaced with a zeal for orthodoxy and a passion for busyness.

Exhortation. The solution to the problem of an abandoned first love took the form of a series of imperatives. "Remember therefore from where you have fallen; repent, and do the works

---

[4] Mounce, *The Book of Revelation*, 88.

you did at first. If not, I will come to you and remove your lampstand from its place, unless you repent. Yet this you have: you hate the work of the Nicolaitans, which I also hate" (2:5-6). Christ first calls the Ephesians to remember. It means a continuous calling to memory. It is a forgetfulness of love that leads to a cold heart. They were to call to mind what God had done in the past among and within the Ephesian Christians.

Christ also commands the church to repent. Remembering is the basis of repentance. It was a call for a change of mind, attitude, and conduct. They were to change their minds toward Christ and their fellow believers.

Christ's third exhortation to the church involved repeating former works. The one thing a person can do to demonstrate the reality of repentance is to live a new kind of life. These believers needed to repeat acts of love for God and for one another.

These three commands end with a sharp warning that if they did not heed Christ's commands, serious consequences could occur. It would mean the removal of the lampstand from its place. The church is essentially a light-bearing community. If it ceases to give light, it ceases to be the church. With all of its doctrinal integrity and extreme busyness, their church was in danger of ceasing to lose its influence.

Almost as an afterthought, John offered another compliment to the church. They hated the work of the Nicoliatans, which Christ also disliked. The evidence for identifying this group is not sufficient to be dogmatic. They are mentioned only in Revelation 2:6 and 2:15. Church fathers have reported that the Nicoliatans were corrupt both in doctrine and in morals. They practiced immorality on the grounds of spiritual liberty.

The message for the church in Ephesus was meant to be heard and obeyed. "He who has an ear, let him hear what the Spirit says to the churches" (2:7). Notice the use of the plural—"churches." The whole church is to receive and live what is said to each one of the seven churches.

Promise. The letter to the church in Ephesus closes with a promise. "To the one who conquers I will grant to eat of the tree of life, which is in the paradise of God" (2:7). The word "conquers" appears in the promise section to each one of the seven churches. It is a military or athletic metaphor that describes superiority and victory over a defeated foe. The church's victory is a participation in Christ's victory. To be a Christian conqueror means a daily walk with God and a dependence on his strength.

The reward for the faithful is striking. They will participate in the blessing intended at creation but never realized for Adam and Eve—"to eat of the tree of life." The word "life" means fellowship with God through Christ here and in the life beyond. The word "paradise" was used by the Persians to describe royal pleasure parks. In the New Testament the word is used three times (Luke 23:43; 2 Cor. 12:4; Rev 2:7) as a synonym for heaven, the abode of the redeemed. This tree symbolizes eternal life which comes only from God and which only those in relationship with God will ever know.

Smyrna
2:8-11

The second message of Christ to the churches goes to Smyrna. The city was located forty miles due north of Ephesus. It is the only one of the seven still in existence as an inhabited city (modern Izmir, Turkey). The city suffered destruction on two occasions, and it was rebuilt after each destruction.

We have no knowledge about the origin of the church at Smyrna. Christians from Ephesus could have come to the city, and people were converted. We do know from this letter to Smyrna in Revelation that Smyrna is one of two churches (the other being Philadelphia) who received no criticism. Also, we know that a man named Polycarp was bishop of Smyrna. In AD 155, some Jews joined with the Romans in accusing him of hostility to the state religion. The Jews helped gather wood to light the fire in which Polycarp was burned to death. Apparently, there was a deep faithfulness to Christ when Revelation was written, and it lasted through subsequent years.

Address. The address is the same as the one to Ephesus. Only the name of the city changed. "And to the angel of the church in Smyrna write" (2:8). Smyrna was a great trade city. It stood on a deep gulf that gave it a magnificent harbor. It was at the end of the road from the valley of the river Hermus, and all the trade of that valley flowed onto its markets and formed an outlet through its harbor.[5]

Smyrna was a beautiful city. It claimed to be "the Glory of Asia." It was built in the fourth century BC, and it was a model of city planning. Straight, spacious streets ran from one end of the city to the other.[6]

Smyrna was a proud city. It boasted of its famous stadium, library, and public theater. The theater was the largest in Asia. One of Smyrna's famous monuments was a monument to Homer, whose birthplace it claimed to be.

Religion thrived in Smyrna. It was evidenced by its temples of Aphrodite, Apollo, Asclepius, Cybele, and Zeus. The residents also sustained a close relationship with Rome and the imperial cult. They built a temple in honor of Emperor Tiberius in AD 26. The city became a center for emperor worship.

Being a Christian in Smyrna was no easy matter. Christians could have been overwhelmed by the heathen splendor

---

[5] William Barclay, *Letters to the Seven Churches* (Louisville: Westminster John Knox Press, 2001), 15.

[6] Ibid.

surrounding them. They could have lived in silence about their relationship with Christ and remained safe. They could have confessed, "Caesar is Lord," and their lives would have been easier. They could have been angry over the unjust slander from the Jews. But, as we shall see, the church remained faithful to Christ amid a secular culture and a plurality of religions.

Identification of Christ. Christ introduces himself to the church with two appropriate titles. "The words of the first and last, who died and came to life" (2:8). These titles were specifically selected to meet the needs of the church in Smyrna. Using the first title, "first and last," he described himself as the eternal Christ. He has always existed and will always exist. This persecuted church needed to hear that Christ will always be preeminent over all things, and he will always be present with his people no matter what they face.

The second title, "who died and came to life," referred to Christ's resurrection. The verb "came" is in the aorist tense, which meant a definite act completed in time. The world took away Jesus' life, but he returned from the grave alive. Persecutors could take away earthly existence, but Jesus guarantees a future life. A church suffering like Smyrna needed the assurance that their ultimate future was secure even though their present lives were lived in great distress.

Commendation. The church at Smyrna received no criticism. Rather than speaking of knowing their work, Jesus tells about knowing their condition. "I know your tribulation and your poverty (but you are rich) and the slander on the part of those who say that they are Jews and are not, but are a synagogue of Satan" (2:9). These believers faced trouble. The word for "tribulation" (*thlipsis*) means pressure. It was a general word that described all the sufferings of the church. This affliction was probably produced by physical persecutions.

Because of the persecution, the church in Smyrna

experienced poverty. In some cases the homes of Christians in Smyrna had been deliberately pillaged and plundered. Also, some had likely lost their jobs because they professed, and it helped produce their poverty. Every time poverty is mentioned in Revelation, it is contrasted in some way with riches. Though the Christians in Smyrna were poor, they had an abundance of true and durable riches.

Jesus also knows the criticism the church received from the Jews. The word "slander" (*blasphemia*) means railing, detraction, and speed injurious to another character. The Jews did not accept Jesus as their Messiah. The Jews slandered the Christians to the Roman authorities, which made the believers appear to be disloyal to Roman law. John gave a stirring denunciation of these Jews' claiming to be the people of God. They said they were Jews, but they were not. These Jews may have called themselves "the synagogue of God,' but John said they were actually "a synagogue of Satan." The choice of the term "Satan" was deliberate, for it depicted this archenemy of God and his people as supremely hostile to God.

Exhortation. Christ's exhortation to the church living under these adverse conditions comes in the form of a prediction and a word of encouragement. "Do not fear what you are about to suffer. Behold, the devil is about to throw some of you into prison, that you may be tested, and for ten days you will have tribulation" (2:10). Oddly enough, the word of encouragement came before the predictions. Christ tells the church to stop being afraid. They were not to be afraid of what they were about to suffer. In the midst of terrible troubles, God's people are called to fearless endurance and witness.

The believers were not to fear imminent and unavoidable suffering. Hardship is "about" to happen. Jesus makes no promises about an easy life for believers. Instead, he assures his people of his comforting presence in the midst of suffering. This imminent suffering was clarified by imminent imprisonment. Some of the believers would be thrown into prison. In the ancient world prisons were not so much places of punishment as places of detention for people awaiting trial. The result could be in release or some sort of punishment, including death.

The purpose of these future persecutions was that they might be tempted for their faith. The oppression would last only ten days. This was a symbolic number that meant the believer would suffer for a brief period of time. The ten days probably served as a comparison with their short time of suffering and the duration of the life forever.

Promise. Christ encourages the church to be faithful even though their faithfulness may lead to death. "Be faithful unto death, and I will give you the crown of life. He who has an ear, let him hear what the Spirit says to the churches. The one who conquers will not be hurt by the second death" (2:10–11). Jesus promises a "crown of life" to those who remain faithful. The crown (*stephonos*) was the crown worn by victorious athletes and warriors. The content of the crown for the Christian is "life." The reward for believers is God's kind of life now, which also continues beyond death and throughout eternity. The call to hear what the Spirit says to the churches is repeated.

Jesus also promises that the believers will never be harmed by the second death. The believers were called conquerors because, while they might lose their earthly lives, they would never experience the second death. The "first death," or physical death, separates one from friends and relations. The "second death" separates one from God. Faithfulness to Christ on earth may bring death on earth, but it brings life in eternity.

The message to the church in Smyrna relates to churches throughout history, as it did to them. Believers will go through hardships brought on by the living of life or by being faithful to Christ amid opposition. Christ's word for Smyrna and other believers is not to fear but to be faithful. The eternal Christ has defeated death. He knows our trials and controls our future.

Pergamum
2:12–17

Sixty-five miles north of Smyrna and fifteen miles from the Aegean Sea lay Pergamum. The city claimed fame in John's day as the capital of the Roman province of Asia. Pergamum did not have the commercial prominence as Ephesus or Smyrna, for its geographical position prohibited it. Though it was inferior in trade, it was superior in historical greatness. The Roman author Pliny reported that it was "by far the most distinguished city in Asia."[7]

There was a church in Pergamum in John's day, but we do not know how it originated. The church, like others in Asia, could have been formed by Paul's converts when he was in Ephesus. These believers lived in the midst of the enormous influence of paganism. Christ has a message to this church about being faithful to the truth.

Address. Jesus addressed the church in Pergamum: "And to the angel of the church in Pergamum write" (2:12). Pergamum occupied a visual prominence overlooking the Caikus Valley. The city had one of the most famous libraries in the world. The library contained more than 200,000 volumes, second in volume only to Alexandria. One of the writing materials of the early centuries of Christianity got its name from Pergamum. It was called parchment from the Latin *pergamena charta* (paper of Pergamum). Parchment was made from animal skins.

Pergamum was a religious city. It was the first place in all the empire to give divine honors to the Roman emperor. In 29 BC an altar was dedicated to Augustus. Emperor worship spread from the city to other places in the province.

---

[7]Mounce, *The Book of Revelation*, 95.

Other religions also flourished in Pergamum. It was a center for worship of four prominent pagan cults of the day—Zeus, Athena, Dionysius, and Asklepios. The shrine of Asklepios, the god of healing, attracted people from all over the world.

The church in Pergamum had to exist in a city proud of its political position. They had to live in an environment of academic pride and religious pluralism. The simple worship of the church took place against the background of the worship of the Olympian gods. Against all of these odds, people in Pergamum held fast to their faith in Christ.

Identification of Christ. Christ identified himself appropriately in light of the church's location: "The words of him who has the sharp two-edged sword" (2:12). This description of Christ came from the Thracian broadsword the Romans used in cavalry charges. This sword became a symbol of Roman might. It was used in Christ's identification probably because the Roman proconsul who lived in Pergamum was in charge of the province. The sword was a symbol of Roman sovereignty, especially to execute enemies of the state. Christ tells the church that he, not the Roman officiate, is the true judge.[8]

This sword is Christ's word of judgment on a church that has grown lax in its attitudes toward pagan practices. This sword emphasizes the penetration of truth. Truth is the only weapon Christ uses in his conflict with evil. It is a weapon or judgment ("two-edged").

Commendation. Christ offers some words of praise to the church at Pergamum. "I know where you dwell, where Satan's throne is. Yet you hold fast my name, and you did not deny my faith even in the days of Antipas my faithful witness, who was killed among you, where Satan dwells" (2:13). Christ commends the church for its strategic location in such a pagan environment.

---

[8]Osborne, *Revelation*, 140.

The Christ with the two-edged sword knows about the wicked place his followers lived. The reference to "Satan's throne" more than likely referred to the fact that it was a center of emperor worship. These believers lived in a city where worship of the emperor took place and where gods and goddesses existed in abundance. Life has placed them where Satan was.

Christ also commends the church for their faithfulness to Christ. They held fast to his name. Much in Pergamum was designed to pry them loose from Christ, but they held on tenaciously to him. They continued with their living relationship with him.

Christ commends the believers for not denying their faith at a tough time. The Greek aorist tense of "deny" points to a particular action completed in the past time. Christians must have remained true during some definite time of crisis in Pergamum.

One martyr of Pergamum was mentioned by name. We know nothing historically about Antipas. He was probably killed for his audacious witness and failure to acknowledge Caesar as lord. Jesus gave Antipas the title "my faithful witness." In Revelation 1:5 Christ called himself "the faithful witness," and that is the title he gave to Antipas. To suffer for Christ is in the end to share in the glory of Christ.

Reprimand. The tone of Christ's message changes. The praise stops and the rebuke begins. "But I have a few things against you: you have some there who hold the teaching of Balaam, who taught Balak to put a stumbling block before the people of Israel, so that they might eat food sacrificed to idols and practice sexual immorality. So also you have some who hold the teaching of the Nicolaitans" (2:14–15). The Pergamum Christians held fast to Jesus' name and did not renounce their faith in him under the pressure of persecution, but they allowed pagan morals to influence them. A group had arisen in Pergamum who held the teaching of Balaam. Balak, the king of Moab, was threatened by the Israelites. He invited the prophet Balaam to curse the Israelites. God restrained Balaam, and to Balak's disgust he blessed them rather than cursing them (Num. 22-24). Afterwards, Israel got involved in harlotry and in idolatrous worship of Baal. This sin was attributed to the advice of Balaam (Num. 31:16). Balaam afterwards became a symbol of those who promote compromises with idolatry and immorality.[9]

The understanding of the phrase "food sacrificed to idols" must be taken from its context. It comes from a single Greek word. It could refer either to meats purchased in the public market that had been sacrificed in a pagan temple, or it could refer to feasts celebrated in the temples in honor of the various gods. More than likely the reference is to participation in the temple feasts, which amounts to worship of a pagan deity. The reference to "practice sexual immorality" could refer to the sexual conduct associated with the feasts.

The mention of the Nicolaitans connects it with the cult of Balaam. These Nicolaitans carried out a project reminiscent of Balaam. Perhaps they advocated that Christians could cooperate with Rome. They rationalized that attendance and participation in the pagan ceremonies could prevent conflict with the system.

Exhortation. The indifference of the church at Pergamum to the practices of the pagan was a matter of considerable concern. Jesus has a strong word for the Pergamum Christians who compromised with pagan practices. "Therefore repent. If not, I will come to you soon and war against them with the sword of my mouth. He who has an ear, let him hear what the Spirit says to the churches" (2:16-17). The entire church is summoned to repent of a problem of which only a few were guilty. The problems of the Pergamum church were tolerance and laxity.

The whole church is to repent of its tolerance. The verb

---

[9] George Eldon L, *A Commentary on the Revelation of John* (Grand Rapids: William B. Eerdmans, 1972), 47.

"repent" means to change previous ways, both spiritually and ethically. Christ wants the believers to change their approach and take a strong stance against the fake teachers. If these believers refuse to repent, Christ will come quickly. This does not refer to the final return but to his judgment in the believers' lifetime. Jesus declares war on the imitators of Balaam and on the Nicolaitans. He will war with them with his word. Christ's words are like a sharp sword. They penetrate deep into the soul.

Christ urges the church to pay attention. Listening to pagan ideas and practicing them are serious matters. To "hear" Christ's exhortation to repentance is to obey, and it is a call to put Christ's exhortation into practice in their church.

Promise. For those who repent Christ promises victory. "To the one who conquers I will give some of the hidden manna, and I will give him a white stone, with a new name written on the stone that no one knows except the one who receives it" (2:17). Christ's promises to the conquerors relate to the situation in Pergamum. The term "hidden manna" relates to a well-known Jewish legend. Many said that Jeremiah had taken the jar of manna from the ark of the covenant and buried it in a cave on Mount Nebo at the time of the temple's destruction in 586 BC. The tradition promised that the manna would be miraculously preserved until the Messiah comes. The manna would become again food for God's people. This picture seems to symbolize the sustenance given by God to his people.[10]

The meaning of the white stone is not as obvious. White stones had a variety of uses in the ancient world. The white stones were used as signs of becoming acquitted in court, tickets of admission to public festivals, and numerous other usages. Probably the meaning that fits is the believer's admission to the Messianic

---

[10] Ibid., 48–49.

feast. It is not clear whether the "new name" refers to the names of Christ or the character given to the holder of the stone. In either case, the white stone means entrance and participation in the Messianic kingdom.

Christ knows the Pergamum believers are surrounded by a pagan society. Throughout history churches face the same problem as the Pergamum church. Believers live in Satan's realm, and they face the pressure to compromise and conform. Christ wants his people to be faithful to him and hold fast to truth both in doctrine and deed.

Chapter 4
The Church during History, Part 2
Revelation 2:18–3:27

Thyatira, Sardis, Philadelphia, Laodicea

Thyatira
2:18–29

THE LONGEST OF THE SEVEN LETTERS is written to the church in the smallest and least important town. It became a Roman city in 190 BC, partly due to its strategic site. It was located in the kingdom of Lydia and situated on a main road from Pergamum to Sardis.

No one can be certain about the origin of the Christian community in Thyatira. Speculations have been made that Lydia, a newborn Christian, returned to her home from a meeting with Paul in Philippi. Some think she returned from Philippi to establish a community of believers in Thyatira. Whether this happened or not, there was a church to whom John wrote Revelation.

Address. Once more the angel of the church is addressed. "And to the angel of the church in Thyatira write" (2:18). Thyatira was located on the Lycus river. Its location made it a city of some commercial importance. It was a manufacturing center and especially famous for its wool trade and its purple dye.

Thyatira had numerous trade guilds. Many of these guilds

were associated with the textile industry. These trade guilds had common meals which were probably dedicated to some pagan deity. These guilds and their practices became a problem for the Christians in Thyatira. In order to participate in a trade, a person had to be a member of the appropriate guild. Questions arose about whether believers should belong and participate in the guilds. Some believers compromised and participated, for they reasoned that the pagan deities did not exist. The problem was compounded because many of these communal guild meals ended in unbridled sexual activity. A small group in the church advocated full participation in heathen social life.

Thyatira did possess a few temples, but it was not a strong center for emperor worship. A few Jews in Thyatira troubled the church. The divine guardian of the city was the god Tyrimnos (identified with the Greek god Apollo). This god was conceived as patron of the guilds and therefore honored in the guild festivals.[11]

Identification of Christ. Christ describes himself as "the Son of God." This is the only place in Revelation where this title is used. "The words of the Son of God, who has eyes like a flame of fire, and whose feet are like burnished bronze" (2:18). The reason for Christ's using this title was most likely in the centrality of Tyrimnos (Apollo) in Thya¹tira. Jesus, not Tyrimnos, is the true Son of God. This is a frequent title in the Gospel of John, and it connotes mystery and divinity. This faltering church needed to center on the true "Son of God."

The next two descriptions of Christ—"eyes like a flame of fire" and feet "like burnished bronze"—come from the inaugural vision of Christ (1:14–15). These images emphasize Christ's all-searching insight and his power to trample down and destroy

---

[1] Mounce, *The Book of Revelation*, 101.

enmity and resistance.

Commendation. Christ's intimate knowledge of both the city and the church prompts him to praise the believers. "I know your works, your love and faith and service and patient endurance, and that your latter works exceed the first" (2:19). Four words are used to commend the church. "Love" comes first on the list. Love is the primary characteristic of those who call themselves children of God. "Faith" appears next in the praise. It describes trust in God and faithfulness in the midst of oppression and pressure from the pagans. "Service" appears only here in Revelation, and it refers to an active life of care and help. It describes charitable deeds and ministry to others. "Patient endurance" comes from one Greek word. It means commitment to an active performance in the midst of pressure and hard times. Christ commends the church for their faithfulness to God and for their care of others.

The qualities praised in the church were not diminishing. "Your last works are greater than the first." They were continuing to grow in their good deeds. This is high praise.

Reprimand. Though the church in Thyatira had commendable qualities, it receives a reprimand.

> But I have this against you, that you tolerate that woman Jezebel, who calls herself a prophetess and is teaching and seducing my servants to practice sexual immorality and to eat food sacrificed to idols. I gave her time to repent, but she refuses to repent of her sexual immorality. Behold, I will throw her onto a sickbed and those who commit adultery with her I will throw into great tribulation, unless they repent of her works, and I will strike her children dead. And all the churches will know that I am he who searches mind and heart, and I will give to each

of you according to your works. But to the rest of you in Thyatira, who do not hold this teaching, who have not learned what some call the deep things of Satan, to you I say, I do not lay on you any other burden (2:20-24).

We cannot be certain about which immoral practices are being censured. The connection of eating may give a clue. There had arisen in the church a woman for whom Jezebel was the symbol. Ahab's queen, Jezebel, supported idolatry, and the woman with her persuasion led some to idolatry in Thyatira. She probably encouraged participation in the local trade guild.

The trade guild's social life included adoration of heathen gods, the offering of foods to these gods in worshipful sacrifice, and a variety of sexual adventures. Jezebel reasoned that one must do whatever one must do to be acceptable in the trade guild.

Christ offers a time for repentance to Jezebel and to those who follow her. Failing to repent would result in severe punishment. She is to be cast into a bed, and her followers will experience great distress. The bed seems to symbolize punishment for her practices. God comes to punish the woman and her followers in some fashion, probably known specifically to him. Jezebel's sins pollute the mind, ruin the body, destroy the conscience, and paralyze the will of those who practice them. This judgment on Jezebel and her followers will let all the churches know about Christ's authority and power in judgment.

Christ turns his attention to the church as a whole to talk about judgment. He has the ability to see the good and the bad in each community of believers. He will reward the good and judge the evil.

Some of the members in Thyatira did not practice the sins of Jezebel. The libertine, or free thinking, lifestyle of Jezebel and her followers assumed that a Christian could take part in heathen practices and remain unaffected. In fact, by participating in these things of Satan, the Christian could supposedly show superiority over them. It is possible that the heretics in Thyatira show an early tendency toward Gnosticism.

Exhortation. Christ gives a simple exhortation to the church in Thyatira. "Only hold fast what you have until I come" (2:25). He calls for believers to keep a firm grasp on the truths of Christian faith and practice. Christ does not give a list of new demands. He merely commands them to continue in their faithfulness to Christ and to avoid the pagan feasts with their idolatrous associations and their immoral practices. The expression "until I come" points to the final coming of Christ. Expecting the imminent return of Christ promotes morality and service.

Promise. Christ has a twofold promise to the victors over Jezebel. "The one who conquers and keeps my works until the end, to him I will give authority over the nations, and he will rule them with a rod of iron, as when earthen pots are broken in pieces, even as I myself have received authority from my Father. And I will give him the morning star" (2:26-28). Those who conquer—that is, overcome the temptations of Jezebel to conform to the pagan culture—will receive power to rule by Christ. This promise fulfills Psalm 2, which tells how the Father gave the Messiah the power to rule over the nations. The reign of Christ is to be shared with his followers. The promise of a greater power to rule is a constant encouragement to suffering Christians.

Christ's power to rule comes from a practice of Egyptian and Mesopotamian kings. They would write the names of their enemies on earthen pots and then smash them. This practice portrayed Christ's sovereignty over his enemies. The followers of Christ share in this power to rule on earth, and they anticipate Christ's ultimate rule beyond history. The next promise is that believers will be given the morning star. The morning star is known for its brightness. It signals the sign of dawn, the promise of a new day. Christ himself is the morning star. He shares light with his followers. This light given by Christ rises over the darkness of the world's persecution and signals a new era, the reign of Christ now and his ultimate reign forever.

Christ concludes his message to the church in Thyatira with a call to listen. "He who has an ear, let him hear what the Spirit says to the churches" (2:29). The challenge for churches is to find a way to be a part of the society in which they live without losing their identity as the people of God. H. Richard Niebuhr, in his book *Christ and Culture*, looked at various approaches the church could take to relate to society. He adopted the position that Christ is the transformer of culture.

The situation in Thyatira is curiously modern. When membership in a business society demands conduct and practice that are not Christian, what is a Christian to do? Many believers in today's world face the compromise with pagan culture as confronted the Christians in Thyatira nineteen hundred years ago.

Sardis
3:1–6

Thirty miles southeast of Thyatira, near Mount Tmolus, lay Sardis. The glory of Sardis was in the past. In the sixth century BC Sardis had been the capital city of Lydia and later a center of Persian government. In New Testament times the city was obscure.

Sardis was located high above Mount Tmolus as an almost impregnable citadel. It jutted out from a northern spur of the mount on a massive, solid-rock pier fifteen hundred feet above the plain. It towered as a testimony to the safety Sardis had built for itself. But, according to history, the residents of Sardis became lax and suffered loss. In 549 BC Cyrus, and in 216 BC Antiochus the Great, slipped into the supposedly safe city and destroyed it.

When John wrote Revelation, a church existed in Sardis. No one knows how the church came into existence. All we know about the church in Sardis is what is written in Revelation 3:1–6.

Address. The address to the church at Sardis follows the same form as the previous four churches: "And to the angel of the church in Sardis write" (3:1). The city of Sardis was a commercial center. The gold-bearing river called the Pactolus ran through it. It was a thriving center for the wool industry. Five major Roman roads going through the city helped make it an important industrial center.

Sardis was an active religious city. Many of the residents were devoted to the nature goddess, Cybele. Sardis was not a center for emperor worship, although it wanted to be. Recent archaeological digs have revealed one of the largest Jewish synagogues in the area. It had the capacity to hold one thousand people. In the latter part of the first century, Saris must have had large and influential communities of Jews. The Christians in Sardis lived primarily in the religious atmosphere of a mystery goddess, the Jews, and emperor worship.

Identification of Christ. As in the other letters, the names of Christ mentioned are critical to Sardis. "The words of him who has the seven spirits of God and the seven stars" (3:1). The "seven spirits of God" refer to the fullness of the Holy Spirit's work. The church at Sardis, which was almost dead, could only be revived by the Holy Spirit.[2]

The "seven stars" symbolize the messengers of the churches (1:16, 20). The verb "has" communicates Christ's control of the churches and his concern and care for them. Although the church had fallen into spiritual complacency, she was still the object of Christ's care.

Reprimand. Christ has no commendation for the church in Sardis. His message begins immediately with criticism. "I know your works. You have the reputation of being alive, but you are

---

[2] George Eldon Ladd, *A Commentary on the Revelation of John*, 55.

dead" (3:1). Christ reprimands the church out of intimate knowledge: "I know." Outwardly the church appeared to be alive. But Christ knew the actual condition of the church. He looks beyond appearance. He said, "You are dead." Indifference to the pagan culture evidently lulled the church slowly into death.

Exhortation. When Christ reprimands a church, he follows with solutions to the problem. "Wake up, and strengthen what remains and is about to die, for I have not found your works complete in the sight of God. Remember, then, what you received and heard. Keep it, and repent" (3:2-3). The Lord gives exhortations to correct the church's deadness: wake up, strengthen, remember, keep, and repent. First, Christ calls the church to spiritual vigilance—"wake up." The church had become like the city. On two occasions Sardis fell because the watchmen were not on the walls, and the enemies climbed the cliffs to take the city.

Second, Christ calls the church to "strengthen what remains." This admonition indicates that the church was not entirely beyond hope. It was not too late to allow God to work with a small minority who showed signs of life.

Christ has found the works of the church inadequate. The church did not seem to be troubled by heresy; it was not concerned over the Jewish opposition. The church had a reputation for its vigorous activity, but in the sight of God their works were mere formality and not infused with the Holy Spirit's life.

The next three imperatives—remember, keep, and repent—came out of the church's incomplete works. The solution for spiritual inadequacy is to remember and repent. The imperative "remember" demands a continual recalling of the past truths they had learned and the past works they had done. The two verbs "received" and "heard" tell the two ways truth came to the church. The next imperative—"keep"—means to obey what they have heard and received. Finally, and that which summarizes the other exhortation, is the call to repentance. They are to change their minds, which will lead to the change of direction in their spiritual lives.

If the church does not awaken to its spiritual lethargy, Christ will visit them in judgment. "If you do not wake up, I will come like a thief, and you will not know what hour I will come against you" (3:3*b*). This does not seem to be a reference to Christ's final coming but a historical visitation in judgment. The final coming is taught in 2:25; 3:11; and 16:15, but this is a warning that Christ will come in judgment unless the church repents.

Promise. Christ precedes his promise to the church with a word of encouragement to the righteous remnant in Sardis. "Yet you have still a few names in Sardis, people who have not soiled their garments, and they will walk with me in white, for they are worthy" (3:4). These people had not conformed to the pagan culture in Sardis. The imagery of soiled clothes comes from one of the sources of wealth at Sardis, the wool industry. By accommodating themselves to the pagan environment, the church had become soiled.

Christ continues the imagery of garments as a symbol for the spiritual life. He promises a new life ("walk") of purity. The evaluation that they are "worthy" does not mean they merited salvation. It means they continue to follow Christ's pattern for life.

Christ makes promises to the conquerors in the church. "The one who conquers will be clothed thus in white garments, and I will never blot his name out of the book of life. I will confess his name before my Father and before his angels" (3:5). The conqueror is the believer who remains faithful in the midst of pressure from the pagans. There are three rewards. First, the conqueror will be clothed in white garments. These garments seem to represent the gradual growth in Christ's character during their lifetime, and the garments they are to be clothed in are their resurrection bodies. Second, the conquerors will not be blotted out of the book of life. In the Old Testament the book of life was a register of those who held citizenship in the covenant community of Israel. God's book of life contains the names of his children. They will never be removed from this book of life.

Third, Christ promises to confess the believers' names before the Father and the angels. He acknowledges to the Father those who have confessed him as Lord in their earthly existence. Faithfulness to Christ during hardships in this life will be rewarded beyond comparison in the life to come.

A repetitive refrain comes at the conclusion of the letter, "He who has an ear, let him hear what the Spirit says to the churches" (3:6). We can hope that the church of Sardis heeded Christ's message. Even if they did not, the church must heed his message today. Just having the reputation for life is not enough. Churches in today's world must possess an inward reality and purity of life pleasing to God. They need a life invigorated by the power of the Holy Spirit.[3]

Philadelphia
3:7-13

Twenty-eight miles southeast of Sardis lay the city of Philadelphia. It had been founded by Attalus the Second in 140 BC. His affection for his older brother, Eumenes II, king of Pergamum at the time, earned for him the title *Philadelphus*, "brother lover." They city was named Philadelphia, "the city of brotherly love."

We have no record about the founding of a church in Philadelphia. In fact, all we know about the church is what appears in Revelation 3:7-13. The church was inwardly faithful, but outwardly it was weak and suffering. The church receives no rebukes. The risen Christ commends and commands it to greater service for him.

---

[3] John R.W. Stott, *What Christ Thinks of the Church* (Wheaton: Harold Shaw Publishers, 1990), 93.

Address. Like the previous five churches, John gives an address to the angel: "And to the angel of the church in Philadelphia write" (3:7). Philadelphia unfortunately had been built on a geological fault. It had frequent earthquakes. In AD 17 a severe earthquake devastated the city.

Philadelphia stood where the borders of three countries—Mysia, Lydia, and Phrygia—met. Because of its position it was called "Gateway to the East." Beyond Philadelphia lay the wilds of Phrygia and the barbarous tribes, and the function of Philadelphia was intended to spread the Greek language, the Greek way of life, and the Greek civilization to the regions beyond.[4]

Though emperor worship was not rampant in Philadelphia, the residents were devoted to Rome. In the early third century AD an imperial temple was built. The main religion of Philadelphia was the cult of Dionysius, the god of wine. It also had many other gods and temples, so many that it was called "little Athens."

Throughout this letter to the church in Philadelphia, the message of Christ came to the people in language and symbols they could understand. Jesus used their history, the things of daily life, and civic practices and spoke his heavenly message.

Identification of Christ. The message to the church begins with two great descriptions of the risen Christ. "The words of the holy one, the true one, who has the key of David, who opens and no one will shut, who shuts and no one opens" (3:7). Christ describes himself in Old Testament terms. In Jewish culture the holy one was a familiar title for God. Christ joins it with "the true one." The Jewish presence in Philadelphia denied Christ as the Messiah. But Christ assures them that he is the authentic Messiah, and he can be trusted to carry his messianic task to completion.

Christ next describes himself as having "the key of David." This was a metaphorical expression depicting complete control

---

[4]William Barclay, *Letters to the Seven Churches*, 67–68.

over the royal household. It means the authority to admit or to exclude. Christ has the absolute power to control entrance to the heavenly kingdom. Perhaps their identification of Christ came because of the claim of some Jews in Philadelphia. They claimed to be the true people of God. Christ claims to be the Messiah of Jewish expectation; he alone allows access into the Messianic kingdom.

Commendation. Christ gives a threefold compliment to the church in Philadelphia. "I know your works. Behold, I have set before you an open door, which no one is able to shut" (3:8). As with Smyrna, there is nothing but approval for the church in Philadelphia. Christ commends the church for its open door. Some think this open door refers to the church's missionary opportunity. Others see this as the entrance to the kingdom. Most of the Jewish Christians had been excommunicated from the synagogues, but Christ has the keys to the kingdom. He opens it, and no one can shut it. Christ first commends the church for walking through the entrance into the kingdom.

Christ next commends the church for its obedience. "I know that you have but little power, and yet you have kept my word and have not denied my name" (3:8). The "little power" probably described the smallness of the congregation. Their true strength is affirmed in that they have obeyed Christ's word. They have not failed under pressure by denying Christ. They gave a faithful witness to him.

Christ commends the Christians in Philadelphia for being victorious over their Jewish opponents. "I will make those of the synagogue of Satan who say that they are Jews and are not, but lie—behold, I will make them come and bow down before your feet and they will learn that I have loved you" (3:9). The Jews earned the title "synagogue of Satan" because they rejected Jesus as Messiah and because they made slanderous accusations of the Christians. The Jews will be made to see that the church is the true Israel. All people, Jews included, must make their submission to Christ and his church. The Jews will ultimately be aware that God's true people are those who believe in his Messiah.

Christ also praises the church for its patient endurance. "Because you have kept my word about patient endurance, I will keep you from the hour of trial that is coming on the whole world to try those who dwell on the earth" (3:10). As a result of this steadfast faithfulness, Christ will help them in their earthly trials. These hardships affect not only believers but all the inhabitants of the earth. Christ is with his people to help them with life's hardships. But he promises more! "I am coming soon" (3:11). Christ's return will end the time of trials and establish the church as a permanent resident of the realized Messianic kingdom.

Exhortation. The church in Philadelphia is to face persecution. In light of their inevitable hardship, Christ encourages the church to keep a firm grip on their faith in Christ. "Hold fast what you have, so that no one may seize your crown" (3:11). What did these believers have? It was, of course, their faith in Christ. The present tense of "hold fast" presents a vivid image. It means to keep on holding to your commitment to Christ.

Christ also exhorts the church to guard its quality of life in Christ. In Philadelphia both pagans and Jews slandered the Christians' relationship with Christ. The "crown" seems to be the believers' participation with Christ. The Lord wants his followers to continue in their intimate fellowship with him.

Promise. Christ promises to victors in Philadelphia an absolute security and an enhanced Christian character. "The one who conquers, I will make him a pillar in the temple of my God. Never shall he go out of it, and I will write on him the name of my God, and the name of the city of my God, the new Jerusalem, which comes down from my God out of heaven, and my own new name" (3:12). Being made a pillar in the temple of God symbolized inclusion into the current as well as the future kingdom of God.

This promise has the absolute security where no one will ever be able to put God's people out of the kingdom.

Christ promises to write on the conquerors in three ways. First, he will write on them the name of God. This is the mark of ownership. Second, he will write the name of the city of God. It is a description of heavenly citizenship. Third, Christ writes his own name on believers. It symbolizes the believer's relationship and fellowship with Christ. Abiding in Christ leads to a character resembling Christ.

As in all other five letters, Christ calls the church to respond appropriately to his messages. "He who has an ear, let him hear what the Spirit says to the churches" (3:13). The message to Philadelphia begins and ends with perseverance. This church as well as all churches were urged to overcome all obstacles to the centrality of Christ. The churches will be vindicated. They will be given the character of Christ and citizenship in his kingdom. But they must be faithful.

Laodicea
3:14–22

The city of Laodicea lay forty-three miles southeast of Philadelphia and about a hundred miles from Ephesus. It was one of three cities located in sight of one another in the Lychus Valley. The city was founded by Antiochus II and had been called Laodicea in honor of his wife.

More than likely the church had been founded by Epaphras of Colossae (cf. Col 1:7; 4:12f). Paul was acquainted with the church, for he wrote a letter to the Laodiceans from Rome (cf. Col. 4:16). The letter could be Ephesians, or it could be a lost letter. From Revelation 3:14–22 we learn that the church in Laodicea was prosperous and outwardly in good condition. The letter does not mention persecution from anyone. It appeared to be a church permeated by complacency. The affluence of the city had a powerful influence on the spiritual life of the church.

Address. As in the other six letters, the angel of the church is addressed: "And to the angel of the church in Laodicea write" (3:14). Laodicea had an impressive geographical position. It was situated where the narrow glen of the Lycus River borders the Meander Valley. It controlled the trade coming down to the river to the seacoast. Three roads came to Laodicea. The city's position made it one of the richest centers of the ancient world. It became a banking center because of its great wealth.

Laodicea had two famous businesses. The city was famous for a beautiful black woolen cloth. A celebrated breed of sheep, featuring rich black wool, was indigenous to the area. Laodicea also had the leading medical facility in Asia. It was prominent in the treatment of eye and ear diseases. It exported a famous eye medication called "Phrygean powder."[5]

Laodicea had a large Jewish population. In 62 BC Flaccus, the governor of the province, became alarmed over the amount of money the Jews exported in the payment of temple taxes. He seized one shipment of the Jewish currency, and according to the amount of money seized, it could be determined that seventy-five hundred male Jews lived in Laodicea in addition to women and children. Christians living in a society so permeated with Jewish influence would face great difficulties.

The religion in Laodicea was typical of the times. It was syncretistic, a combination of local and Roman gods. The Phrygian god, Men Karou, was its chief deity, although it was a center for emperor worship.

Identification of Christ. The names of Christ in the in the introductory formula are significant. "The words of the Amen, the faithful and true witness, the beginning of God's creation" (3:14).

---

[5] William Barclay, *The Revelation of John, vol. 1* (Philadelphia: Westminster Press, 1959), 175.

The title "the Amen" probably came from Isaiah 65:16 where God is described as the God of truth, or the God of the Amen. This word "amen" is used to affirm and to guarantee a statement as absolutely true and absolutely trustworthy. To say that Jesus is "the Amen" is to say that Jesus is the personification and affirmation of the truth of God.

Jesus also calls himself "the faithful and true witness." This title amplifies the title "the Amen." It clarifies the trustworthiness of Christ. The final title of Christ is "the origin of God's creation." Jesus is the source, the origin, the moving cause of all creation. To be sure, the Christ who is trustworthy in character and the beginning of creation deserves to be heard and heeded by the believers in Laodicea.

Reprimand. The Laodiceans received no commendation from Christ. Instead, they received the most scathing rebukes of all the churches. Christ first criticizes the church for its lukewarmness. "I know your works; you are neither cold nor hot. Would that you were either cold or hot! So, because you are lukewarm, and neither hot nor cold, I will spit you out of my mouth" (3:15–16). The threefold repetition of the church's being neither cold nor hot indicates the seriousness of the church's condition. The imagery of water temperatures used here would have been understandable to the residents of Laodicea. Six miles to the north was Hierapolis, noted for its natural hot springs. Ten miles to the east was Colossae, where the cold waters of the Lychus River flowed. Hot water flowed from Hierapolis to Colossae, but it became lukewarm by the time it reached Laodicea. Lukewarmness stood for being indifferent, nominal, complacent. Christ would have been pleased with either a fiery zeal or a rigid coldness but not a nauseous lukewarmness.[6]

Christ also criticizes the church for its arrogant spirit. "For

---

[6] Osborne, *Revelation*, 205.

you say, I am rich, I have prospered, and I need nothing" (3:17). Notice the appearance of first-person singular in this claim: "I am . . . I have . . . I need nothing." Their boastful pride and self-sufficiency led them to be blind to the truth. The church that is prosperous materially can easily fall into the self-deception that her outward prosperity is the measure of her spiritual prosperity.

Christ characterizes the church as "not realizing that you are wretched, pitiable, poor, blind, and naked" (3:17). Their state is described by four adjectives that can be separated into two groups. The first two adjectives (wretched and pitiable) describe their general situation, and the next three adjectives (poor, blind, and naked) give a specific description. "Wretched" means extreme unhappiness. "Pitiable" means to have pity on a church that depends on herself rather than on God.

The next three adjectives (poor, blind, naked) come out of the church's association with the city of Laodicea. This condition introduces the exhortation that comes in 3:18–19. These three adjectives described the lack of a vital relationship with Christ.

Exhortation. Christ's council for the church comes from conditions existing in Laodicea. "I counsel you to buy from me gold refined by fire, so that you may be rich, and white garments so that you may clothe yourself and the shame of your nakedness may not be seen, and salve to anoint your eyes, so that you may see" (3:18). Each element in the triple counsel Jesus gives to the church stands as a counterpart to something of which the city of Laodicea boasted. First, in contrast to the Laodicean banking center, the church needs to become rich by buying from Christ gold refined by fire. Of course that means increasing in openness to Christ. Second, though the city prided itself on producing textiles made from the special wool, the church needs from Jesus white garments. This indicates the righteousness of Jesus. Third, in a region known for its eye salve, the church needs an anointing from Christ to help them see spiritual realities.

Christ reminds the Laodicean church that the reprimands come from his love. "Those whom I love, I reprove and discipline, so be zealous and repent" (3:19). Those who fail in their walk with Christ experience a divine love that leads to discipline. Christ's attitude toward the church is not punitive but corrective. The two verbs "reprove" and "discipline" relate to each other. The first verb refers to a rebuke that points to a problem. The second goal refers to training and guidance. Christ's call to repent indicates there is still hope for this church.

The loving compassion exemplified in 3:19 is now exemplified in an invitation. "Behold, I stand at the door and knock. If anyone hears my voice and opens the door, I will come in to him and eat with him, and he with me" (3:20). This invitation is for a lukewarm church to open themselves to Christ and invite him into their lives. If they do so, Christ will enter into a deeper fellowship with them. A shared meal in the ancient Jewish world had a great significance. It was a symbol of affection, of common beliefs, and of intimacy. Real repentance leads to the most intimate fellowship possible with Christ.[7]

Promise. Christ makes a promise to those who repent. "The one who conquers, I will grant him to sit with me on my throne, as I also conquered and sat down with my Father on his throne" (3:21). The conqueror's role is analogous to that of Jesus and the Father. Jesus took his place on the throne by conquering. Jesus defeated sin and death. His victory was the basis of his throne. The victory of believers is based on their overcoming the world and its evil through the power of Christ.

The call to listen and obey appropriately closes the letter to the Laodiceans. "He who has an ear listen, let him hear what the Spirit says to the churches" (3:22). It is the Spirit speaking, not just

---

[7] Ibid., 213.

John's message. Lukewarmness is not to be taken lightly. The message for Laodicea is for every church in every age suffering from complacency.

Chapters 2 and 3 contain a record of what Christ knows about seven churches and what he says to them. What he said, he continues to say. The churches of the first century faced pressure from pagan practices, opposition from local Jews, and the appeal of emperor worship. There were also false teachers within the church. Churches had lost heir first love, experienced death, and suffered from lukewarmness. These churches were in need of a word from Christ. The words of Christ to the churches do not need to be locked in the past. They need to be shared with today's churches.

Chapter 5
The Controller of History

Revelation 4:1–11

FOR SEVERAL DECADES THE WORLD has watched and listened to launches of spacecrafts from Cape Canaveral, Florida. You would think the guidance of these launches would be in a control room at Cape Canaveral. Also, you would think that after the spacecraft attained its orbit around the earth, the astronauts on board would control the craft.

Actually, the control of the spacecraft takes place hundreds of miles from Florida in Houston, Texas. The Mission Control Center at the Johnson Space Center guides all spacecraft missions. From the moment of liftoff to landing, the Mission Control Center controls the flight of the shuttle. The familiar term used for the management of the spacecraft is "Houston Control."

When John wrote Revelation from the island of Patmos, he did not know anything about spacecrafts. But he did get a picture in Revelation 4 of the sovereign God in full control of the affairs of human history. G. B. Caird called Revelation 4 a vision of "the control room of Supreme Headquarters."[1] The persecuted

---

[1] G. B. Caird, *The Revelation of St. John the Divine* (New York: Harper & Row Publishers, 1966), 60.

History Under Control

Christians in Asia cried out, "Who is in charge of the world?" From all appearances the Romans held sovereign sway over the world. John received a vision behind the scenes of the "Control Room of History," and he assured his readers that God is in control. John's vision made the readers vividly conscious of the absolute sovereignty of God.

The opening word of Revelation 4:1 indicates a new vision—"after this." The first vision in 1:10-20 depicted Christ caring for and protecting his churches. It was a vision of the Supreme Christ. Now the second vision communicates the ultimate and eternal reality of God enthroned and ruling his universe. However fearful the apparently uncontrolled forces of Roman power might have been, Rome could not eclipse the greater fact that behind the scene God is governing the universe. This second vision prepares the readers for the conflict and suffering seen in subsequent visions. While they read and experienced hardships, they had this vision in Revelation as a point of reference. Behind the shadows of suffering, God is on the throne keeping watch over his own.

God gave a revelation to John. "After this I looked, and behold, a door standing open in heaven!" (4:1*a*). The expression "after this" introduces new visions in Revelation (7:1, 9; 15:5; 18:1; 19:1). John sees an open door in heaven. The term "heaven" evidently meant "God's dwelling." The open door represents what God chose to reveal to John. Robert Mounce says, "A true insight into history is gained only when we view all things from the vantage point of the heavenly throne."[2]

After seeing a door open to heaven, he hears a voice. "And the first voice, which I had heard speaking to me like a trumpet, said, 'Come up here, and I will show you what must take place after this'" (4:1). John receives an invitation to gain greater insight

---

[2]Mounce, *The Book of Revelation*, 133.

into spiritual realities. God pulls back the curtains and shows John the real focus of the world's power. The emperor may sit on his throne in Rome, but it is no match for God's throne.[3] It seems certain that the voice is that of the glorified Christ whom he heard in 1:10. The voice calls John to come up to heaven, and he will show John what must take place. The word "must" is important. John does not write about matters of chance but about events which will certainly occur. The second use of "after this" serves as a structuring devise calling attention to a new vision John has received.

John describes his condition when he received God's revelation to come and view the dwelling of God. "At once I was in the Spirit" (4:2). The expression "in the Spirit" describes a supernatural state of receptivity. John's ability to see truth from God's perspective was his condition of being in touch with God. Once again John joins the prophetic tradition by hearing and seeing God's message, and then he communicates it to his readers.

The first thing John sees in heaven is a throne. "A throne stood in heaven, with one seated on the throne" (4:2). John mentions the throne seventeen times in Revelation 4 and 5. He uses the word for "throne" forty-seven times out of a total of sixty-two uses in the New Testament. John's readers knew about earthly thrones, and they were troubled about Caesar's throne. John does not let them forget that there is a throne above every throne.[4]

God takes John on a tour of the dwelling place of God, the heavenly throne room. John describes what he saw on the tour. He describes the One on the throne with great reserve. John does not name the One on the throne. He uses symbolic suggestions rather than literal descriptions to identify the One on the throne. John

---

[3] Mitchell G. Reddish, Revelation, 92.

[4] Morris, The Revelation of St. John, 86.

reports that everything in the vision centers on the One on the throne. John describes the universe's supreme government to be God. The message of the vision is obvious: Who rules the universe? Who alone is worthy of worship? The believers in Asia needed assurance. Here it is! God has not abdicated his throne in favor of Domitian or any other ruler. In the center of John's vision is the sovereign God on his throne.

The Occupant on the Throne
4:2-3

While on tour of the throne room, John first sees an Occupant on the throne. He refuses to name the One on the throne. Rather than name him, John describes him with graphic apocalyptic symbols. John avoids all anthropomorphic or human language. Instead, he uses the brilliance of precious jewels to describe him. The symbols convey the idea of a Being, perfect in holiness, goodness, majesty, supremacy, and mercy. The description of the One on the throne fills us with the radiant glory and the unfathomable mystery of God.

The Symbol of God's Sovereignty

"A throne stood in heaven, with one seated on the throne" (4:2). The throne symbolizes one who rules or is in control. The psalmist wrote, "God reigns over the nations; God sits on his holy throne" (47:8). John sees the One on the throne in charge of the universe. The mere mention of the word "throne" suggests someone who is sovereign. John did not use a literal statement by saying, "God is sovereign." Instead, he used the symbol of a throne, and readers knew the One John describes is sovereign.

The Occupant on the throne is never named. Obviously, the One on the throne is God. The image communicates the power and rule of God. In spite of the lofty claims of the emperor, the emperor is not the one on the throne. John leads his readers to see that the power structures of the world are illusionary and temporal. The true course of history resides with the One on the throne. He directs history and brings it to a close because he is absolutely sovereign.

The Symbol of God's Majesty

John likens the One on the throne to precious jewels: "And he who sat there had the appearance of jasper and carnelian" (4:3). Instead of describing God, John used a comparison to indicate that which he is not allowed to describe. The jasper and carnelian are not to be taken literally. They symbolize the majesty of God.

Jasper is a clear stone like quartz crystal or diamond. It probably symbolizes the sanctity and purity of holiness. Carnelian is a dark reddish stone capable of flashing brilliance. It is often interpreted as a symbol for God's wrath or judgment. It seems best to see the jewels as part of an overall description. They symbolize the majesty of God, resplendent and clothed in brilliant light. Mitchell G. Reddish thinks that the jewels "function to overwhelm and awe the readers with a sense of the majesty and mysteriousness of God."[5]

The Symbol of God's Mercy

"And around the throne was a rainbow that had the appearance of an emerald" (4:3). This rainbow around the throne alludes to God's covenant which he established with Noah (Gen. 9:12–16). It represented a pledge of God's mercy and faithfulness to restrain his wrath from sinful human beings.

The word "rainbow" (*iris*) is an unusual term. It can mean either a rainbow or a halo. Nearly all commentators think that rainbow is meant, but it has an unusual shape in that it encircles the

---

[5] Reddish, *Revelation*, 94.

throne. The promise never to destroy the world with water probably prepares for the judgment scenes in the rest of the book. The description of the rainbow as an emerald probably suggests the glory surrounding God on his throne.

The Twenty-Four Elders Around the Throne
4:4

As soon as John sees One on the throne, he sees twenty-four elders. These elders are seated on thrones. They are dressed in white robes, and they wear golden crowns on their heads. "Around the throne were twenty-four thrones, and seated on the thrones are twenty-four elders, dressed in white garments, with golden crowns on their heads" (4:4).

The Identity of the Twenty-four Elders

Who are these twenty-four elders? Some think this is a reference to the twenty-four shifts of priests who are to minister in the temple. Robert Mounce thinks John experiences heaven as a massive temple where God is continuously worshipped.[6] He thinks the key to this interpretation views the primary function of the elders as that of worship.

Some think the twenty-four elders represent special angelic beings. They think human beings seem out of place in this heavenly scene around the throne of God. They understand the elders to be angelic attendants for God.

Others identify the twenty-four elders as the whole people of God. They think John uses the Jewish symbolism of numbers. Twelve was the number for organized religion. There were twelve tribes of Israel and twelve apostles of Jesus. Consequently, the twenty-four elders seem to represent all of redeemed humanity who

---

[6] Mounce, *The Book of Revelation*, 135–36.

are with God.[7]

The Garments and Crowns of the Elders

John pictures the twenty-four elders dressed in "white garments." The white robes symbolize purity. The image depicts the perfection of their character. The picture could have been used to describe God's people in their resurrected state.

John also portrays the twenty-four elders wearing golden crowns on their head. Crowns suggest a reign. The twenty-four elders have reigned on the earth in an imperfect manner, but now in the vision the people from the Old Testament era and the people from the New Testament era reign perfectly with God.

The sight of the twenty-four elders clothed in white robes and wearing golden crowns communicated comfort for the threatened readers of Revelation. They faced the possibility of death. Naturally, they would ask, "What then?" The vision tells them that they will be with God reigning with him.

The Action from the Throne and the Scenes before the Throne
4:5-6

John stays focused on the throne. He has written about the One on the throne and the twenty-four elders around the throne. Now he reports actions from the throne and scenes before the throne. "From the throne came flashes of lightning, and rumblings and peals of thunder, and before the throne were burning seven torches of fire, which are the seven spirits of God, and before the throne there was as it were a sea of glass, like crystal" (4:5-6). Both

---

[7]M. Eugene Boring and Fred B. Craddock, *The People's New Testament Commentary* (Louisville: Westminster/John Knox Press, 2004), 4.

the action from the throne and the scenes before the throne symbolize some great aspects of the character of God.

The Presence of God

John reports the sight of lightning and the sound of voices of thunder coming from the throne. Readers were reminded of the great appearance of God at Sinai when God descended in fire and smoke accompanied by thunder and lightning (cf. Exod. 19:16ff). The imagery is connected with the presence and power of God. The presence of God is so awesome to John that he could only portray it with natural phenomena. The scene of God's presence creates a sense of awe.

The Perfection of God

Seven torches of fire burn before the throne of God. The lamps give light. Seven is the perfect number. The seven spirits depict the Holy Spirit. Here the Holy Spirit joins in the activity of God. What is symbolized in the image is a disclosure of God's sovereignty and the perfect operation of the Holy Spirit in his work of illumination and revelation to human beings about the things of God.

The seven torches are identified as the seven spirits of God. The number seven symbolizes the fullness of the work of the Holy Spirit in convicting the world, producing Christians, comforting the hurting, teaching truth, gifting believers, and many other activities. The perfect Spirit is the means by which God works in the world.[8]

The Transcendence of God

Before the throne there was "a sea of glass, like crystal." Whatever else this may represent, it suggests the vast distance

---

[8] Summers, *Worthy Is the Lamb: An Interpretation of Revelation*, 132

which intervened between John and the Occupant on the throne. When Moses and the elders of Israel went up Mount Sinai and appeared before God, they saw under his feet something like a pavement made of sapphire and clear as the sky (Exod. 24:9–10). A great gulf separates a holy God from sinful human beings. God is unlike anything we have known in our familiar world of time, space, and matter. The "crystal sea" adds to the majesty of God's great difference from his creation.

The Four Living Creatures Around and on Each Side of the Throne
4:6–9

The scene in the throne room shifts to a vision of four creatures around and on each side of the throne. John draws his symbolism of these creatures from the vision of Ezekiel described in chapter 1. However, John modifies Ezekiel's imagery. Ezekiel's creatures had four faces each, but in John's vision each creature had only one face.

The Identity of the Four Creatures

Who are these strange creatures John describes? "And around the throne, on each side of the throne, are four living creatures, full of eyes in front and behind: the first living creature like a lion, the second living creature like an ox, the third living creature with the face of a man, and the fourth living creature like an eagle in flight" (4:6–7). Ray Frank Robbins says, "There have been at least thirteen interpretations of the phrase, 'four living creatures.'"[9] We shall examine only the two major interpretations of the four living creatures. First, some think these creatures represent attributes of God to depict his eternal vigilance on behalf

---

[9] Robbins, *The Revelation of Jesus Christ*, 88.

of his people.[10] By this theory the lion symbolizes bravery, the ox represents strength, the man represents intelligence, and the eagle represents speech. This is an attractive view, but in 4:8 the living creatures are seen worshipping God.

Second, others think that the four living creatures represent the fourfold division of animal life so that all God's creatures are worshipping him. Four was the number used to symbolize the material world of God's creation. John's choice of the specific creatures may have symbolized the entire created order of God—birds, wild animals, domestic animals, and humans. The symbol seems to depict all of creation fulfilling its proper function: waiting upon God, fulfilling his will, and setting forth his glory.

The Description of the Four Creatures

John gives a vivid description of the four living creatures. He describes them as "full of eyes in front and behind." This picture suggests that the creatures are alert and knowledgeable. Nothing escapes their notice. John further describes the creatures as the first like a lion, the second like an ox, the third with a human face, and the fourth like a flying eagle. The lion was considered the king of wild beasts. The ox represented domesticated animals, the man's face represented human beings, and the eagle represented the totality of God's creation.

John gives an additional description of the four living creatures. "And the four living creatures, each of them with six wings, are full of eyes all around and within" (4:8). Most commentaries point out that the three pairs of wings symbolize reverence, humility, and obedience (cf. Isa. 6:2). The animals are around the throne so that each one can face the One of the

---

[10] H. E. Dana, *The Epistles and Apocalypse of John* (Dallas: Baptist Book Store, 1937), 115.

throne.[12] The eyes "all around and within" make it possible to see them surrounding the throne.

The Action of the Four Living Creatures

John emphasizes the chief action of the four living creatures to be the worship of the One on the throne. "And day and night they never cease to say, "Holy, holy, holy is the Lord God Almighty, who was and is and is to come!" (4:8). The two expressions—"day and night" and "never cease" place a double emphasis on the continuous activity of their creatures. They praise God for his lordship over creation.

The four living beings celebrate three things about God: his holiness, his omnipotence, and his eternality. They begin with the thrice repeated "Holy, holy, holy." John draws from the throne room scene of Isaiah 6:3. The holiness of God points to his separation from this created order. He is the "Wholly Other." The threefold repetition of "holy" places greater stress on his holiness.

Praising God for his holiness leads naturally to the celebration of his power. John used the title "Lord God Almighty." Real power is not with evil but with the God who is holy. Robert Mounce wrote, "To churches about to enter a period of severe testing and persecution a declaration of God's unlimited might would bring strength and encouragement."[11] Nothing lies beyond the control of God because he is Almighty.

Finally, the living creatures celebrate the eternity of the One who is holy and omnipotent. "Who was, and is, and is to come." The God who is sovereign controls past, present, and future. God exists eternally. There has never been a time when God did not exist, and there will never be a time when he does not exist.

---

[11] Mounce, *The Book of Revelation*, 139.

The Twenty-Four Elders Worship the One on the Throne
4:9–11

The twenty-four elders join the four living creatures in worshipping God. "And whenever the living creatures give glory and honor and thanks to him who is seated on the throne, who lives forever and ever" (4:9). The terms "glory" and "honor" celebrate God's perfection. "Thanks" celebrates God's gift of creation and redemption. The four living creatures sum up two major aspects of God given in chapter 4. First, he is seated on the throne, which symbolizes that God is the sovereign ruler of the universe. Second, he is eternal. He is the One who lives forever and ever. John shifts from describing the worship of the living creatures to the worship of the twenty-four elders.

The Significant Gestures

As we read the action of the twenty-four elders, we notice two significant verbs—"fall" and "cast." "The twenty-four elders fall down before him who is seated on the throne and worship him who lives forever and ever. They cast their crowns before the throne" (4:10). To fall before the One on the throne communicates the acknowledgment of God's holiness, sovereignty, and eternity. In the secular realm it was common for subjects to fall before the king. This gesture demonstrates that homage belongs only to God. God alone is worthy of much obeisance. Ultimately all the world will bow before Christ and acknowledge him as Lord (Phil. 2:10–11).

The second gesture involves casting their crowns before the throne. In the secular world lesser kings would lay their crowns before higher kings. All earthly kings eventually acknowledge the absolute sovereignty of God. The earthly rulers realize that their authority is delegated and temporal.

The Significant Singing

The song of the twenty-four elders provides an appropriate climax to the vision of the throne room. "Worthy are you, our Lord and God, to receive glory and honor and power, for you created all things, and by your will they existed and were created" (4:11). The praise of the elders differs from that of the living creatures in that the elders address praise directly to God.

There are two parts to the hymn, centering on the worthiness of God and celebrating his creative work. Grant R. Osborne thinks "Worthy are you" comes from the political language of the day. As the Roman emperor entered a city, such acclamation was given to him.[12] John makes clear that only God is worthy of worship. The superiority of God to all earthly rulers is seen in the expression "our Lord and God." Only God, not the emperor, is worthy of the title "Lord."

Since God alone is worthy of worship, he must receive "glory, honor, and power." Notice that one word differs in the acclamation of the elders, and that is "power" instead of "thanks." The word "power" refers to miracles in the Synoptic Gospels. The elders celebrate God's power to bring creation into being and to sustain it.

Three verbs appear in the elders' singing which call attention to God's creative work: "created," "existed," and "created." God, according to the elders, brought all created things into existence. Due to his will and to his will alone creation came into being. But God did not create the world and then abandon it. Throughout history God has been sustaining his creation. He works to bring creation toward a consummation where it will be perfected.

God gave John a vision of the throne room. John reports about what he saw and heard. His report is written in symbolic,

---

[12] Osborne, 240.

apocalyptic language. He means for the truths to mean more than the language. He uses jewels to describe the majesty, holiness, and sovereignty of the One on the throne. He describes how the people of God and the entire creation worship God by figures of twenty-four elders and four living creatures. He emphasizes the presence, perfection, and transcendence of God with images of natural phenomena, flaming torches, and a crystal sea. John wants the theological truths communicated in the language to comfort those in crisis and to give hope for the future to the perplexed. The main message of Revelation 4 is that God is forever on the throne.

Chapter 6
The Redeemer of History

Revelation 5:1-14

JOHN'S VISION OF THE THRONE room continues through chapter 5. In the previous chapter John focused on the throne of God and its surroundings. He has also mentioned "the seven spirits of God" or the Holy Spirit. But now in chapter 5, John centers his attention primarily on the Lamb. John shifts from the first and third persons of the Holy Trinity to the second person, namely Jesus Christ.

John's book, the Revelation, demonstrates the traits of a great drama. The great drama begins in the throne room. John notices in the right hand of the One on the throne a scroll. It has writing on both sides and is sealed with seven seals. He hears a voice asking, "Who is worthy to open the scrolls and break its seals?" A tension in the drama arises when no one is found to open the scroll. It causes John to weep.

A turn occurs in the dramatic story when one of the elders tells John that the Lion of the tribe of Judah has conquered, so he can open the scroll and break its seals. As soon as the elder tells John this good news, John sees a Lamb standing between the throne and the four living creatures. John describes the Lamb as having seven horns and seven eyes. The Lamb appears to have been slain, but yet he stands at the center of the throne.

Dramatic actions take place by the Lamb. The Lamb now begins to move. He comes to the One on the throne and takes the scroll from his right hand. When this happens, the four living creatures and the twenty-four elders fall prostrate before the Lamb, and they sing a new song. They sing of his worthiness to take the scroll and redeem the human race. The Lamb's actions cause millions of angels to join in the new song. The action comes to a dramatic crescendo when every creature throughout the universe ascribes praise to the One on the throne and to the Lamb.

The vision of the heavenly throne room serves a strategic purpose in the overall dramatic story of the apocalypse. Through this vision John assures his readers that God controls the universe and that the Lamb has successfully brought God's plan and purpose to fulfillment. Before writing about scenes of suffering, judgment, and destruction, John reminds the readers of the centrality of the throne room in heaven. He further reminds them that Christ conquered evil by his death on the cross. Christ's work brings meaning and purpose to life and death. Christ's redemptive work holds the keys to history's meaning and destiny. The readers can face life with assurance, knowing that Christ has the ultimate outcome of the world in his hands. The scene of the Redeeming Lamb recorded in Revelation 5 deserves our careful consideration.

The Sight of a Scroll
5:1–4

The expression "then I saw" (*kai eidon*) appears three times in chapter 5 (v. 1, "then I saw"; v. 2, "and I saw"; v. 6, "I saw"). The usage of this expression lends dramatic imagery to the various scenes in the chapter. In the first scene (vv. 1–4), God sits on the throne and holds a double-sided scroll in his right hand. Seven seals secure the protection of the scroll. John's eyes focus on the scroll. "Then I saw in the right hand of him who was seated on the throne a scroll written and on the back, sealed with seven seals" (5:1).

The Identity of the Scroll

John gives several qualities about the scroll. He sees the scroll in the right hand of the One on the throne. The right hand symbolizes power and authority. Whatever the scroll contains in context is in the control of God. This scroll is written on both sides. Papyrus scrolls in John's day were usually inscribed only on one side. The fact that it is written on both sides suggests the fullness of its contents. The scroll is completely full of the declaration of God's will. It had no room for additions to be written.

The scroll is sealed with seven seals. This figure means the scroll is fully or completely protected. Its ownership rests in the authority of God. In apocalyptic writings the seals kept the content secret until the time of fulfillment. Daniel writes, "Seal up the vision, for it pertains to many days from now" (8:26). When the time has fully come, the seals will be removed, and history will move swiftly to a climax.

Obviously the seals stress the secrecy of the scrolls' content. There are several speculations about what was written in the scroll. Some think it was the Lamb's book of life, which would presumably reveal the names of the redeemed at a future time (cf. Rev. 13:8; 17:8; 20:12, 15; 21:27). Others think the scroll is the Old Testament. Jesus went into the synagogue at Nazareth, and after a reading from Isaiah, he announced, "Today this Scripture has been fulfilled in your hearing" (Luke 4:21). Thus Christ is the One who can bring the Old Testament prophetic hope to its fulfillment.

Some think the scroll contains a record of events soon to take place. There is a question as to why the delay until AD 95 if Christ had won the right to open the seal in AD 29 or 30.[1] In this

---

[1] Caird, *The Revelation of St. John the Divine*, 71.

writer's opinion the scroll contains God's redemptive plan. The sealed book contains the destiny of the world and the purposes and plan of God for all creation. God's plan for the world is accomplished through Jesus, the slain Lamb.

A Question about the Scroll

John sees a strong angel. This strong angel appears three times in Revelation: the question of the strong angel (5:2), at the presentation of the little scroll (10:1-2), and at the announcement of the destruction of Babylon (18:21). These three references represent crucial events. Probably the idea is that only one supremely strong angel could issue a challenge to all creation. The angel's voice reaches heaven, earth, and what is under the earth. A dramatic tension arises in the scene of the scroll. The strong angel looks for someone worthy to break the seal of the scroll and reveal its contents. "And I saw a strong angel proclaiming with a loud voice, 'Who is worthy to open the scroll and break its seals?' And no one in heaven or earth or under the earth was able to open the scroll or to look into it" (5:2-3). No one in all of God's creation (heaven, earth, and under the earth) can disclose the content of the scroll. God's ways can never be known to human beings except by revelation.

John weeps over the news that no one is worthy to open the scroll and reveal its contents. "And I began to weep loudly because no one was found worthy to open the scroll or to look into it" (5:4). The word "weep" suggests a profound experience of mourning. John weeps that no one can explain life to him. He wants to know its meaning and its destiny. No one seems capable of such explanation, and John grieves greatly.

The Introduction of the Lion/Lamb
5:5–6

Dramas often take a turn in extreme tense situations. This story takes a new direction with the appearance of one of the elders on the scene and with his announcement. "And one of the elders said to me, 'Weep no more; behold, the Lion of the tribe of Judah, the Root of David, has conquered, so that he can open the scroll and its seven seals'" (5:5). This turns the story from sorrow into joy, from despair into hope. The answer to John's question comes from two figures which clearly symbolize Christ.

The Lion of the Tribe of Judah

The strong angel announces about One who had conquered. He qualifies him to break the seals. The elder uses Old Testament language to describe the One who conquered. "The Lion of the tribe of Judah" alludes to one of the first messianic prophecies in Genesis 49:9–10. Jacob singles out the tribe of Judah as a "lion's whelp." Jacob further promises that the rule would not depart from Judah. The figure of the Lion applies to the greatest of all members of the tribe, namely Jesus Christ. The picture in Genesis depicts not a suffering Messiah, but One who wields the scepter of a ruling king.

The strong angel uses another expression from Isaiah 11:1 to refer to the Messiah. Isaiah looked forward to an ideal king from the line of David. The royal family of David, the son of Jesse, is likened to a fallen tree. Isaiah prophesied that from the tree's stump would come a new tree to restore the rule of David. Isaiah gives a picture of this king's rule: "But with righteousness he shall judge the poor, and decide with equity for the meek of the earth; and he shall smite the earth with the rod of his mouth, and with the breath of his lips he shall kill the wicked" (Isa. 11:4). This prophecy pictures a king divinely endowed who will destroy all evil, deliver

God's people from affliction, and establish a new order of righteousness.

John tells us that the Lion has "conquered." The word points to Christ as completely triumphant. The tense of the verb indicates a victory once and for all.[2] His character and conquest make Christ worthy to open the scroll and break the seals.

The Slain and Living Lamb

John turns to see the Lion, but instead he sees a Lamb. "And between the throne and the four living creatures and among the elders I saw a Lamb standing, as though it had been slain, with seven horns and with seven eyes, which are the seven spirits of God sent out into all the earth" (5:6). Notice the position of the Lamb in the vision. God occupies the throne at the center. Four living creatures and twenty-four elders surround the throne. The Lamb stands in the midst of the throne, the four living creatures, and the twenty-four elders. The imagery places the Lamb with God at the center.

John uses a beautiful mixed metaphor to describe Christ—the Lion/Lamb. The final picture is the Lamb, not the Lion. The Lion of Judah has conquered not through military might but through the sacrifice of the Lamb. The Lamb is the main designation of Christ in Revelation. It is found twenty-nine times in the book. The Lamb John sees is not an ordinary Lamb. It bears the marks of execution: "standing, as though it had been slain." The Lamb clearly refers to Jesus who died on the cross for the sins of the world. John sees the Lamb as a victorious figure who conquered by self-sacrifice. This Lamb bears the marks of past wounds, but he is not dead. The mutually antagonistic metaphors convey the truth that though Christ died, he lives.

The seven horns on the Lamb symbolize the power and

---

[2]Morris, *The Revelation of St. John*, 96.

strength of the Lamb. He is no helpless victim but a victorious Lamb. The seven eyes represent God's presence and knowledge. He has God's power and God's insight. John combines images of death and defeat with symbols of power and authority. The Lamb conquers through love and self-sacrifice, not through violence.[3] What John appears to be saying in his different symbols is that Jesus Christ, of the tribe of Judah and the line of David, is supremely powerful and all-knowing. He has won the victory by his sacrificial death and resurrection.

The Action of the Lamb
5:7–10

The drama takes another interesting turn. The Lamb, who stands at the center of the throne, takes the scroll from the right hand of God. The focus shifts from the character of the Lamb to the work of the Lamb. Because of the Lamb's worthiness, God allows the Lamb to take the scroll. Christ's work of redemption comes through clearly in the actions in the apocalyptic imagery.

The Taking of the Scroll

"And he went and took the scroll from the right hand of him who was seated on the throne" (5:7). God allows the Lamb to take the scroll from his right hand. The action expresses the perfect harmony between the will of God and the will of Christ. No one else could take the scroll—only the lamb qualified to be the Redeemer of history.

The verb "took" has a vividness which is difficult to translate in the English. The verb pictures the whole action of Christ in one verb. The Lamb existed throughout eternity with the Father. He did not hold to his position, but he became a man and

---

[3]Reddish, *Revelation*, 110.

took on the form of a servant. In this servant role Christ died for the sins of the world. He rose again and ascended back to the Father. He reigns in heaven, and at a day appointed by the Father, the Lamb will return to vindicate his followers and to judge the world.

The Celebration of the Lamb's Action

The Lamb's action evoked a great outburst of praise and worship. All the hosts of heaven anticipate what the breaking of the seven sealed book will be. "And when he had taken the scroll, the four living creatures and the twenty-four elders fell down before the Lamb, each holding a harp, and golden bowls full of incense, which are the prayers of the saints" (5:8). Prostration before God appears throughout the Bible as a gesture of worship. The creatures and elders acknowledge the majesty, power, character, and work of the Lamb.

Each of the heavenly beings hold two objects of worship—harps and bowls of incense. Harps played a significant role in temple worship. They were instruments of praise to God. They accompanied the singing of psalms. John sees the harps providing accompaniment for the new song.

The "golden bowls of incense" pictured the incense the priests offered to God every morning and evening in the temple. The incense smoke symbolized the prayers of the saints rising to God.

The four living creatures and the twenty-four elders join together to sing a new song to the Lamb. "And they sang a new song, saying, 'Worthy are you to take the scroll and to open its seals, for you were slain, and by your blood you ransomed people for God from every tribe and tongue and people and nation, and you have made them a kingdom and priests to our God, and they shall reign on earth'" (5:9–10). The song to the Lamb is a "new song" because the covenant established through his death is a new covenant. The Lamb's action of taking the scroll created a new situation and thus elicits a new outburst of praise.[4]

The new song has three parts: the celebration of the worthiness of the Lamb (5:9*b*), the saving work of the Lamb (5:9*c*), and the creation of a new community (5:10). The first part ascribes worthiness to the Lamb. His worthiness has been noticed in his character, but now his worthiness comes with his death. The idea of the unity of God and Christ appears in the celebration. The angels' chorus in the second part of the new song celebrates Christ's saving work. John uses two words to describe Jesus' death—"slain" and "ransomed." John emphasizes the tremendous cost of ransom with the expression "by your blood," which means "by his death." The word "slain" pictures a violent scene used in association with a slaughtered animal. John's use of this term could suggest an interpretation of the death of Jesus as the Passover Lamb. The word "ransomed" depicts the practice of buying the freedom of slaves or prisoners of war. Christ's death freed people from the bondage of sin and from the enslaving power of evil. The word "ransom" could picture the liberation of the Hebrews from Egyptian bondage.

John picks up expressions to show that the redeemed come from all over the world—"tribe, tongue, people, nation." The church comes from every station and walk of life. The church recognizes no gender, political, cultural, or racial boundaries.

The third part of the new song discloses that the Lamb has created a new community. What God promised to the Israelites at Sinai, he creates in the establishment of the church through the death of Christ. "You shall be to me a kingdom of priests and a holy nation" (Exod. 19:6). The term "kingdom" suggests that the church reigns partly with God now, but they shall reign perfectly in the end of history. The term "priests" pictures God's people

---

[4] Morris, *The Revelation of St. John*, 98–99.

serving. Through the death of Christ the church has rulers serving with Christ.

The Sight and Sounds of an Angelic Chorus
5:11–14

After the new song by the four living creatures and the twenty-four elders, a chorus of angels lifts their voices in praise to the Lamb. Two verbs communicate this scene—"looked" and "heard." John saw unnumbered hosts of heaven and heard their hymn of praise.

The Sight and Sounds of Many Angels
"Then I looked, and I heard around the throne and the living creatures and the elders the voice of many angels, numbering myriads and thousands of thousands" (5:11). The angels encircle the throne and the living ones and the elders. They occupy a strategic plan but not the center. John piles expression on expression to emphasize their number—"myriads of myriads and thousands of thousands." These expressions symbolize a countless multitude.

John introduces the words of the angels with "saying," which indicates that he heard what they sing. "Worthy is the Lamb who was slain, to receive power and wealth and wisdom and might and honor and glory and blessing!" (5:12). The basis for the outburst of praise is the sacrificial death of the Lamb. The Lamb receives a sevenfold praise. The worship which has been given to God extends now to Christ. The seven attributes can be divided into a pattern of four celebrating the attributes of Christ—power, wealth, wisdom, might—and three celebrating the worship due him as a result—honor, glory, and praise. Christ has won the praise because of his self-sacrifice.

The Praise of Creation

John tells of hearing the four living creatures and the twenty-four elders praising the redemptive work of the Lamb. He tells also about an innumerable host of angels praising the worthiness of the Lamb. Now he tells about how the whole creation joins in the praise. "And I heard every creature in heaven and on earth and under the earth and in the sea, and all that is in them, singing, 'To him who sits on the throne and to the Lamb be blessing and honor and glory and might forever and ever!'" (5:13). The song of praise addressed the One on the throne and the Lamb. Christ is adored in complete equality with God the Creator. All creation bursts forth in praise to God and the Lamb. John specifies the created order as that which is in heaven, on earth, under the earth, and on the sea.

The praise of creation is fourfold—blessing, honor, glory, might. The creation repeats three elements of the previous seven praises (5:12). The word for "might" differs. Probably the fourfold ascription corresponds to the fourfold division of creation. The hymn represents the fervent outpouring of praise for all that God has done through the Lamb. The song links the One seated on the throne with the Lamb. There cannot be any doubt that the Lamb is to be reckoned with God and as God.[5]

The vision closes with the four living creatures and the twenty-four elders. "And the four living creatures said, 'Amen!' and the elders fell down and worshiped" (5:14). The four living creatures begin the chorus of praise (4:8), and they close it. As the four creatures say, "Amen!" the elders prostrate themselves in worship.

God uses the vision of the throne room and the Lamb to assure the readers that he controls the universe and that the Lamb brings God's plans and purposes to fulfillment. Regardless of what

---

[5] Ibid., 102.

happens in history, the readers can face life with assurance, knowing that the ultimate outcome of history is not in doubt.

Chapter 7
A Pageantry of Suffering Throughout History

Revelation 6:1-17; 8:1-5

THE ACTION OF THE GREAT DRAMA continues as the Lamb takes the scroll from the hand of God and proceeds to break the seals one by one. The scroll contains insights into God's divine will. It symbolizes God's will and purpose for humanity and the principles of God's government in his creation. It is a book of the world's destiny.

The Lamb has the answer to the problems raised by human history. The seven seals indicate that the scroll is completely sealed. Only Christ has the authority to break the seals and reveal the contents of the scroll. He holds the meaning of history and directs it to its conclusion.

Of course the question arises, What does the opening of these seals mean? The dramatic action seems to depict the subject of suffering, an experience well-known to the readers. Edward A. McDowell calls the vision of the seals "History's Pageant of Suffering."[1] The seals portray what was happening in John's day. They also represent what has happened since the beginning of human rebellion in the garden and what is happening today. The

---

[1] McDowell, *The Meaning and Message of the Book of Revelation* , 87.

vision of the seals characterizes the entire course of history from the ascension of Christ until his return in glory.

The seals may be divided into four parts around the common subject of suffering. The first four seals dramatize the presence of suffering with four horsemen riding across the stage of history. The horses bear the colors of white, red, black, and pale green. They symbolize conquest, war, famine, and death. These actions have been the scourge of humankind throughout history. They appear and reappear in history in the order in which they come in the vision. Someone comes with the ambition to conquer the world. They implement their ambition with war. The war brings severe famine, and the ultimate outcome is death. These are hard, inescapable facts of history. John sees the horses riding in his day with Domitian's desire to dominate the world. He sees the suffering caused by this self-absorption. John knows these horses will continue to ride again and again across history. These horses are not signs of the end but signs of the time.

The second part of the seal vision depicts another insight about suffering. It involves people's weariness with hardships. The martyrs for the cause of Christ call for God's help and ask, "How long will this suffering last?" Suffering happens to God's people, and it causes weariness and raises serious questions.

The question of the martyrs about "How long?" seems to prompt the action of the sixth seal. The great earthquake, followed by appalling convulsions seems to be the conclusion of history. The end represents a time of vindication of God's people and judgment of the ungodly. All of John's images portray a historical crisis or the final crises. God takes his hands off, and the cosmos collapses in on itself. That is what the wrath of God is, letting people persist in their own self-will, self-trust, and self-assertion. No wonder that after the sixth seal the cry comes, "Who is able to stand?" Of course only those who have the seal of the living God can stand, which is the theme of Revelation 7.

History Under Control

The fourth part of the seals' pageantry would seem to picture what happens to suffering after the end of history. The seventh seal simply portrays silence in heaven for one-half hour. The seal does not tell us explicitly what happens to suffering after the end, but it does tell us implicitly. Silence seems to communicate the absence of the cries of suffering and the absence of the questions of why.

The pageantry of the seals has created intense interest and helpful insight. Act I pictures what has happened in history. Horsemen have ridden, and they will continue to ride. Act II pictures God's people hurting and agonizing over the presence of suffering in their lives. Act III takes us to the dramatic resolution of suffering when history ends. Act IV presents the serene scene of silence. The drama tells us that God takes care of some suffering immediately during history, but ultimately, he eliminates all suffering.

The Four Horsemen Riding Across History
6:1–8

John watches as the seals break one by one. After each of the first four seals breaks, one of the living creatures shouts in a voice like thunder, "Come!" and behold, a horse and its rider appear. "Now I watched when the Lamb opened one of the seven seals, and I heard one of the four living creatures say with a voice like thunder, 'Come!'" (6:1). The pageantry begins with four horsemen riding across the stage of history. The volume of the creatures' voice calls for the readers to pay special attention to the action and for the riders to come on the scene and go forth on the earth.

The White Horse

The first horseman on a white horse responds to the living creatures' invitation to come. "I looked, and behold, a white horse! And its rider had a bow, a crown was given to him, and he came out conquering, and to conquer" (6:2). The white horse symbolizes military conquest. The white represents an evil force attempting to defeat and oppress believers. The crown he is given symbolizes his victory over enemies. The rider has a bow which is a weapon of warfare.

John explicitly states that the purpose of the horseman is to conquer. This horseman joins with the horsemen of the next three seals to depict destruction and death. The expression "was given to him" reflects the common Jewish idiom called "the divine passive." That means God is understood to be the unexpressed subject of the verb. God controls everything, and only by the permissive will of God is the white horse allowed to conquer.[2]

The Red Horse

The second seal opens, and the second living creature calls for the horseman on the red horse to ride. "When he opened the second seal, I heard the second living creature say, 'Come!' And out came another horse, bright red. Its rider was permitted to take peace from the earth, so that people should slay one another, and he was given a great sword" (6:3-4). The red horse naturally follows on the heels of the white horse of conquest. The color of the second horse is appropriate, for it symbolizes bloodshed.

The rider is allowed to do three things: take peace from the earth, cause people to kill one another, and use a sword to slaughter people. These three actions are governed by the usage of the expression "was permitted." Evil can only operate under the sovereignty of God. Evil takes peace away, and human beings do

---

[2] Trafton, *Reading Revelation*, 70.

the damage to one another. The word "slay" has the meaning of butcher. The horrors of the rider on the red horse indicate internal strife, civil war, international conflict, and anarchy.

The Black Horse
When the Lamb opens the third seal, a rider on a black horse rides across the stage. "When he opened the third seal, I heard the third living creature say, 'Come!' And I looked, and behold, a black horse! And its rider had a pair of scales in his hand. And I heard what seemed to be a voice in the midst of the four living creatures, saying, 'A quart of wheat for a denarius, and three quarts of barley for a denarius, but do not harm the oil and the wine'" (6:5-6). The pair of scales points to the fact that when conflict and war assert themselves, food will have to be weighed and restored. A quart of wheat met the need for one person for one day. A denarius represented one day's wage. In other words, the bare necessities cost a whole day's wage. The alternative would be to spend the day's wages on barley to make inferior bread. The scourge of the third horsemen represents famine, which follows naturally in the wake of conflict and war.

The famine conditions did not affect the olive oil and the wine. These were not necessities of life. They symbolize the luxury and extravagant lifestyle of the wealthy. It symbolizes greed and selfishness.

The Pale Green Horse
The Lamb breaks the fourth seal, and the fourth living creature invited the pale green horse to ride. "When he opened the fourth seal, I heard the voice of the fourth living creature say, 'Come!' And I looked, and behold, a pale horse! And its rider's name was Death, and Hades followed him. And they were given authority over a fourth of the earth, to kill with sword and with famine and with pestilence and by the wild beasts of the earth"

(6:7–8). The Greek *chloros* denotes a yellowish green. This rider's name is Death. Hades follows Death. The imagery of Hades following him pictures Hades gathering the corpses left by pestilence and death as they struck victim after victim.

Once more God "gave" the evil force power to inflict suffering on humanity. They are given power only over one-fourth of the earth to kill. This is the first use of a fraction in Revelation. The fraction symbolizes the limited power of evil. The four methods evil uses are: sword, famine, pestilence, and wild animals. These represent typical ways of describing the horrors of war.

What do these first four seals seem to mean? These seals describe the conditions in the Roman Empire as revealed to John. He sees a vast world power, outwardly victorious and eager for fresh conquests. Conflict leads to war which leads to famine and ultimately results in death. The four horsemen rode, and they ride again and again. From creation to consummation, there plays the pageantry of suffering.

The Souls Martyred During History
6:9–11

The first four seals have to do with happenings on the earth. The fifth seal takes place in heaven. Apocalyptic writers, including John, often shift scenes back and forth from earth to heaven. John sees underneath the altar in the throne room those who died in faithfulness to the Lamb. The souls of these martyrs cry out to God for vindication. The scene of the sixth seal pictures God's people asking questions about suffering.

The Scene of the Martyrs
"When he opened the fifth seal, I saw under the altar the souls of those who had been slain for the word of God and for the witness they had borne" (6:9). To be under the altar of glory is to be in the

presence of him who sits on the throne. John sees the martyrs under the watchful eye of God.[3] Some have argued for two altars in heaven, the altar of burnt offering and the altar of incense. Robert H. Mounce thinks the theme of sacrifice would suggest the altar of burnt offering, and the prayers (v. 10) seem to indicate the altar of incense. Mounce concludes, "There is no reason in John's vision the two should not blend together as one."[4]

The martyrs have given up their lives because of the Word of God and their testimony. These are people who, like Antipas of Pergamum, were faithful witnesses to Christ. Although the scene is in heaven, it is the results of actions that occurred on earth. The expression "under the altar" symbolizes a place of prestige and honor. They are near God.

The Cry of the Martyrs

From beneath the altar of God, the martyrs' cry for vindication arises. "They cried out with a loud voice, 'O Sovereign Lord, holy and true, how long before you will judge and avenge our blood on those who dwell on the earth?'" (6:10). The "loud voice" represents the anguished cry for God to stop the suffering and to do something about evil. The martyrs address God with reverence and meaning. The expression "Sovereign Lord" comes from a Greek word which is not the usual word for Lord in the New Testament. John uses the word *despotes*, which pictures one with absolute rule over all things. The martyrs also address God as "holy and true." The term "holy" pictures the God who transcends all evil, and "true" indicates that God will be faithful to his promises of vindicating his people.

The martyrs seem weary with the believer's suffering on

---

[3] Beasley-Murray, *The Book of Revelation*, 133–34.

[4] Mounce, *The Book of Revelation*, 157.

earth. They ask, "How long?" They want to know how long God will tolerate resistance to his will. They want to know how long it will be before God will "judge and avenge" the blood shed by the martyrs. This could be seen as a cry for revenge, but it seems to be more a cry for vindication. The martyrs want God to vindicate their commitment to him, and they want God to vindicate his will on "those who dwell on the earth." This designates human beings in hostility to God.

The Response to the Martyr's Cry

God responds to the cry of the martyrs. "They were each given a white robe and told to rest a little longer, until the number of their fellow servants and their brothers should be complete, who were to be killed as they themselves had been killed" (6:11). Before God answers the martyrs' cry, he describes the martyrs with him as clothed in "a white robe." The white robe symbolizes purity and victory. In a way God shows his vindication, for God shows the martyrs experiencing the victory by God.

God also tells the martyrs to "rest a little longer." The imminence of the end of history is strongly emphasized in the expression "a little longer." Throughout the book of Revelation, God is seen in the process of bringing the world to an end in his own time. During the time between Christ's ascension and his return, believers are not only to wait but to "rest." This term "rest" means that the martyrs are to enjoy their blessed state until the end of history comes. Church history proves God's Word is true. Martyrdom continues today. Ultimately, God will say, "That's enough!" He will then end history and vindicate his ways.

The Cataclysmic Events at the End of History
6:12-17

The four horsemen ride continuously. The pageantry of suffering seems never to end. "How long?" continues to be the question. Justice seems incredibly slow in coming, but in the sixth seal John pictures God's vindication arriving. The seal portrays the end of the age. With the opening of the sixth seal, the scene shifts back to the earth.

The Cosmic Upheavals

Although the principle of sin and retribution sometimes seems incredibly slow in coming, John pictures vindication coming at the end of history. "When he opened the sixth seal, I looked, and behold, there was a great earthquake, and the sun became black as sackcloth, the full moon became like blood, and the stars of the sky fell to the earth as the fig tree sheds its winter fruit when shaken by a gale. The sky vanished like a scroll that is being rolled up, and every mountain and island was removed from its place" (6:12-13). The upheavals number seven: earthquake, sun, full moon, stars, sky, mountains, and islands. All of these images appear throughout the Bible either to portray a historical crisis of judgment or to portray the final judgment. For example, Isaiah prophesies of Babylon's judgment on Judah with the images of the desolation of the earth and upheavals of the moon and sun, mountains and hills (24:3). Jesus speaks of the Roman destruction of Jerusalem with images of earthquakes, the sun darkened, the moon failing, and the stars falling (Mark 13:8, 24).

Some think that the judgment pictured in the sixth seal refers to the destruction of Rome. This writer thinks it can portray both the destruction or judgment on an ungodly world power and the picture of the final judgment at the end of history. It depicts the consequences of sin during any and every era of history. But, because of the expression "great day of their wrath" in 6:17, the picture in the sixth seal seems to be the final judgment at the end of history.

John's apocalyptic images picture the end of the entire universe as we know it. They symbolize the end of social and political structures. These images depict a "universe shattering" event, not just an isolated event in Palestine. In the drama of the seals, the end of history has come. It is time for God to judge the world and to vindicate his will.

The Response of the World to the End

The end of history represents a day of terror for the world. "Then the kings of the earth and the great ones and the generals and the rich and the powerful, and everyone, slave and free, hid themselves in the caves and among the rocks of the mountains, calling to the mountains and rocks, 'Fall on us and hide us from the face of him who is seated on the throne, and from the wrath of the Lamb, for the great day of their wrath has come, and who can stand?'" (6:15-17). Oddly enough, John's list of catastrophes include seven, and he names seven classes of people. The terror struck by these people is understandable, for they realize the judgment of God has arrived. At the end of history, everyone who has stood against God will react with terror.

The response of these seven groups involves both action and words. First, they hide themselves in caves and among the rocks of the mountains. Then they cry for the mountains and rocks to fall upon them. Henry B. Swete says, "What sinners dread most is not death, but the revealed presence of God."[5] Since Adam and Eve rebelled and hid themselves from the presence of God, the guilty conscience makes people fugitives from God. According to this

---

[5] Henry B. Swete, *The Apocalypse of St. John* (Grand Rapids: William B. Eerdmans Publishing, 1951), 94.

picture, humans can no longer hide. God confronts them in judgment.[6]

The "wrath of the Lamb" strikes the reader as a paradoxical expression. A lamb is a meek, nonviolent animal. But the Lamb in Revelation is also the Lion of Judah, the Messiah, and the figure of judgment. The wrath of God appears throughout the New Testament. It is neither personal vindictiveness nor an impersonal process of retribution. It is the response of God's holiness to persistent and impertinent rebellion. When God appears in judgment and tears away human masks and deception, people will sense the terror of having rejected Christ.

John describes the end as "the great day of their wrath." It is a day of reckoning for evildoers. The judgments of God inevitably come upon those who sin. The expression describing the end depicts the tragic consequences of sin.

When the sixth seal has been opened, the reader expects the opening of the seventh seal. No, the cataclysmic description of the end elicits a questions, "Who can stand?" John interrupts the action to insert an interlude (7:1-17). The seventh seal does not open until 8:1. The interlude provides an answer to the question, "Who can stand?" John offers words of assurance and comfort for God's people. He pauses in the dramatic action to assure the faithful that they would not suffer God's wrath at the final judgment. In Revelation 7 John describes two groups: the people of God on earth (7:1-8) and the people of God in heaven (7:9-17). The first scene is on earth, and the second scene is in heaven. We shall go on in our study of the seventh seal and return in the next chapter to discuss this interlude of comfort.

---

[6] Mounce, *The Book of Revelation*, 63.

The Dramatic Silence at the End of History
8:1-5

The interlude ends. Readers anticipate the opening of the seventh seal. They think it will give them a picture of what lies beyond history. When the Lamb opens the seventh seal, the reader does not see the end or beyond the end. Instead, silence confronts the readers. The opening of the seventh seal brings a great hush over the worshipping hosts of heaven. Martin Kiddle says the silence is "a brilliant device for deepening the suspense."[7] "When the Lamb opened the seventh seal, there was silence in heaven for about half an hour. Then I saw the seven angels who stand before God, and seven trumpets were given to them" (8:1-2).

The Silence of Heaven

An impressive silence occurs. We could think this silence indicates information about the end. Instead, the silence launches a new series of visions heralded by angels with trumpets. This is typical of John's method. He goes over the ground again and again, each time teaching us something new.[8] John wants us to know that there is more to history than suffering, and he gives us visions to bring out some other facet of history.

The silence clearly depicts a solemn and impressive moment. The reader expects some type of judgment scene or further insight into what happens beyond history. Readers do not expect the silence. Habakkuk reported the silence in heaven: "The LORD is in his holy temple; let all the earth keep silence before him" (2:20). The fact of silence indicates that God is in his holy

---

[7] Martin Kiddle, *The Revelation of St. John* (London: Hodder and Stoughton, 1940), 114.

[8] Morris, *The Revelation of St. John*, 119.

temple. The silence seems to be a dramatic suspense builder for the readers.[9] The sixth seal depicts the end of history, and one would expect insight into what happens after the end of history. But no information comes, only awe-inspiring silence.

The silence lasts for "half an hour." This expression continues to build suspense. The half hour represents a dramatic, short period of time. With the breaking of the seventh seal, John sees seven angels who are given seven trumpets. Another angel takes incense from the altar and casts it to the earth. The seven angels prepare to blow their trumpets. The dramatist has created expectation. Something else is about to happen.

The Seven Angels

After telling about the silence in heaven, John introduces seven angels. They had not been mentioned before 8:2. Apparently these seven angels were known to John's readers. "Then I saw the seven angels who stand before God, and seven trumpets were given to them" (8:2). These seven angels occupy the throne room along with the four living creatures, the twenty-four elders, and the countless number of other angels. Some think these angels constitute the "angels of the Presence" who are mentioned in the apocryphal documents of Tobit and Enoch. These angels receive the seven trumpets, which figure in the next vision.

Evidently, God gave the angels the seven trumpets. We do not know for certain the identity of these angels, but we can be certain of their role. These seven angels prepare to sound the trumpets. In the Old Testament, trumpets sounded to signal divine visitation. The apocalyptic writers adopted the trumpet as their favorite instrument to get people's attention. Before the trumpets sound, another angel appears.

---

[9] Ashcraft, "Revelation", 292.

Another Angel

In the seventh seal vision, another angel appears in the role of a priest's function. "And another angel came and stood at the altar with a golden censer, and he was given much incense to offer with the prayers of all the saints on the golden altar that is before the throne, and the smoke of the incense, with the prayers of the saints, rose before God from the hand of the angel. Then the angel took the censer and filled it with fire from the altar and threw it on the earth, and there were peals of thunder, rumblings, flashes of lightning, and an earthquake" (8:3–5). John brings an angel he has not mentioned. The angel is simply called "another angel." We have no means of identifying this angel, and we do not know who gave the angel the incense.

The other angel appears in the vision holding a golden censer. This censer was a metal ladle or shovel used in handling live coals. The angel receives a great quantity of incense to offer with the prayers of the saints on the golden altar. John echoes the picture of the golden altar of incense which stood in the holy place before the veil in the Jewish temple. The priest burned incense every morning. The smoke from the incense symbolized the rising of prayers to heaven. With this image John communicates that God hears and answers the prayers of his people.

After burning the incense, the angel takes the censer filled with fire from the altar and throws it to the earth. This action seems to symbolize the earthly effects of prayer. T. F. Torrance interprets the action of the fire thrown to the earth: "What is it that we see? Where are the real master-powers behind the world and what are the deeper secrets of our destiny? Here is the astonishing answer: the prayers of the saints and the fire of God. That means that more potent, more powerful than all the dark and mighty powers let loose in the world, more powerful than anything else, is the power of prayer set ablaze by the fire of God and cast upon the earth."[10] God not only hears the prayers of the saints, but he answers them with actions. Prayer makes a difference to the world.

The silence ceases in the drama, and sights and sounds happen. "And there were peals of thunder, rumblings, flashes of lightning, and an earthquake." With these phenomena John implies that God responds to the prayers of the saints. Maybe John also uses these happenings to introduce another series of visions—the trumpets. In these trumpets God calls people to pay attention and think of him.

The seven seals present a pageantry of suffering. Four horsemen representing conflict, war, famine, and death ride across the course of history, and they produce sadness in the drama. God's people cannot tolerate the presence of suffering passively. They actively ask God, "How long do you intend to allow this suffering to take place?" After the question about suffering, God gives a picture of the end of history. This picture portrays righteousness vindicated and unrighteousness judged. The reader curiously wants to know, "What's next after the end?" The answer comes with dramatic silence. This silence communicates that God is in his holy temple and history and eternity belong to him. Readers receive assurance that these prayers are heard, and these prayers have tremendous results.

---

[10] Thomas F. Torrance, *The Apocalypse Today* (Grand Rapids: William B. Eerdmans Publishing, 1959), 60.

Chapter 8
A Pause in the Suffering for Comfort

Revelation 7:1–17

SUSPENSE BUILDS AS EACH of the seals opens. When the first four seals open, readers see suffering as a part of history from its beginning to its end. The sixth seal opens, and people ask questions about suffering and pray for deliverance. When the sixth seal opens, John uses apocalyptic images to describe the close of a cosmic world system.

The opening of the sixth seal brings a variety of cosmic activities. An earthquake happens to symbolize the visitation of God. John sees many cosmic convulsions. The sun darkens, and the moon turns blood red. Stars fall like figs in a gale wind. The sky rolls up like a scroll. Mountains and islands become dislodged. People of every class and condition hide themselves in caves and call for mountains to fall upon them and hide them from the wrath of the One on the throne and the Lamb: "For the great day of their wrath has come, and who can stand?" (6:17).

The sixth seal brings the reader to the time of God's judgment. It is the Day of the Lord. It is a day from which none would escape and of which all will be terrified. The rhetorical question comes, "Who can stand?" The readers prepare for the seventh seal to open, which surely must fully describe God's day of judgment. Instead the readers get a surprise. They get an unexpected answer to the question, "Who can stand?" So, between the sixth and seventh seals, John pauses to help God's people.[1]

The interlude in 7:1–17 consists of two scenes. The action in the scenes takes place at different times and different locations, but the scenes belong together. The first scene in 7:1–8 takes place on earth. In this scene the people struggle with suffering, but they are sealed by God to enable them to persevere in life's hardships. The second scene in 7:9–17 takes place in heaven. In this scene an innumerable multitude assembles before God. Their sufferings have ceased, and God's people celebrate victory in heaven.

The two scenes picture two groups. The first group numbers 144,000 and comes from the twelve tribes of Israel. The second group involves a huge, unnumbered multitude drawn from all nations, languages, and tribes. Some attempt to distinguish between the two groups. But it seems clear that both groups represent the redeemed community of God. The first group symbolizes the redeemed in the struggle of suffering during history. It is the church militant on earth. The second group is the church triumphant in heaven. The purpose of this interlude is to picture the people of God being helped during their tough times in history and to picture them in heaven celebrating the end of suffering.

God's People Sealed During Suffering
7:1–8

The interlude opens with "after this I saw." These words indicate a new and important vision John sees. It introduces the actions of four angels and another angel. The vision pictures the people of God on earth; 144,000 people receive the seal of God. This seal symbolizes their help from God during tough times on

---

[1] Trafton, Reading Revelation, 77.

earth.

The Sealing of God's Servants

John sees four angels standing at the four corners of the earth, holding back the four winds of destruction. Apocalyptic writers picture the forces of nature under the charge of angels. "After this I saw four angels standing at the four corners of the earth, holding back the four winds of the earth, that no wind could blow on earth or sea or against any tree" (7:1). Winds bring good rains or pleasant breezes, but they can also bring evil desert siroccos or plagues of locusts. In this reference the winds symbolize evil powers standing in restrained readiness. These angels keep the winds from damaging the earth, sea, or any tree. The four corners do not refer to the shape of the earth. Instead they symbolize the whole earth. The vision of the four angels controlling the four winds depicts God's holding back punishment of his people.

Another angel enters the vision. John sees an angel coming from the east ("from the rising of the sun") with instructions from God to delay the blowing of the winds until the faithful "servants of our God" receive protection. "I saw another angel ascending from the rising of the sun, with the seal of the living God, and he called with a loud voice to the four angels who had been given power to harm earth and sea, saying, 'Do not harm the earth or the sea or the trees, until we have sealed the servants of our God on their foreheads'" (8:2-3). The angel seals the 144,000 from the tribes of Israel, and the angel comes from the direction of Palestine.

The angel brings "the seal of the living God." The sealing of God's servants comes from Ezekiel 9. God instructs a man with an inkhorn to place a mark on the forehead of all those who deeply grieve over Jerusalem's sin. This mark protects them from the judgment coming on the city. The purpose of the seal is to protect believers from coming judgments. It protects God's people from the ultimate consequences of God's judgment.

The seal serves another purpose in addition to protection. It enables believers to survive during great tribulation. G. K. Beale thinks "the sealing enables them to respond in faith to the trials through which they pass, so that these trials become the very instruments by which they can even be strengthened in their faith."[2] The seal strengthens faith and protects God's people from experiencing the judgment of God. In no way does the sealing of God's servants mean immunity from tribulation but rather enablement during tribulation. Eugene Boring said, "Faithful Christians are preserved through (not from) the great persecution that is about to be unleashed upon them."[3]

The servants of God do not represent a selected group singled out from among the rest to receive the seal of God. They stand for every believer. The angel's designation to them as servants of God implies that both believers on earth and angels in heaven participate in the service of God.

The Identity of the People of God

John does not describe the actual sealing of the faithful, but he does hear how many are sealed. The number of those sealed is 144,000, composed of 12,000 from each of the twelve tribes of Israel. Some interpret this number 144,000 as a literal reference to the nation of Israel. Others think that the 144,000 are Jewish Christians, and these interpreters think the group mentioned in 7:8-17 consists of Gentile Christians. Still others do not think the 144,000 represent all faithful believers but a special group in the church who experience martyrdom for Christ.

---

[2] G. K. Beale, *The Book of Revelation: A Commentary on the Greek Text* (Grand Rapids: William B. Eerdmans Publishing, 1999), 404–5.

[3] M. Eugene Boring, *Revelation: A Bible Commentary for Teaching and Preaching* (Louisville: John Knox Press, 1989), 128.

History Under Control

The number 144,000 is obviously symbolic. Twelve (the number of tribes) is both squared and multiplied by a thousand, a twofold way of emphasizing completeness.[4] The number 144,000 symbolizes the complete church. Later John identifies them as those "who had been redeemed from the earth" (14:3). The reason they are represented as the twelve tribes of Israel is that throughout the New Testament the church is seen as "the Israel of God," "the circumcision," and "a chosen race, a holy nation, a people for his own possession" (Gal. 6:16; Phil. 3:3; 1 Pet. 2:9).

> "And I heard the number of those who were sealed, 144,000, sealed from every tribe of the sons of Israel: 12,000 from the tribe of Judah were sealed, 12,000 from the tribe of Reuben, 12,000 from the tribe of Gad, 12,000 from the tribe of Asher, 12,000 from the tribe of Naphtali, 12,000 from the tribe of Manasseh, 12,000 from the tribe of Simeon, 12,000 from the tribe of Levi, 12,000 from the tribe of Issachar, 12,000 from the tribe of Zebulun, 12,000 from the tribe of Joseph, 12,000 from the tribe of Benjamin were sealed" (7:4-8).

Several irregularities appear in John's listing of the twelve tribes. He begins with Judah rather than Reuben, Jacob's firstborn son. The reason for the change is obvious. Christ belonged to the tribe of Judah. John omits the tribe of Dan and includes Manasseh, one of Joseph's sons. Why did John leave out Dan and add Manasseh? No definite answer can be made. Perhaps the inclusion of Manasseh was to bring back the total number to twelve.

John does not seem to have any particular reason for the order in which the tribes are given. The tribes are listed in eighteen

---

[4] Mounce, *The Book of Revelation*, 168.

different orders in the Old Testament. None of the orders agree with the sequence of listing in Revelation. The various irregularities of the list of the tribes in Revelation do not affect the interpretation of the 144,000. This symbolic number represents the complete number of God's people, made up of Jews and Gentiles. The people have been sealed during their life on earth so that they can cope with the crises of life. The church of Jesus Christ, purchased by the blood of the Lamb, constitutes the new Israel.

God's People Celebrating after Suffering
7:9–17

Another transition appears in Revelation 7:9 with the words, "After this I looked." The scene shifts from earth to heaven. John again looks in the throne room and sees a great multitude from every nation and cultural background standing before the throne of God. They wear white robes and wave palm branches of victory. They sing songs of worship, ascribing salvation to God and to the Lamb. The angels, elders, and living creatures join the worship. The scene pictures God's people triumphant over suffering and evil in heaven.

The Description of the Great Multitude
Instead of seeing 144,000, John sees an innumerable multitude. "After this I looked, and behold, a great multitude that no one could number, from every nation, from all tribes and peoples and languages, standing before the throne and before the Lamb, clothed in white robes, with palm branches in their hands, and crying out with a loud voice, 'Salvation belongs to our God who sits upon the throne, and to the Lamb!'" (7:9-10). This vision fulfills God's promise to Abraham in which God told Abraham that he would become a great nation and through him "all the families of the earth shall be blessed" (Gen. 12:2-3). God said that

Abraham's offspring would eventually become as numerous as the stars in the sky, the dust of the ground, and the sand on the seashore (Gen. 13:16; 15:5; 22:17; 26:4; 28:14). This promise has now been fulfilled according to the vision in Revelation. A great multitude appears in heaven which no person can count. This innumerable crowd comes from every racial, ethnic, political, and linguistic background.

John further describes the great multitude by telling of their existence in heaven. They stand before the throne and the Lamb. God has been with his people during their crises. Now his people abide with him in ultimate intimacy with freedom from evil and suffering. God gives John the privilege of looking beyond history to the see the ultimate triumph of God's people. The scene resembles Jesus' transfiguration, where he revealed his coming glory to the disciples (Mark 9:2–8).

The description of the great multitude around the throne pictures a celebration scene. The multitudes wear white robes and wave palm branches. The white color symbolizes victory and purity. The white robes also symbolize what God has done in Christ's sacrificial death. Later, in 7:14, John describes these robes becoming white by virtue of being washed in the blood of the Lamb. The palm branches symbolize celebration. The great multitude breaks out in a loud song of praise to God and to the Lamb. "Salvation belongs to our God who sits upon the throne, and to the Lamb!" (7:10). Salvation comes from the sovereign plan of God and the redemptive activity of the Lamb.[5]

Salvation concerns all the heavenly inhabitants. The angels, elders, and living creatures join the jubilant song of the multitude. "And all the angels were standing around the throne and around the elders and the four living creatures, and they fell on their faces before the throne and worshiped God" (7:11). They cry out,

---

[5] Ibid., 172.

"Amen! Blessing and glory and wisdom and thanksgiving and honor and power and might be to our God for ever and ever! Amen!" (7:12). The angelic host first says, "Amen!" which agrees with the cry of the multitude in 7:10. The angels' act of worship happens because of their joy over God's saving act. Their song to God and to the Lamb involves a sevenfold celebration. They ascribe seven qualities to God with each quality preceded by an article in the Greek. It means "the blessing," not "a blessing." It communicates the blessing, the glory, the wisdom, the thanksgiving, the honor, the power, and the might above all others. The expression "forever and ever" sounds a celebrative conclusion which puts all these qualities in the realm of eternal verities. The angels end, as they started, with an enthusiastic "Amen!" to affirm the reliability of it all.[6] The heavenly habitants direct praise to God, where all praise belongs.

The Identity of the Great Multitude

When John sees the great multitude, one of the elders engages John in a dialogue. The elder raises the question about the identity of the great multitude described in verses 9 and 10. "Then one of the elders addressed me, saying, 'Who are these, clothed in white robes, and from where have they come?'" (7:13). Prophets often used the question-and-answer format to explain their visions. For example, after Zechariah gives the vision of the golden lampstands and the two olive trees, an angel asks, "Do you not know what these are?" The prophet answers, "No, my lord" (Zech. 4:5). In the vision of Revelation 7:9–10, John either does not know the answer to the elder's question or is reluctant to reply. John simply says, "Sir, you know" (7:14).

The elder asks two questions: "Who are these, clothed in

---

[6] Leon Morris, *The Revelation of St. John: An Introduction and Commentary* (London: The Tyndale Press, 1973), 117.

white robes?" and "From where does the great multitude come?" The elder seems to answer the last question first—"From where have they come?" "And he said to me, 'These are the ones coming out of the great tribulation. They have washed their robes and made them white in the blood of the Lamb'" (7:14). The elder identifies the origin. The multitudes are those who are coming (present tense) out of the great tribulation. What does John mean by "the great tribulation" (*mega thlipsis*)? The word "tribulation" comes from the Greek word *thlipsis*, which refers to tribulation in general. This word includes all the hardships, trials, afflictions, sufferings, and persecutions of God's people—the constant trials of life which are the result of evil's warring against God. R. H. Charles interprets the scene as one in which the great multitude represents all of God's people who have died during history, all the ones dying, and the ones who will die. In other words, Charles thinks John pictures people continually coming out of the ordeals of life and entering into the bliss of heaven.[7]

In John's mind tribulation began with the birth, life, ministry, death, resurrection, and ascension of history. Jesus' reign collides with the kingdom of humanity in rebellion against God. The great tribulation has existed since Jesus came. It has continued throughout church history. It exists today. The New Testament seems to say that it will intensify as we get closer to the end. Any time the kingdom of God comes up against and clashes with the kingdom of humanity in rebellion, a great tribulation occurs.

Those who make up the great multitude are not just martyrs but the whole number of the elect. They arrive safely out of their great tribulation into glorious triumph. All that the redeemed have passed through in their life on earth is now completed. The elder gives John a picture of the future church triumphant.

---

[7] R. H. Charles, *The Revelation of St. John*, vol. 1, (Edinburgh: T & T Clark, 1930), 213

The elder's second question seems to be, "Who are these, clothed in white robes?" He answers the question by identifying them: "They have washed their robes and made them white in the blood of the Lamb" (7:14). The people dressed in white robes are the ones who have come out of the great tribulation. In startling imagery John states that these people have washed their robes in the blood of the Lamb, and their robes have become white. John uses symbolic language to describe the cleansing effect of the blood of Christ. Their clean clothing depicts a cleansed or purified life that is acceptable before God. The background for John's symbol comes from the concept of blood as a means of atonement. The blood represents the life of the victim (cf. Lev. 17:11).[8]

The "blood of the Lamb" refers to Christ's death. Through Jesus' sacrificial death, he defeated the powers of evil and made possible the victory of the faithful. These people have been "washed by the blood," which indicates that they have committed their lives to the way of Christ. They align themselves wholeheartedly to him and refuse to yield to the attractions and demands of the political power structures and cultures around them. Their salvation is made possible only by the work of Christ. It is his blood, his sacrifice that makes them whole. Who are these people dressed in white robes? They are the faithful in Christ.

The Results of the Great Multitude's Relationship to Christ

A transition occurs in 7:15 with the hinge word, "therefore." Because of the great multitude's intimate relationship with Christ, the elder or someone in the heavenly host offers a hymn of praise for the great multitude's perseverance and purity. The hymn has three parts.[9] First, praise comes because of the great

---

[8] Reddish, *Revelation* (Macon: Smyth and Helwys, 2001), 151.

[9] Osborne, *Revelation*, 321.

multitude's presence and service before God. "Therefore they are before the throne of God, and serve him day and night in his temple; and he who sits on the throne will shelter them with his presence" (7:15). Because of their relationship to Christ, they qualify to stand in God's presence. These people worship and serve God continuously. The word "serve" means both worship and service. "Day and night" seems to be an idiomatic expression to convey the idea of ceaseless worship and service. John does not envisage heaven with the scene of holy inactivity.[10] This worship and service takes place where God dwells.

God's presence shelters his people. The image "shelter" involves a protecting presence. The verb "shelter" (*skenosei*) evokes memories of the tabernacle in the wilderness. The Israelites carried the tabernacle, and it symbolized God's presence in their midst. In eternity there will be no distance between God and his people.

The second part of the hymn portrays God's abundant provisions for his people. "They shall hunger no more, neither thirst any more; the sun shall not strike them, nor any scorching heat" (7:16). This picture comes from Isaiah 49:10, which described the exiles returning from Babylon. The Israelites lacked food and water during their sojourn in Babylon. Their trip back involved the scorching sun and the dry east wind. The elder uses these needs to depict that God takes care of the needs of his people when they come out of the great tribulation of existence on earth. All their met needs come because the Lamb serves as their shepherd. "For the Lamb in the midst of the throne will be their shepherd, and he will guide them to springs of living water" (7:17). In Psalm 23, we learn that the shepherd provides for the necessities of his sheep. Likewise, Jesus, who has sustained the faithful through the great tribulation, will lead and nurture his own.

The third part of the elder's hymn praises God for

---

[10] Morris, *The Revelation of St. John*, 118.

deliverance from pain and suffering. "And God will wipe away every tear from their eyes" (7:17). Their earthly existence has been filled with suffering and sorrow. It has been a pilgrimage of pain during the great tribulation. But these experiences are over. God delivers his people from suffering, and they enjoy fellowship with him forever.

The six seals have depicted history as a time full of suffering. John pauses between the sixth and the seventh seals to offer comfort and hope to Christian communities struggling to maintain their commitment to Christ during difficult circumstances. This pause assures the readers that God will sustain them during their earthly sufferings and will provide abundant reasons for celebrating with him throughout eternity.

Chapter 9
The Attempts for Attention during History

Revelation 8:6–9:20; 11:14–19

A FRIEND OF MINE SUFFERED a severe heart attack. The doctors discovered four blocked arteries, and they did emergency surgery for four bypasses. The initial attack almost cost him his life, and the ensuing pain and discomfort made him depressed. He thought he was going to die, and if he did not die, he wondered what quality of life he would have.

Several weeks after his surgery, he seemed to be making good progress. I made a visit to my friend. At first we talked small talk about current news events, sports news, and mutual friends. Ultimately he turned the conversation to his illness. Quite bluntly, he said, "I don't think God sent the heart attack on me. I think it came as a result of fatty foods, stressful living, and lack of exercise." Thankfully I paused in silence, for he had more to say that I needed to hear. He continued, "But the heart attack got my attention. It warned me that I had to make some lifestyle changes. I have resolved to adopt new eating habits, live life with a lot less stress, and participate in a reasonable exercise program."

My friend's evaluation seemed more than a personal illness report. It certainly had insights about health, but it also exposed theological insights. It said that God does not send bad things to people, but bad things do happen. We do not know the causes of some of these bad things, and many bad things mystify us about their causes. Oddly enough, at the time of the conversation with my friend, I was struggling to understand the vision of the seven trumpets in Revelation. Catastrophic occurrences happen in the vision of the seven trumpets. John does not say that God sent these happenings. Instead, he seems to emphasize the blowing of trumpets simultaneous with the occurrences. The message of the trumpets does not seem to be about what causes natural tragedies, evil actions, or collapse of emperors; but the message seems to be an attempt to gain people's attention when these things happen. Life events have a way of getting our attention about life and its meaning, as well as its brevity. God can use these events to awaken people to him and to repent.

With my friend's experiences and insights in mind, let us proceed with an exegesis of the vision of the seven trumpets in Revelation 8:6-9:20; 11:14-19. Before examining words and phrases, maybe we need to hear the dramatic narrative about the seven trumpets. When the seventh seal opens (8:1-5), John introduces us to seven angels. The angels stand before God, and they are given seven trumpets. The angels prepare to blow the trumpets. Seven angels, one after another, blow their trumpets. The trumpet, which is better known as the shophar, figured prominently in Israel's life. The Israelites blew the trumpet in times of war, at the dedication of the temple, and when a king was enthroned. Trumpets called the people to repentance in times of natural disaster. The Jews blew the shophar to call people to worship. In Jewish life, there were at least twenty-one blasts of the trumpet daily in the temple, and on feast days as many as forty-eight.[1] Simply stated, the trumpet in Hebrew life called for people's attention and called for some type of action such as going

---

[1] Osborne, *Revelation*, 342–43.

to battle, preparing for worship, celebrating a feast, and numerous other actions. John's trumpet vision serves the same purpose. The trumpets sound in the vision to call people's attention to God and to act in repentance.

Each of these seven angels puts his lips to the trumpet ready to blow it. The first four trumpets sound one after the other. The trumpets affect the earth, sea, rivers/springs of water, and the luminaries of the sun, moon, and stars. Fire falls upon the earth. A great mountain is thrown into the sea. A star falls in the river and springs of water. The sun, moon, and stars become dark. These four trumpets seem to describe with apocalyptic catastrophic occurrences in nature. The trumpets represent attempts to get people's attention when natural disasters happen.

The fifth trumpet sounds, and a plague of locusts comes from the bottomless pit. These locusts have a king over them whose name is Abaddon, or Apollyon, which means destroyer. John uses apocalyptic imagery to describe the locusts. The leader and his army symbolize evil actions committed by people. These evil actions motivate people to stop and think about the reality of evil in the world. Evil people doing evil deeds call attention to the inevitability of God's judgment.

When the sixth trumpet blows, an angel hears a voice from the four horns of the golden altar before God. The voice commands the sixth angel to ask for the release of four angels bound at the Euphrates River. Both the Jews and the Romans viewed the Euphrates River as the last barrier for the invasion of dreaded enemies. This trumpet seems to communicate that ungodly rulers and nations are invaded by other rulers and countries. Seeing kingdoms rise and fall with regular monotony should get people's attention that no earthly ruler or kingdom lasts permanently.

The action becomes so intense with natural disasters, evil actions, and released restraints for enemies to invade that John offers an interlude (10:1–11:14). Sometimes life becomes so hard for

History Under Control

God's people that a pause needs to come to reflect on God's truth. Just as there was an interlude between the sixth and seventh seals, so now an interlude appears before the sounding of the seventh trumpet.

John sees in the interlude visions of a mighty angel, a little scroll, a measured temple, and two witnesses. The mighty angel comes from heaven with a little scroll in his hand. The angel tells John to eat the scroll. John eats it, and it becomes sweet as honey in his mouth, but in his stomach it becomes bitter. The images picture the "sweet" possibility of repentance and the "bitter" possibility of a refusal to repent.

John also sees a measured temple and two witnesses who appear to be killed, but they return to life. In the scene of the measured temple, John communicates that the church will be protected not from physical harm but from ultimate spiritual harm. The death of the two witnesses and their subsequent resurrection symbolize that, throughout history, evil powers persecute God's people. The cause of Christ, at times, seems to be dead, but it cannot be stopped. It rises again!

The vision of the trumpets closes with the sounding of the seventh trumpet. John hears the heavenly chorus celebrating victory. The scene pictures Christ's cause as ultimately triumphant. The seventh trumpet seems to be an appropriate place to stop. Instead, John has other visions which give different insights from the seals and trumpets. John has brought the readers from the beginning to the conclusion of the gospel era. In 12:1, another new cycle begins.

Now that we have seen the flow of the dramatic narrative, we can proceed to look closely into the vision of the seven trumpets. The trumpets focus on natural disasters, evil actions, invading enemies, and the end of the world. The trumpets use these historical events to get the world's attention. Various happenings in life may be events to cause the world to think about God, to evaluate life, and to make decisions for lifestyle changes.

Natural Occurrences Get Attention
8:6–12

The first four trumpets depict the elemental forces of nature. They bring partial destruction to the world indicated by the fraction "a third." They represent woes upon nature in its fourfold aspect. In John's day people classified nature into land, sea, fresh waters, and luminary bodies. John's descriptions of the natural catastrophes correspond in some measure to the ten plagues sent upon Egypt (Exod. 7–10).

Grant R. Osborne concludes that the plagues on Egypt had a threefold purpose: to prove the sovereignty of God, to show the powerlessness of the Egyptian gods, and to show Pharaoh he could not win.[2] These plagues called attention to God and to the need for Pharaoh to let Israel return to Canaan. The plagues and the trumpets seem to have a corresponding purpose. John R. W. Stott says, "The purpose of these plagues in Egypt was to bring Pharaoh and his court to repentance."[3] God allows natural disasters to happen to drive people to repentance before it is too late.

The First Trumpet

The first angel sounds the trumpet. "The first angel blew his trumpet, and there followed hail and fire, mingled with blood, and these were thrown upon the earth. And a third of the earth was burned up, and a third of the trees were burned up, and all green grass was burned up" (8:7). This trumpet affects the earth. It resembles the seventh plague in Egypt (Exod. 9:13–35). Thunder,

---

[2] Ibid., 339.

[3] Stott, *What Christ Thinks of the Church*, 191.

hail, and fire rain down on crops, people, and livestock. John adds "fire mingled with blood." Also he indicates the natural disasters only affected a "third of the earth." These afflictions did not happen universally.

John seems to use three images from the seventh plague to depict natural calamities. Bruce M. Metzger says, "His visions may be in part suggestion by storms, earthquakes, and eclipses of the first century."[4] Land disasters may be the means God uses to warn the wicked. These disasters happen throughout history, and they serve as agents of getting the world's attention.

Think of all the terrible disasters which have affected the earth: tornadoes, floods, earthquakes, and tsunamis. These events call attention to the uncertainty of life. They record the loss of lives. These disasters cannot be prevented, and in many cases they cannot be avoided. The trumpet sounds and depicts natural disasters and calls people's attention to God.

The Second Trumpet

The blowing of the second trumpet affects the sea. Whereas the first trumpet referred to environmental disasters, the second trumpet alludes to economic distress. "The second angel blew his trumpet, and something like a great mountain, burning with fire, was thrown into the sea, and a third of the sea became blood. A third of the living creatures in the sea died, and a third of the ships were destroyed" (8:8-9). This trumpet parallels the first Egyptian plague where the water in the Nile turned to blood (Exod. 7:14-21). In John's vision something like a burning mountain falls into the sea.

When something like a burning mountain falls into the sea, devastating results occur. People dependent on the sea economically could appreciate how terrible this was to the original

---

[4] Metzger, *Breaking the Code*, 64.

readers. The effect on the sea is threefold. First, one-third of the sea becomes blood. Second, one-third of the creatures in the sea die. Finally, a third of the ships are destroyed. Something has happened to interrupt sea trade. It has created an economic catastrophe. The sea lanes were called the lifeblood of Rome because the Romans depended on the sea for food and transportation. It is a partial destruction (one-third). It should cause people to stop, think, and repent.

The Third Trumpet

The blowing of the third trumpet calls attention to the rivers and springs of water. "The third angel blew his trumpet, and a great star fell from heaven, blazing like a torch, and it fell on a third of the rivers and on the springs of water. The name of the star is Wormwood. A third of the waters became wormwood, and many people died from the water, because it had been made bitter" (8:10–11). A great star "blazing like a torch" falls from the sky. The star affects the rivers and springs of water. This trumpet alludes again to the first Egyptian plague. John turns from the waters of the sea to the fresh waters on the land.

A great star named Wormwood fell into these fresh waters. The star made the streams bitter. The name "wormwood" comes from a plant which has a bitter taste. The plant came to be associated with bitterness and sorrow (cf. Prov. 5:3–4; Lam. 3:19). G. B. Caird views wormwood as the star of Babylon to which Isaiah referred (Isa. 14:12–20). Babylon made the life of God's people bitter and full of sorrow. Perhaps John sees Rome poisoning the springs with her idolatry.[5] Rome's idolatry and its results suggest the people's need to pay attention and to turn from these gods to the true and living God.

---

[5] Caird, *The Revelation of St. John the Divine*, 115.

The Fourth Trumpet

The fourth trumpet sounds over the problem with the celestial bodies—the sun, the moon, and the stars (8:12). "The fourth angel blew his trumpet, and a third of the sun was struck, and a third of the moon, and a third of the stars, so that a third of their light might be darkened, and a third of the day might be kept from shining, and likewise a third of the night" (8:12). The trumpet resembles the ninth Egyptian plague, in which darkness covers the land of Egypt for three days (Exod. 10:21-23). Throughout the Old Testament darkness symbolizes judgment. Amos speaks of the Day of the Lord as a day of darkness rather than light. Joel also speaks of the Day of the Lord as "a day of darkness and gloom, a day of clouds and thick darkness" (Joel 2:2). Jesus quotes Isaiah in saying, "But in those days, after that tribulation, the sun will be darkened, and the moon will give its light" (Mark 13:24).

John uses the effects of the sun, moon, and stars to emphasize that the actions of the heavenly bodies get people's attention, especially in John's day. When people observed strange phenomena in the heavens, they were puzzled, amazed, and even frightened. Eclipses of the sun and moon did not have scientific explanation. Meteor showers also mystified people. Even while I write, a meteor shower seen in Howard County, Iowa, terrified people. It got their attention. Just as Bruce M. Metzger says, the visions in the first trumpet could have been suggested by storms and earthquakes, so the eclipses of the sun and moon as well as the falling stars could have suggested the fourth trumpet. Readers of Revelation need to get the message of the vision more than paint a picture of the vision.

Four trumpets have sounded. Natural occurrences have sounded to get the world's attention and to lead them to repentance. Now John makes a dramatic transition to describe yet another happening which God may use to get people's attention.

Evil Actions Get Attention
8:13–9:12

The fifth trumpet does not follow immediately after the fourth. John pauses before he introduces a new sight and a new voice into the scene. "Then I looked, and I heard an eagle crying with a loud voice as it flew directly overhead, 'Woe, woe, woe to those who dwell on the earth, at the blasts of the other trumpets which the three angels are about to blow!'" (8:13). The three utterances of "woe" stress the fact that the last three trumpets communicate bad news. The woes are directed toward "those who dwell on the earth." The bad news applies specifically to the ungodly.

The English Standard Version translates *aetos* as "eagle." It could mean "eagle" or "vulture." If "eagle" is John's intention, the emphasis is on the bird's swiftness and strength. It serves as a powerful communicator of bad news. The threefold repetition of woe corresponds to the three trumpets yet to blow.

The fifth trumpet becomes the first woe. When the trumpet blows, a plague of demonic locusts comes from the bottomless pit. These locusts have a leader whose name is Abaddon, the destroyer. As king of the demonic locusts, his mission is to destroy. What does this fifth trumpet communicate to John's readers? It seems to say that evil actions always get people's attention. School shootings, mass murders, terrorist bombings, and sexual abuses continue to make front-page headlines and lead-in stories on the evening news. John describes the power and influence of the demonic world. Perhaps John intends to teach that God uses evil actions to warn, to get attention, and to call to repentance.

The Opening of the Bottomless Pit

Following the blowing of the fifth trumpet, John focuses his attention on the "bottomless pit." "And the fifth angel blew his trumpet, and I saw a star fallen from heaven to earth, and he was given the key of the shaft of the bottomless pit" (9:1). Who is this star? Numerous identities have been attributed to this star. We shall examine what appears in the text. This star seems to be a person, for he receives a key to the bottomless pit, and he opens the pit. Isaiah pictured the king of Babylon as a daystar fallen from heaven. In apocalyptic writings such as 1 Enoch 21:6, the fallen stars represent those who transgressed the commandment of God. Jewish thought symbolized living beings as stars. Some interpret this "star fallen from heaven" to be a fallen angel. Ray Frank Robbins interprets the fallen star to be Satan.[6] Robert Mounce thinks it is more likely that the fallen star is one of the many divine agents who carry out the will of God.[7] This writer agrees with Robbins and thinks John is referring to Satan, the archenemy of Jesus Christ.

Someone gives the key to the bottomless pit to the fallen star. Who gives it? "Was given" represents another way John teaches the sovereignty of God. This star angel had no independent authority. John does not want his readers to underestimate the power of evil, but he does not want them to overestimate the power of evil.

The fallen star angel opens the bottomless pit. "He opened the shaft of the bottomless pit, and from the shaft rose smoke like the smoke of a great furnace, and the sun and the air were darkened with the smoke from the shaft" (9:2). The bottomless pit represents the underworld of evil. It was the dwelling place of demons, evil spirits, and everything else considered to be evil. Opening the bottomless pit means to unleash a new plague of evil on the earth. When the angel opens the shaft, a large cloud of smoke billows out

---

[6] Robbins, *The Revelation of Jesus Christ*, 123.

[7] Mounce, *The Book of Revelation*, 142.

of the bottomless pit, and the sun and air become darkened. This picture symbolizes the evil actions happening as a result of the angel opening the shaft to the bottomless pit. Evil darkens the world.

The Coming of the Locusts

Out of the smoke came locusts. "Then from the smoke came locusts on the earth, and they were given power like the power of scorpions of the earth. They were told not to harm the grass of the earth or any green plant or any tree, but only those people who have not the seal of God on their foreheads. They were allowed to torture them five months, but not to kill them, and their torture was like the torment of a scorpion when it stings someone. And in those days people will seek death and will not find it. They will long to die, but death will fly away from them" (9:3-6). People of the ancient world knew about the terror of locusts. In the Bible locusts appear as symbols of destruction and divine punishment. Probably John uses the eighth Egyptian plague as the primary source for his imagery (Exod. 10:1-20). John uses the symbolism of a locust plague to depict the devastation wrought by sin. He shows how God points to evil actions to bring the world to its senses.

John shows how the locusts are under the ultimate control of God. Their power centers on three divine passives.[8] First, "they were given power like the power of scorpions of the earth." Scorpions are known for their painful sting. John will elaborate on the scorpions' sting in 9:10. Second, the locusts were told to harm only those people who do not have the seal of God on their foreheads. The locusts were also ordered to leave all vegetation unharmed. This surprises the readers, for plants and trees are what locusts would be expected to harm. Third, the locusts are allowed

---

[8] Trafton, *Reading Revelation*, 96.

to torture them for five months but not to kill them. What is the significance of the five months? Some say this represents the life span of a locust. Probably the number symbolized a short, limited time.

John speaks of the pain from the locusts "like the torment of a scorpion." More than likely, John uses this expression to describe the consequences of unforgiven sin. John describes the frustration of wicked people as they seek death but are unable to find it. Physical death does not remedy the "sting" of an evil conscience. John graphically shows evil actions coming from inner decay.

The Description of the Locusts

After John describes the origin and purpose of the locusts, he gives a vivid description of the locusts. This description makes clear that the prophet portrays the demonic character of the destructive forces of evil. "In appearance the locusts were like horses prepared for battle; on their heads were what looked like crowns of gold; their faces were like human faces, their hair like women's hair, and their teeth like lions' teeth; they had breastplates like breastplates of iron, and the noise of their wings was like the noise of many chariots with horses rushing into battle. They have tails and stings like scorpions, and their power to hurt people for five months is in their tails" (9:7-10). Notice the number of times the word "like" appears in the description of the locusts. John intends to compare not to give literal descriptions. The message matters more than the pictures.

John gives seven distinct comparisons of the locusts. First, the locusts appear like horses prepared for battle. They depict demonic forces ready to do battle with good. Second, the locusts appear to have crowns on their heads. This means that evil appears to be in complete control at the time, but it never is. It only seems that way. Third, John describes the locusts with human characteristics: human faces and long women's hair. This image shows the desire of human beings to usurp God's creation for themselves and become the crown of creation, the place humankind holds.[9]

Fourth, the locusts have teeth like lions' teeth. Lions and locusts have a fierce appetite. These demonic creatures have an insatiable desire to destroy God's ways. Fifth, these locusts wear what appears like iron breastplates. These enemies have protection, and they are hard to destroy. Sixth, the locusts make noise like many chariots rushing to battle. Obviously this image conveys the widespread influence of evil in the world. Seventh, the description of the locusts returns to 9:5 where the focus is on the sting of scorpions. Again John uses vivid imagery to depict how evil never satisfies. It brings torment.

Real locusts do not have a king, but these locusts do. "They have as king over them the angel of the bottomless pit. His name in Hebrew is Abaddon, and in Greek he is called Apollyon" (9:11). "Abaddon" in Hebrew means destruction, and "Apollyon" in Greek means destroyer. The name sums up and personifies the character of the one who bears it. The king who leads the malicious spirits for the work of destruction is Satan. This picture of evil and evil actions affecting the world should get people's attention. It should show the world the discomfort of evil as well as the limited time evil has.

What seems to be the message of these locusts coming out of the smoke of the bottomless pit? It seems to be the evil actions of the demonic world. William Hendriksen sees the description as "the operation of the power of darkness in the soul of the wicked during the present age.... The entire symbolic picture emphasizes

---

[9] Osborne, *Revelation*, 370.

this one idea: terror and destruction, for that is Satan's work!" [10] Evil manifests itself throughout the course of history. It has power in this present age, but it is a limited power. Ultimately God will bring history to a close, and evil will be eliminated.

John announces three "woes" in 8:13. He describes the first "woe" in 9:1–11. He announces that two more woes are to come. "The first woe has passed; behold, two woes are still to come" (9:12). The powers of evil do not exhaust themselves in one kind of manifestation. Greater manifestations are coming.

Collapsing Kingdoms Get Attention
9:13–21

The sixth trumpet resembles the tenth plague in Egypt. That plague results in the death of the firstborn throughout the land. That is the only plague in which humans die. Likewise, the sixth trumpet is the only one in which people die. The first four plagues affect the earth. People are only influenced indirectly. The locusts in the fifth trumpet vision attack and torture people, but they are prohibited from killing them. When the sixth trumpet sounds, death comes to the human population.

The Removal of Restraint

John hears a voice from the golden altar. The identity of the voice is not stated, but the fact that it comes from the golden altar indicates that it comes with divine authority. "Then the sixth angel blew the trumpet, and I heard a voice from the four horns of the golden altar before God" (9:13). The voice comes from the same altar where the prayers of the saints and incense were offered (8:3–4). The actions which follow indicate that the prayers of God's

---

[10] William Hendriksen, *More Than Conquerors: An Interpretation of the Book of Revelation* (Grand Rapids: Baker Book House, 1967), 147.

people are being answered.

The voice makes a command to the sixth angel. "Saying to the sixth angel who had the trumpet, 'Release the four angels who are bound at the great river Euphrates'" (9:14). These four angels are not the same as those who restrained the four winds in 7:1. These angels seem to be evil angels since they have been bound. They are probably the leaders of the demonic activity. Leon Morris says, "They are evil beings who have been restrained until now."[11] These angels have been bound at the great river Euphrates. It is the ancient boundary between Israel and her enemies of Assyria and Babylon to the east. Also, the eastern boundary of Rome was the Euphrates, and her enemy at the time was the Parthians.

John pictures God's restraint removed. "So the four angels, who had been held prepared for the hour, the day, the month, and the year, were released to kill a third of mankind" (9:15). In apocalyptic thought God has fixed the time for every event. Specifying the hour, the day, and the month indicates that God has control of historical events. Invasion happens only under the permissive will of God. God's control is further indicated in that he allows the armies to kill only "a third of mankind." No world power can take complete control of the world.

The Invasion of the Army

After removing the restraint at the Euphrates River, a large number invades the land. What invasion did John have in mind? More than likely he refers to the removal of restraint against Rome. He feels that Rome will ultimately be invaded by an enemy. But John's reference is not restricted to Rome. It means, then, any godless ruler and world power will have the restraint removed by God, and the ungodly nation will be invaded by an enemy.

John describes the invasion of the enemy in vivid detail. He

---

[11] Morris, *The Revelation of St. John*, 133.

sees an enormous number of soldiers coming. "The number of mounted troops was twice ten thousand times ten thousand; I heard their number" (9:16). The size of the army is so large that he had to be told the number. Two hundred million horsemen ride at the command of the four angels (9:16). The number seems to communicate the power of the invading enemy. There is strength in numbers.

The size of the army strikes terror, but also the physical appearance of the army brings shock. "And this is how I saw the horses in my vision and those who rode them: they wore breastplates the color of fire and of sapphire and of sulfur, and the heads of the horses were like lions' heads, and fire and smoke and sulfur issued from their mouths. For the power of the horses is in their mouths and in their tails, for their tails are like serpents with heads, and by means of them they wound" (9:17-19). John reminds us that all of this is seen in a vision. He reminds us of the strong symbolic element in the description. The riders wear breastplates the same color as fire, sapphire, and sulfur. These symbols describe the terrifying nature of this demonic cavalry. There is a close parallel between the demonic locust swarm in 9:7-10 and the demonic cavalry in 9:17-19. Both have grotesque supernatural appearances. The heads resemble the heads of lions. This majestic and terrible image of the lion conveys the viciousness of the enemy. Fire, smoke, and sulfur come from the mouths of these creatures. These are symbols of punishment and destruction.

The horses of the army are abnormal. They are fire-breathing monsters. These horses have power to harm in their mouths and in their tails. The descriptions of these horses conjures associations with Satan. Like the locusts in the preceding vision, these horses represent more than an earthly army. They are demonic forces. God allows these demonic powers to be released against the oppressors of his people. The continuous falling of evil empires should get the attention of the world and motivate them to turn to the true and living God.

The Refusal to Repent

The blowing of the trumpets intends to bring about repentance. Natural disasters, evil actions, and collapsing empires call for attention and action. But none of these attention-getting incidents bring repentance. Like the stubborn pharaoh of Egypt, humanity remains stubborn and obstinate, unchanging in its rejection of God. "The rest of mankind, who are not killed by these plagues, did not repent of the works of their hands nor give up worshiping demons and idols of gold and silver and bronze and stone and wood, which cannot see or hear or walk, nor did they repent of their murders or their sorceries or their immorality or their thefts" (9:20-21). The survivors witness events which should get their attention, but they continue to worship idols. John is amazed that people will give their lives to a god they cannot see, hear, or walk. "The works of their hands" means their actions, their deeds. Loyalty appears by what people do, not by what they say.

In addition to their idol worship, the survivors continue in their sins. John gives four representations of their sins: murders, sorceries, immoralities, and thefts. Three of these vices are prohibited in the Ten Commandments. Sorcery refers to witchcraft and the use of deception into evil.

The "rest of mankind" refuses to heed God's warnings. Six trumpets did not lead them to repentance. Probably the saddest words in the trumpet visions are these: "The rest of mankind . . . did not repent." Human response defies explanation. People continue to do what they want to. They continue to center life on self rather than on God.

After the six trumpets blow, we expect the seventh one to bring the end. But John holds us in suspense and intrudes into the drama with an interlude between the sixth and seventh trumpets

(10:1–11:14). This interlude focuses on "a little scroll," which undoubtedly is the Word of God. John eats the "little scroll," and then he prophecies to many people, nations, tongues, and kings. This means that between Christ's ascension and his return, the Word of God is to be preached everywhere. In this interlude John turns his attention to the responsibility of God's people to preach the Word until the end of history comes. This interlude with the vision of the two witnesses in chapter 11 describes the role of the faithful during the troubles and persecutions in history.

Announcing the End Gets Attention
11:15–19

After a lengthy interlude in 10:1–11:14, John returns to the seven trumpets. Six trumpets have sounded. The seventh trumpet waits to be blown. The seventh trumpet blows, and a heavenly chorus proclaims the universal sovereignty of God. The vision is a consummation scene. It announces the end of the world.

One problem with the seventh trumpet concerns the relationship to the three woes announced in 8:13. The three woes were to be the final three trumpet blasts. The first two woes coincide with the fifth and sixth trumpets. But the third woe does not seem to fit the seventh trumpet. The events following the seventh trumpet are not woe but celebration and praise. Evidently, John intentionally or unintentionally omits the third woe.

Though John takes us to the end in the seventh trumpet, he does not stay long or say much about the end. Once again he sues a literary device known as "characterization and climax." He has used this method in the vision of the seals. In the seals he characterizes history as filled with suffering, but with the opening of the seventh seal, he pictures a peaceful world free from suffering. In the trumpets he characterizes history as a time for issuing warnings and calls to repentance. When the seventh trumpet blows, he pictures the end of history. He does not give extensive information about the end. Instead John announces the end, celebrates the end, and gives the agenda for the end.

The Announcement of the End

The seventh trumpet begins with an announcement. "The seventh angel blew his trumpet, and there were loud voices in heaven, saying, 'The kingdom of this world has become the kingdom of our Lord and of his Christ, and he shall reign forever and ever'" (11:15). Heavenly voices make an astonishing announcement. They declare an event that has already happened—"The kingdom of this world has become." The verb is in the past tense. Like an Old Testament prophet, the heavenly voices announce God's ultimate rule as if it had already happened. It stresses the certainty by looking at future events as completed action.

This announcement has in it the reversal of rulers. The earthly rulers are replaced by the divine ruler. The kingdoms of the world have conspired against the Lord, but the Lord reverses the rules. God rules at the end!

This announcement made by the heavenly voices relates how the reign would be forever, not just temporary. Earthly rulers come and go, but Christ rules now in the hearts of his followers, and he will rule in the end over everyone forever. What an announcement!

The Celebration of the End

Upon hearing the announcement of God's ultimate reign, the twenty-four elders celebrate with a song. "And the twenty-four elders who sit on their thrones before God fell on their faces and worshiped God, saying, 'We give thanks to you, Lord God Almighty, who is and who was, for you have taken your great power and begun to reign'" (11:16–17). The elders include the character of God in their worship—"Lord God Almighty." This title for God appears nine times in Revelation. It describes God as the awesome ruler and Lord of the universe. These elders celebrate the God who has ended the world order and has begun the eternal order.

These elders also celebrate the eternity of God—"who is and who was." Earlier in Revelation the elders describe God as the one "who is and who was and who is to come" (1:4, 8; 4:8). Now the elders address God as "who is and who was." The element of "who is to come" is not needed because the kingdom of God has finally been realized. The elders celebrate God's rule in the past and in the present. They acknowledge that there has never been a time when God did not exist or rule.

The elders also celebrate the action of God—"that you have taken your great power and begun to reign." God takes his great power and puts it to use as a natural aspect of his character as the "Almighty." God's sovereign might has overpowered all opposition and set up his eternal rule.

The Agenda of the End

The song of the twenty-four elders not only depicts celebration of the end, but these elders also include the agenda for the end. "The nations raged, but your wrath came, and the time for the dead to be judged, for rewarding your servants, the prophets and saints, and those who fear your name, both small and great, and for destroying the destroyers of the earth" (11:18). God's two agendas at the end involve rewarding and destroying. God rewards his people at the end. The rewards go to three groups—servants, prophets, and saints. These groups make the rewards comprehensive.

God's agenda also involves destroying. God repays in kind, and for those who wreak havoc upon the earth, there is reserved the wrath of a righteous God. John has in mind the rulers of the

Roman Empire who, with their power and authority, corrupt the earth. But these destroyers may be applied to any evil power at any time. These destroyers are ultimately destroyed. The wages for destroying the earth is their own destruction.[12]

The seventh trumpet vision closes with a glimpse of the heavenly temple, which is a counterpart of the Jerusalem temple. "Then God's temple in heaven was opened, and the ark of his covenant was seen within his temple. There were flashes of lightning, rumblings, peals of thunder, an earthquake, and heavy hail" (11:19). Inside the heavenly temple John sees the ark of the covenant. The ark symbolized the presence of God with his people. When the Babylonians invaded Jerusalem, the ark disappeared. A tradition found in 2 Maccabees claims that Jeremiah hid the ark in a cave on Mount Nebo where it would remain until God gathers his people together again. John probably draws on the belief that the ark will be restored in the last days. When John sees the ark in the temple, he feels that the end has arrived, and God has gathered his people. This scene of the heavenly temple is a gracious reminder that God will carry out his promises of rewarding and destroying.

The phenomena accompanying the glimpse of the heavenly temple typify the sign associated with God's appearance. The vision of the end has not told us everything. It does tell us of God's rewarding his people and destroying the ungodly. At the present time John thinks this is enough. More about the end comes later in the book.

The seven trumpets have sounded. They will not remain silent. They continue to blow down the course of history until the end. God's interest is not in human destruction but human redemption. God attempts in various ways to get the world's attention. Trumpets blow during times of natural disasters. Floods, earthquakes, erupting volcanoes, tsunamis, and hurricanes happen

---

[12] Ashcraft, "Revelation," 306.

during history. C. S. Lewis says, "God whispers to us in our pleasures, speaks to us in our conscience, but shouts in our pain."[13] God uses these events to call people's attention to the uncertainty of life.

Trumpets blow when evil actions occur. Mass murder, sexual abuses, terrorist attacks, embezzlements, and numerous other acts call attention to the presence and power of evil in the world. We are not to underestimate the power of evil—"on earth is not his equal," says Martin Luther—but neither are we to overestimate the power of evil. People cannot win over evil without the power of God. Thinking about our own actions and the evil actions of others should drive the world into admitting their need for God.

Trumpets blow when kingdoms collapse. History books are full of rising and falling empires. Domitian, Alexander, Napoleon, Hitler, Stalin, Saddam Hussein, and others provide examples of collapsing evil empires. These historical occurrences alert the world to the fact that no earthly king or kingdom exists forever.

The trumpet blows announcing the certainty of the world's end. God will bring this age to an end. He will reward the faithful and destroy the ungodly. The inevitability of the end calls the world to repent and turn to the true and living God.

---

[13] C. S. Lewis, *The Problem of Pain* (New York: Macmillan, 1944), 81.

Chapter 10
The Faithful Sharing of God's Word throughout History

Revelation 10:1–11:13

DO YOU REMEMBER THE VISION of the seals? Six seals open one after the other. They portray the pageantry of suffering during the course of history. When the sixth seal opens, John describes with vivid apocalyptic language the end of history and the full realization of the kingdom of God. It reflects a terrifying time. You recall the question, "Who can stand?" which comes at the end of the sixth seal. John delays the action of the seventh seal opening to answer that question. He gives an interlude of comfort between the sixth and seventh seal. In two visions he pictures God's people sustained during suffering while they lived on earth, and he sees peoples celebrating freedom from suffering either when they die or when the Lord returns.

Now in the trumpet vision, John uses the same literary technique as he did in the seals. Between the sixth and seventh trumpets John inserts an interlude. The sixth trumpet has sounded, and John sees a vision of the end of the age. George Beasley-Murray thinks the interlude answers a question implicit at the close of the sixth trumpet, "What is the task of the church in these troublesome times?"[1] The trumpet interlude answers that question of what God's people are to be and do in the light of the coming end. Between Christ's ascension and his return, God's people are to be holy and to share faithfully the Word of God.

The second interlude features five vivid images: the mighty angel, the little scroll, the angel's oath, the measured temple, and the two witnesses. Each image communicates some aspect of the Word of God. Also, the theme of prophecy runs throughout the interlude. Three terms for prophetic activity occur a total of five times (10:7, 11; 11:33, 6, 10): "prophets," "prophecy," "prophesying." God involves John and others in prophetic activity. This prophetic ministry involves God giving his word and his servants sharing that Word. The main idea in this interlude is the Word of God.

The Origination of God's Word
10:1-4

The interlude opens with "then I saw." This expression "I saw" appears more than forty times in Revelation. It indicates the overwhelming visual nature of the book. This means readers need to read Revelation with visual imagination, watching the scenes unfold. In this first scene in the interlude, John sees a mighty angel come from heaven. The angel has a distinct appearance as well as a distinct sound. He has a little scroll open in his hand. The scroll comprises the main feature of the vision. This symbolizes the open Bible and its sovereign power. When the angel speaks, the sound is like a lion's roar, which indicates the call for attention. The fact that the angel comes from heaven indicates the divine origination of the Word of God. The most important attribute of the angel is the object he carries—"a little scroll open in his hand." The image

---

[1] Beasley-Murray, *The Book of Revelation*, 168.

of the mighty angel conveys the divine origination of the Word of God.

The Angel Bears Unique Characteristics

John sees "another angel" as he did in 8:3, and again the angel is described as being "mighty" or strong. John sees the angel coming from heaven. Up to this point little has been said about the appearance of angels. It has focused on what they did and said. But John describes this angel fairly fully. 'Then I saw another mighty angel coming down from heaven, wrapped in a cloud, with a rainbow over his head, and his face was like the sun, and his legs like pillars of fire" (10:1). Each one of these characteristics has connection with God or with Christ, so this makes the angel clearly important.

John gives a vivid description of the mighty angel. The angel wears a cloud for clothing. He has a rainbow over his head, which causes his face to shine like the sun. His legs resemble pillars of fire. He has a little scroll opened in his hand. Clouds in apocalyptic literature symbolize heavenly messengers. The rainbow over his head symbolizes a heavenly dignity and glory. The fact that the angel comes down from heaven indicates that he is a heavenly messenger. His legs were like pillars of fire. Fire symbolized God's presence with his people in the wilderness (Exod. 23:21*ff*).

John also sees a little book open in the angel's hand. The little book is not the sealed scroll given to the Lamb in chapter 5. It is "little," which means it does not contain all the counsels of the scroll given to the Lamb. The scroll is open. If the words "little scroll" has diminutive force, the significance would be that the "little scroll" contains part of God's revelation, not the full revelation of God's plan seen in chapter 5. The "little scroll" rests in the angel's hand, and it is open. It is not concealed, and it is not likely ever to be.²

The angel does a unique action. "And he set his right foot on the sea, and his left foot on the land, and called out with a loud voice, like a lion roaring. When he called out, the seven thunders sounded" (10:2-3). Placing one foot on the land and the other on the sea probably indicates that the angel's message is for the whole world. The angel also cries with a loud voice like the roar of a lion. This image suggests that the voice of the angel demands the attention of those who heard. When he speaks, seven thunders sound.

The Angel Brings God's Message

Undoubtedly the most important attribute of this angel is the object he carries—"a little scroll open in his hand." This scroll lies open in the hand of the angel. The scroll seems to be the essential feature of the vision. Leon Morris sees the "little scroll" to be the Word of God.³ The "little scroll" figures significantly in the dramatic narrative of the interlude.

The vision of the mighty angel discloses that the Word of God comes from heaven. The mighty angel comes down from heaven to earth. Readers get the sense that the angel's message did not arise from human or angelic invention but from God.

The mighty angel's speaking like the roar of a lion indicates the divine authority of the Word of God. When God's Word is shared, people need to listen to it. The message relates to their needs.

When the mighty angel spoke, seven thunders sounded. "And when the seven thunders had sounded, I was about to write, but I heard a voice from heaven saying, 'Seal up what the seven

---

[2] Morris, *The Revelation of St. John*, 137.

[3] Ibid., 136.

thunders have said, and do not write it down'" (10:4). John heard the message of the seven thunders, and he was about to write about it. But a voice of divine origin forbids John to write about the seven thunders. This voice tells John to "seal up what the seven thunders have said." It means to keep the message hidden. Of course human nature wants to know the contents of the seven thunders. Numerous suggestions have been made. What these seven thunders were is idle conjecture.

In John's vision of the mighty angel, the minds of the readers have been stimulated. These visuals make us conclude that God's message comes from him. It originates with him, not with an angel. When the angel speaks God's message, we hear a word with authority. The vision of the angel standing with the right foot on the sea and the left foot on the land tells us that God's message is intended for the entire world. The mighty angel "coming down from heaven" represents a symbolic way of saying that the message originated with God.

The Attestation of God's Word
10:5-7

John turns from the seven thunders to the mighty angel. This angel stands astride sea and land and lifts his hand to heaven and makes an oath. The angel attests to the truth of God's Word. People can trust the reliability of God's Word. John refers to God's eternity and omnipotence to attest the certainty of the prophecy which follows.

The Means of the Angel's Oath

In the Old Testament the lifting of the hand was a part of oath making. "And the angel whom I saw standing on the sea and on the land raised up his right hand to heaven" (10:5). Abraham declined the spoils of battle. "I have lifted my hand to the LORD,

God Most High, Possessor of heaven and earth, that I would not take a thread or a sandal strap or anything that is yours" (Gen. 14:22-23). The angel in Revelation lifts his hand to heaven and solemnly swears that the period of delay is over. When the seventh trumpet sounds, God's purpose in creation and redemption is to be brought to completion.

God's people often reflect lack of patience with God when God's Word does not happen immediately. Daniel asked the question, "How long?" in his last vision (Dan 12:6). Daniel has been told by the means of an oath by "him who lives for ever" (Dan. 4:34) that the end would come after "a time, times, and half a time" (Dan. 7:25). But he was ordered to seal this information until the end. John now announces that the time has come. It will come when the seventh trumpet sounds.

Sometimes God's people need an oath. John thinks as a theologian, writes as an apocalyptic poet, and addresses his thought and style to human needs as a pastor. More than likely John's readers needed to see and hear an oath to the truth of God's Word. The secular culture, the religious pluralism, and the moral relativity of the times caused doubts to enter the minds of the readers. The mighty angel lifts his right hand to attest to the truth of God's Word.

The Basis of the Angel's Oath

The angel lifts his right hand to God to make the oath. "And swore by him who lives forever and ever, who created heaven and what is in it, the earth and what is in it, and the sea and what is in it" (10:6-7). The angel singles out God's eternity and his activities in creation. God's character demonstrates the certainty of the fulfillment of the message which follows. The God who brings all things into being can carry them through in fulfillment of his redemptive purpose.

The truth of God's Word rests on his character. The angel

announces the imminence of the end in the name of the eternal God. The end will happen because God is the eternal and sovereign one who ultimately rules and overrules all things in the universe. The basis of the angel's oath rests on God's character.

The Content of the Angel's Oath

The content of the angel's oath involves the coming of the end of history. "That there would be no more delay, but that in the days of the trumpet call to be sounded by the seventh angel, the mystery of God would be fulfilled, just as he announced to his servants the prophets"(10:6–7). The announcement of no further delay comes as welcome news. The martyrs under the altar (6:9–12) had to wait a while. The seven thunders would have involved yet another delay had they not been silenced. Now nothing stands in the way of the final dramatic period of human history. The delay is over, and the events of the end are irrevocably set in motion.[4]

John specifies the end as the blowing of the seventh trumpet. Throughout the ages God has planned to bring the people to salvation. John sees God's purpose coming to its culmination. It involves the judgment of evil and the vindication of God's people. Instead of further delay, the seventh angel blows the trumpet, and the trumpet announces "the mystery of God." By "mystery," John means something formerly concealed but now revealed. It seems here to denote "the whole purpose of God," the joyous solutions of all the problems of history, the consummation of the divine promise of ultimate blessing for the world. It is the message of the Old Testament and New Testament prophets that God plans to bring his people to salvation. However, before the blessed consummation occurs, God's people will experience the hardships of being a Christian.

---

[4] Mounce, *The Book of Revelation*, 211.

The Assimilation of God's Word
10:8-11

After the mighty angel's oath to the truthfulness of God's Word, the attention returns to the scroll in 10:1-4. The voice John heard from heaven to seal the message of the seven thunders speaks again to him. This time the angel commands John to take the little scroll and eat it. John obeys the angel's commands, and the content of the little scroll becomes both sweet and bitter to John.

The Appropriation of the Scroll
The scene in the interlude moves back from heaven to earth. "Then the voice that I had heard from heaven spoke to me again, saying, 'Go, take the scroll that is open in the hand of the angel who is standing on the sea and on the land'" (10:8). John becomes a participant in the vision not just a spectator. This voice from heaven underscores the authoritative nature of the command. Once again the angel stands on sea and earth. This expression seems to symbolize God's concern and dominion of the entire world.

John obeys the angel immediately. "So I went to the angel and told him to give me the little scroll. And he said to me, 'Take and eat; it will make your stomach bitter, but in your mouth it will be sweet as honey.' And I took the little scroll from the hand of the angel and ate it. It was sweet as honey in my mouth, but when I had eaten it my stomach was made bitter" (10:9-10). John now writes about experiences that happen on earth. Actually the angel gave two commands: take the scroll and eat it. Both Jeremiah and Ezekiel had similar experiences. Jeremiah ate God's words, and they became joy and delight (Jer. 15:16). Ezekiel ate a scroll, and it became sweet like honey in his mouth (Ezek. 3:1-3). Neither Jeremiah nor Ezekiel experienced bitterness in the belly as John did.

The second command of the angel involves an interesting

verb—"eat" (*kataphage*). It means "to devour it," to "eat it down." It means to make the contents of the little scroll completely your own. It means the appropriation of prophetic revelation. The angel wants John to assimilate the content of the scroll before communicating it to others.[5]

John tastes both bitterness and sweetness. The scroll is sweet because John knows the good news that in Christ the victory has been won over sin, Satan, and death. The Lamb, through his sacrifice, has brought salvation to the world. The message of the little scroll contains hope, comfort, and assurance. All that Christ has done makes the message of the little scroll extremely sweet.

But John confesses that there is a bitter side of the message he has assimilated. John knows from personal experience that to be a messenger for God is a costly experience. He has tasted the bitterness of exile on the island of Patmos. He reports the bitterness of the martyrdom with Antipas (2:13). John expects more outbreaks of persecution. He also knows that life in Christ involves a fight with evil until the finish of history. The sweet message became bitter by the realization of the cost it entails.[6]

John realizes that his message is not completely one of salvation. It contains a message of judgment for those who refuse to repent and turn to God. John believes in a holy God, a God opposed to evil, a God who expects righteousness. Those who refuse God's attempt to get attention and ignore God's gracious offer of grace experience God's judgment. John, like other messengers of God, has the joy of knowing God's Word, but the messengers have sorrow over unheeded warnings and inevitable

---

[5] Morris, *The Revelation of St. John*, 142.

[6] Reddish, *Revelation*, 199–200.

doom.[7]

The Communication of the Scroll

After eating the scroll and experiencing the effects, John hears a voice speaking to him again. "And I was told, 'You must again prophesy about many peoples and nations and languages and kings" (10:11). John's prophetic ministry is a divine compulsion—"must." It is a necessity in light of the seriousness and relevancy of the message. John has been commissioned two other times in this book (1:19 and 4:1). The commission to prophesy again builds on both of these previous commands. It represents a re-commissioning of his prophetic ministry. In light of what John has to tell, he needs the assurance that his commission comes from God.

John's prophetic ministry is to be "about many peoples and natures and languages and kings." The word translated "about" (*epi*) is critical. If it is translated "about," it is a positive message addressed to the church in its mission to the nations. Some translators render the preposition *epi* as "against," which makes it a negative proclamation of judgment against the nations. It seems that "about" is a better translation, but it needs to be taken as containing both positive and negative elements. Witnessing and warning do not exist as separate elements in the prophetic ministry.[8] Prophesying involves calling to the whole world the opportunity to repent but telling the world the consequences of not repenting.

---

[7] Ibid, 20.

[8] Osborne, *Revelation*, 404–5.

The Continuation of God's Word
11:1-14

In this interlude John continues to share images he received. "Then I was given" is a divine passive which emphasizes the divine impetus behind the giving of these images. This part of the interlude in 11:1-14 contains two different but connected scenes. The first image describes the measuring of the temple (11:1-2), and the second image presents the picture of the two witnesses (11:3-13). Verse 14 functions as a transition between the sixth and seventh trumpets. Both of these images symbolize both the preservation of the church from Christ's first coming to his final coming and the church's continuation of communicating God's Word between these comings. The church will be protected not from physical harm but from ultimate spiritual harm.

The Measuring of the Temple

John's role as a passive spectator again changes to an active participant in this part of the interlude. "Then I was given a measuring rod like a staff, and I was told, 'Rise and measure the temple of God and the altar and those who worship there'" (11:1). Someone gives John a measuring rod and tells him to measure the temple, its altar, and its worshipers. Many commentators note that the measuring of the temple is difficult to interpret. The difficulty stems from the literal or symbolic interpretation of the apocalyptic language. Many interpret the action of the measuring of the temple in a straightforward, literal approach. They think the temple will exist during a seven-year tribulation, the two witnesses are special persons, and the altar will be a place where sacrifices are renewed. Others interpret this apocalyptic language in a highly symbolic sense. They think the measuring of the temple symbolizes the sustenance of the church from Christ's first to his final coming. The subsequent image of the two witnesses symbolizes the apparent death of the church's message but the constant resurrection throughout the course of history. John seems to say that the church will be here until Christ comes and no one can destroy the church's message of the Word of God.

More than likely, John draws the image of measuring the temple from Ezekiel 40:1–42:20 and Zechariah 2:1–5. These references signify God's ownership and protection of his people. John stresses in the measuring of the temple God's sustenance during the course of history. What did John mean when he was given a measuring rod and told to measure the temple of God and the altar and those who worship there? He certainly did not refer to the standing temple in Jerusalem, for John writes twenty-five years after the temple had been destroyed. John appears to be using symbolic language and thinks of the temple not as a building but as God's people. Such a use of "temple" appears elsewhere in the New Testament. Paul, for example, asks the Corinthian believers, "Do you not know that you are God's temple?" (1 Cor. 3:16). Later he says, "We are the temple of the living God" (2 Cor. 6:16). The measuring of the temple happens constantly. It means that God protects and preserves his people during persecution and the judgments of God.

The heavenly messenger tells John to measure only the inner court. The Jerusalem temple had three inner courts—the court of the women, the court of the Jews, and the court of the priests. It had a large outer court which was known as the court of the Gentiles. The part John measures is only the inner court, namely the altar and those who worship there. This inner court symbolizes the church. The action pictures care during times of calamities and persecution. This image of the measuring of the temple has the same message as the sealing of the 144,000 in chapter 7. Both scenes reassure God's people that even in times of pain, suffering, and persecution, God helps them through the worst ordeals. This corporate protection of the church resembles Jesus' promise that "the gates of hell shall not prevail against it" (Matt. 16:18).

The heavenly messenger tells John not to measure the outer court. "But do not measure the court outside the temple; leave that out, for it is given over to the nations, and they will trample the holy city for forty-two months" (11:2). Interpreters have a difficult time with this image. The court outside the temple seems to symbolize the pagans of society. They did not respect the court of the temple even though it had been provided especially for them to learn about God. Jesus himself declared that Jerusalem would be "trampled underfoot by the Gentiles" (Luke 21:24). These in the outer court persecute the church.

In God's permissive will, the pagan society can persecute the church for forty-two months. Is this time period to be taken literally or symbolically? This period of forty-two months comes from Daniel 9:27 and 12:7. Daniel refers to the time of the defilement of the temple by Antiochus Epiphanes, the king of Syria. He put an image of the Greek god in the temple, and he had a pig slaughtered on the altar. This desecration lasted from 167 to 164 BC. This period became a conventional symbolic expression to indicate an indefinite onslaught of evil on God's people. Sometimes the period is reported by months (11:2), or days (11:3), or years (12:14). The period is indefinite in time but definite in the truth that the persecution will come to an end.

John reports the action of the pagan society with the words, "They will trample the holy city for forty-two months" (11:2). This period covers the entire duration of the church's history on earth. In John's imagery "the holy city" represents another description of the church. The word "trample" symbolizes the harsh treatment God's people receive from the pagans. The earthly struggle between Christians and their enemies has been a theme throughout the book, and it will continue to be so.[9]

The Two Witnesses

The heavenly messenger tells John about two witnesses who prophecy during the church age. "And I will grant authority to my two witnesses, and they will prophesy for 1,260 days, clothed in sackcloth" (11:3). The period of witnessing coincides with the period of suffering and persecution. The two witnesses bear faithful testimony to the world about God. They prophesy, which means to be God's spokespersons. The dress of the two witnesses in sackcloth indicates the context of their message. They mourn over the sin of the people and the result that sin brings.

John further identifies the two witnesses with imagery drawn from Zechariah 4:2-6. "These are the two olive trees and the two lampstands that stand before the Lord" (11:4). Zechariah had a vision of two olive trees standing one on each side of the lampstand of the temple to supply it with a perpetual stream of oil. In Zechariah the two trees symbolized Joshua and Zerubbabel, the anointed religious and civil leaders. The exiles returning from Babylonian captivity were shown that a divine strength like a stream of oil would make them victorious over their enemies. John uses this same idea by reminding the church that the two witnesses were channels through which divine strength flowed to the people. God's strength is available to the church when it relies not on might or power but on God's Spirit (Zech. 4:6).

The two witnesses encounter opposition. But no one can destroy God's witnesses before the mission has been accomplished. Those who try succeed only in bringing destruction upon themselves. "And if anyone would harm them, fire pours from their mouth and consumes their foes. If anyone would harm them, this is how he is doomed to be killed" (11:5). This fire needs to be

---

[9] Trafton, *Reading Revelation*, 107.

interpreted figuratively. John draws the image from Jeremiah 5:14: "Behold, I am making my words in your mouth a fire, and this people wood, and the fire shall consume them." The fire of their witness refines and purifies and convinces some. But it is also the fire of judgment which follows those who reject their testimony. No one can harm God's witnesses until their mission has been accomplished. Those who try bring destruction upon themselves.

John proceeds to identify the two witnesses. "They have power to shut the sky, that no rain may fall during the days of their prophesying, and they have power over the waters to turn them into blood and to smite the earth with every kind of plague, as often as they desire" (11:6). The histories of Moses and Elijah supply the background. Moses had power from God to turn water into blood. Elijah had power from God to close the sky to prevent rain. John's images express the truth that God's prophets in every age have the resources of the power of God.[10]

John shifts his emphasis to the future, to a time when the two witnesses finish their testimony. "And when they have finished their testimony, the beast that arises from the bottomless pit will make war on them and conquer them and kill them" (11:7). Abruptly, John refers to the beast which he will write extensively about in chapter 13. This beast is *the* beast" not "*a* beast." It introduces an evil being prevalent throughout the rest of Revelation. The beast comes from "the bottomless pit," which indicates the place of evil. The two witnesses need to be regarded as a mighty host, not as individuals. The beast does three things to the witnesses: "war on them and conquer them and kill them" (v. 7). The death of the witnesses symbolizes the triumph of the ungodly power and the silencing of the testimony of the witnesses. However, the assault and victory by the beast does not last long. During the time between Christ's ascension and his return, the

---

[10] Morris, *The Revelation of St. John*, 149.

church experiences fierce opposition from the power of Satan. At times Satan seems to have won the battle.

After the beast kills the two witnesses, he leaves their corpses in the street. "And their dead bodies will lie in the street of the great city which that symbolically is called Sodom and Egypt, where their Lord was crucified" (11:8). Refusing burial of the dead offered a great insult. It pictures the universal scorn heaped upon the witnesses after they are martyred. "The great city" symbolizes what is ungodly of the world. John identifies the city in three ways. First, it is allegorically called Sodom. This name in Hebrew writings represented great wickedness. Second, it is allegorically called Egypt. In Hebrew writings this place stood for oppression. Third, it is the place where Jesus was crucified. Some link this to Jerusalem. Sodom, Egypt, and Jerusalem symbolize any people that resist God's witness. It communicates human beings having the spirit of slavery, wickedness, oppression, and murder, which has characterized the evil power persecuting the church.

John further describes the scorn and contempt of evil power toward the church. "For three and a half days some from the peoples and tribes and languages and nations will gaze at their dead bodies and refuse to let them be placed in a tomb, and those who dwell on the earth will rejoice over them and make merry and exchange presents, because these two prophets had been a torment to those who dwell on the earth" (11:9–10). The three and a half days corresponds to the 1,260 days of prophetic activity mentioned in 11:3. It symbolizes a brief period of time. John repeats the refusal to allow the dead to be buried. This describes graphically the scorn and contempt the evil powers have toward the church.

John continues to describe the reaction of the ungodly to the "death" of the two witnesses. They rejoice, make merry, and exchange presents. The expression, "those who dwell on the earth," designates the pagan world. The testimony of God's faithful witnesses has harassed the consciences of evil people. The silencing of God's witness always brings rejoicing to the evil ones.

Then the drama takes a radical turn. The three and a half days end. An unusual event takes place. The two witnesses come to life again. "But after the three and a half days a breath of life from God entered them, and they stood up on their feet, and great fear fell on those who saw them" (11:11). Truth that seemed to be dead rises to new power and life. History has often seen the church oppressed to the verge of extinction, but it always rises again. The resurrection of truth indicates that God possesses ultimate authority and control. Each resurrection strikes fear into the hearts of the oppressors. The image John uses follows Ezekiel 37, in which God sends the breath of life into the valley of the dry bones. There bones come to life and stand on their feet. John pictures the church's perseverance during times of persecution and martyrdom.

At the command of a heavenly voice, the two witnesses ascend into heaven out of sight of their enemies. "Then they heard a loud voice from heaven saying to them, 'Come up here!' And they went up to heaven in a cloud, and their enemies watched them. And at that hour there was a great earthquake, and a tenth of the city fell. Seven thousand people were killed in the earthquake, and the rest were terrified and gave glory to the God of heaven" (11:12-13). The fate of the two witnesses is the same as Christ's. They are triumphantly vindicated and glorified. John seems to be saying that the same God who transformed Christ's death into life can transform the church's defeat into victory. The church wins through the power of Christ.[11]

The time of victory for the two witnesses becomes the time of judgment for the ungodly. The earthquake symbolizes God's punishment to the ungodly world for their rebellion against God and for their mistreatment of God's messengers. The numbers "a

---

[11] Robbins, *The Revelation of Jesus Christ*, 141–42.

tenth" and "seven thousand" seem to symbolize a partial judgment, not a total one. John seems to be saying that throughout the course of history, the truth of God seems to die, but God brings it back. Also, throughout the course of history, God judges partially but not entirely. Ultimate elimination of evil comes at the final close of history. More than likely John thinks of this partial judgment as the fall of Rome. Rome did fall, but afterwards other evil empires appeared.

The response of the people to the judgment has been interpreted differently. "And the rest were terrified and gave glory to the God of heaven." Some think the people respond only with terror and dread. Others think these people respond in reverential fear. This fear leads them to give glory to God and suggests their repentance. If this is the case, the work of the witnesses produces repentance.

The interlude closes with an ominous pronouncement. "The second woe has passed; behold, the third woe is soon to come" (11:14). After the lengthy interlude, John returns to the trumpets. Six trumpets have sounded, and the seventh trumpet waits to be blown. The first six trumpets have sounded warning of God upon the earth—natural disasters, evil actions, and falling kingdoms. The seventh trumpet sounds and announces the absolute sovereignty of God. The first six trumpets depict the situation on earth, and the seventh trumpet pictures a scene of celebration in the heavenly throne room. When the seventh trumpet sounds, God's judgment is not partial. It is ultimate.

Christ calls the world to repentance (chapters 8–11). The trumpets sound to get people's attention. The scroll and the two witnesses represent the church's faithful preaching of the gospel. At times the Word seems to fail, but it always rises again. John has once again brought us full circle from the beginning to the conclusion of the gospel era. With 12:1 the whole cycle will begin again with another distinctive characteristic prevalent in history.

Chapter 11
The Evil Intruder into History

Revelation 12:1-17

THE DRAMA OF HOLY SCRIPTURE opens with phenomenal beginnings. Out of nothing God creates a vast universe and a big earth. Then God creates man and woman and places them in this lovely garden. It is an idyllic scene. The man and woman have a perfect relationship. Also, no enmity exists between the two human beings and the other created things. This man and woman have the freedom to eat of every tree in the garden but one. But what is one prohibition amid the proliferation of so many good things! The garden is a paradise. Life is so good. It is a place of perfection.

As the drama of Holy Scripture unfolds, an intruder enters the garden. An uninvited and un-welcomed snake enters the story. The snake speaks in this theological drama, and each one of the snake's lines invokes slander and question of God's Word. In a subtle manner the snake tempts the two human beings to rebel against God. The pair succumbs to the solicitation of the snake. The decision of these two people influences the course of history. The drama of the human story leads to alienation from God, animosity to each other, and enemies with their physical environment.

In a unique way the divinely inspired writer of Genesis 3 introduces the intrusion of evil into the world. The rest of Scripture follows the story line of the conflict of good and evil. Strange as it many seem, the Genesis fact does not discuss the explicit origin of evil. Instead, the Genesis writer states the facts people need to know. He tells that there would be a struggle between the evil intruder in the garden and the human race. The intruder with slander, lies, and opposition to God would do great damage. Along with this entrance of evil into the world, the Genesis writer tells of the ultimate destruction of evil (cf. Gen. 3:15). God communicates through the human author of Genesis that evil would bother human beings throughout history, but God announces that he will defeat evil and banish it forever.

Interestingly, Jesus has the same theology reflected in the garden story. He tells about a master who tells his workers to sow a field with wheat: The workers sow the field, and after some time passes, these workers notice the presence of weeds growing amid the wheat. The workers go to the master and tell him about the situation. The master says, "An enemy has done this" (Matt. 13:28). He instructs the workers to allow the weeds and the wheat to grow together until the harvest day. At the harvest the wheat will be separated from the weeds and kept, but the weeds will be destroyed.

Jesus' parable has the intrusion of an enemy. Like the intruder in the Genesis story, this enemy seeks to destroy the good. The farmer does not deal with the situation immediately. He waits for the weeds and wheat to grow together for a period of time. Then he tells the workers to separate the wheat from the weeds on harvest day. Jesus implies that evil enters history and exists along with good until an appointed time. At the end of time, Jesus' story implies the reward for good and the destruction of evil.

Oddly enough, the last book in the Bible continues to report the story line of an evil intruder into history. Rather than report this story line in an imaginative narrative account like Genesis or in a parabolic method like Jesus, John uses apocalyptic images to tell about the evil intruder's entrance and influence on the human race. In Revelation 12 three characters appear: a pregnant woman in labor, a male child, and a red dragon.

These three actors engage in apocalyptic activity which yields great theological meaning. As the woman goes into labor, the dragon stands over her to devour her child the moment he is born. When the woman gives birth to the male child, her son is snatched up to God and his throne. The woman then flees to the desert to a place prepared for her by God. She will be taken care of for 1,260 days, which symbolizes the period from Christ's first coming to his final coming.

There can be no doubt of the identity of the dragon, for John refers to him in 12:9 as "that ancient serpent, who is called the devil and Satan." Also, the male child is one who will "rule all the nations with a rod of iron." He is the Messiah, the King of kings (12:5 and Ps. 2:9). The woman is Israel. The woman is also the church, the new Israel. This lady seems to be a symbol of the people of God who exist from Christ's first coming to his final coming.

The vision of the woman, the child, and the dragon condenses the marvelous story from the Messiah's birth in fulfillment of the Old Testament to his resurrection and ascension. The imagery depicts an age-long enmity between the serpent and the Messiah and his people. In John's apocalyptic images he tells how this intruder tries to destroy Christ. The intruder's attempts fail, and Christ defeats the intruder. When the enemy fails to destroy Christ, he turns his evil ways on the followers of Christ. Believers win over the evil intruder by their relationship to Christ.

The Evil Intruder Seeks to Destroy Christ
12:1-6

John's story about the evil intruder begins on Christmas Eve.[1] Revelation 12 is an apocalyptic form of the Christmas story. Eugene Peterson writes, "This is not the nativity story we grew up with, but it is the nativity story all the same. Jesus' birth excites more than wonder; it excites evil."[2] John tells how the woman gave birth to the male child. As soon as he is born, the dragon tries to kill the child. Matthew writes the same version of the Christmas story. When Herod heard of the birth of the "King of the Jews," he ordered all boys two years old and younger to be killed (Matt. 2:16-18). John tells of the same event with apocalyptic images. The story of the evil intruder begins in Revelation 12 with the dragon trying to destroy the male child.

The Sign of a Woman and a Child

The pageant opens with the appearance of a great marvel in the sky. "And a great sign appeared in heaven: a woman clothed with the sun, with the moon under her feet, and on her head a crown of twelve stars. She was pregnant and was crying out in birth pains and the agony of giving birth" (12:1-2). The word "sign" translates *semion*, a word rendered "sign" or "miracle" in the fourth Gospel. John seems to use the word *semeion* to refer to a significant person rather than a significant happening. A woman appears arrayed with the sun, crowned with twelve stars, and standing on the moon. This woman does not appear to be Mary, the mother of

---

[1] Darrell W. Johnson, *Discipleship on the Edge: An Expository Journey through the Book of Revelation* (Vancouver: Regent College Publishing, 2004), 222.

[2] Eugene H. Peterson, *Reversed Thunder: The Revelation of John and the Praying Imagination* (San Francisco: Harper & Row, 1988), 12.

Jesus, but the messianic community, the true Israel. Out of faithful Israel Messiah will come. The woman comes to signify the church (12:17). Robert H. Mounce says, "The people of God are one throughout all redemptive history. The early church did not view itself as discontinuous with faithful Israel."[3] In the Old Testament God's people were known as Israel, and in the New Testament God's people were known as the new Israel.

The sun, moon, and stars that adorn the woman indicate her status. She is clothed in light from head to toe. God told Israel that they were "a light for the nations" (Isa. 42:6). Jesus told his followers that they "are the light of the world" (Matt. 5:14). Light represents God's character. God's people reflect the character of God to the world about them. The "twelve stars" seem to represent the whole people of God. The church represents light in constant warfare with the darkness.

This radiant woman prepares to give birth to a child. She cries out in travail and pain to be delivered. The Old Testament frequently pictured Israel as a woman in travail (Isa. 26:17; Mic. 4:10). The time of birth is near. Israel is about to give birth to the Messiah. The language vents Israel's expectancy for a coming Messiah and the agony of wanting the Messiah to come.

The Sign of a Dragon

At the time when the male child was about to be born, John sees another portent in the sky. "And another sign appeared in heaven: behold, a great red dragon, with seven heads and ten horns, and on his heads seven diadems. His tail swept down a third of the stars of heaven and cast them to the earth" (12:3–4). John leaves no doubt as to the identity of this dragon: he is "that ancient serpent, who is called the devil and Satan" (12:9). In the Old Testament dragons were associated with the enemy of God and his people.

---

[3] Mounce, *The Book of Revelation*, 236.

Pharaoh is called "the great dragon that lies in the midst of his streams" (Ezek. 29:3). Isaiah referred to both Assyria and Babylon as a dragon (Isa. 27:1). Readers of John's vision would immediately understand the dragon to represent the archenemy of God and his people.

John has a vivid description of the dragon. His color is red, which symbolizes the murderous character of Satan. Jesus said to the Jews, "You are of your father the devil. . . . He was a murderer from the beginning" (John 8:44). This dragon John describes has seven heads, which symbolize complete wisdom and cunning for the execution of his plans. The dragon also has ten horns. In apocalyptic literature horns symbolized power or strength, so the ten horns symbolized complete human power. The seven diadems on the dragon's head symbolize his dominion over the domain of evil. This dragon represents a composite creature of malevolent spiritual powers arrayed against God. These characteristics symbolize the dragon's destructive intent and power.[4]

The dragon's evil character leads to evil actions. "His tail swept down a third of the stars of heaven and cast them to the earth" (12:4). This cataclysmic action emphasizes the size and the awesome power of the dragon. "A third of the stars" stresses that the dragon does not have complete power. He destroys, but he cannot destroy all. Because of the dragon's evil nature, he has evil actions.

The dragon's primary purpose is to destroy the child about to be born. "And the dragon stood before the woman who was about to give birth, so that when she bore her child he might devour it" (12:4b). Satan has been hostile to Jesus since his birth. Remember Eugene Peterson's words, "Jesus' birth excites evil."[5]

---

[4] Robbins, *The Revelation of Jesus Christ*, 148.

[5] Peterson, *Reversed Thunder*, 121.

Satan sought to destroy Jesus from the moment of his birth. The male child of the messianic community met violent antagonism during the years of his life on earth. It began with the determination of Herod to murder the Christ child (Matt. 2). It continued throughout the dangers and temptations of his earthly life. The opposition of the dragon culminates with the crucifixion.

The Birth of the Male Child

The radiant woman gives birth to a son, a male child. "She gave birth to a male child, one who is to rule all the nations with a rod of iron, but her child was caught up to God and to his throne" (12:5). In this verse John relates the story of the incarnation and its impact with strong, figurative language. John sums up the entire earthly ministry of Jesus, his birth, crucifixion, and resurrection to show that the dragon's power and craft are futile. Satan tried hard to destroy Christ, but he did not succeed. John jumps in verse 5 from Jesus' birth to his ascension to the throne in heaven to show Christ's victory and Satan's failure. The evil designs of the devil failed by the successful completion of Christ's ministry. The child is caught up to God and to his throne. This expression "caught up to God" refers to Christ's ascension.

The words "rod of iron" comes from the description of the Messiah's rule predicted in Psalm 2:9. This male child was destined for world dominion. Satan sought to destroy this male child because Satan wanted the nations as his subjects. But Satan could not destroy Christ while he was on earth. This symbolic action stresses that in the incarnation, Jesus has decisively defeated the devil. With the incarnation completing itself with Jesus' ascension, spiritual evil has been completely defeated.

Just as God protected his Son during his earthly life, so also will the Son protect his followers. "And the woman fled into the wilderness, where she has a place prepared by God, in which she is to be nourished for 1,260 days" (12:6). John shifts in symbolism by the woman in this verse becoming the personification of the Christian church. Since Satan could not destroy Christ, he could still try to destroy the church. The "wilderness" echoes the Exodus story, to the Hebrews fleeing from Pharaoh. The wilderness became a place of safety and liberation. It also represented a place of divine nourishment and provision. The woman's stay in the wilderness lasts one thousand two hundred and sixty days. This term symbolizes a short period for the domination of evil. Like Israel, the church on earth has been delivered from bondage but has not yet arrived in the promised land. During this indefinite period of trial and persecution, from Christ's ascension to his return, God protects and provides for his church.

Christ Defeats the Evil Intruder
12:7–12

John moves from the vision of the woman and the male child to a vision of two armies engaged in battle. John R. W. Stott says, "This second vision does not depict events subsequent to those of the first, but is superimposed on it as its heavenly counterpart."[6] Michael, a leading archangel mentioned in Daniel, together with his army of good angels, engages the dragon and his demonic forces in war. The dragon and his forces are soundly defeated.

This second vision in Revelation 12:7–12, like all of Revelation, is told in apocalyptic language. John intends to communicate spiritual truth, not to paint a literal picture. In most cases Revelation will interpret itself. Readers see in verses 7–12 the terms "defeated," "thrown down," "conquered," and they get the idea that the evil intruder has been defeated. With an apocalyptic mind-set, we shall examine this unique vision about a war in

---

[6] John R.W. Stott, *The Incomparable Christ* (Downers Grove, IL: InterVarsity Press, 2001), 199.

heaven and its implications.

A War in Heaven

John sees a fierce war taking place. "Now war arose in heaven, Michael and his angels fighting against the dragon. And the dragon and his angel fought back" (12:7). John sees a war in heaven between Michael and his angels and the dragon and his angels. Notice that this war takes place after the ascension of Christ. Therefore, this passage does not seem to depict a battle waged in heaven before creation. That idea comes from John Milton's *Paradise Lost*, Book VI. Nothing in the Bible deals with such a premundane battle. The story of the origin of evil never appears in Scripture. The biblical writers speak about the presence of evil, its characteristics, and its ultimate defeat, but not its origin.

Michael is the name for an angel mentioned in Daniel 12:1, who champions the cause of the Jewish people. He is mentioned twice in the New Testament (12:7; Jude 9). In Daniel 10:56, Michael denotes a chief among the angels appointed to watch over the Jewish people. In Daniel 10:13, 21, Michael is represented as the guardian angel of Israel, and he fights for her against the guardian angels of other nations. While Michael occupied the role of guardian angel of Israel, Christians assigned that place and function to Jesus Christ and to him alone. John uses Michael as a representative of Christ, who appears himself as the leader of his armies.[7]

While it may seem odd to modern readers, an apocalyptic worldview conceived of earthly realities has a heavenly counterpart. Thus, in Daniel the struggle between Israel and her enemies were told in terms of a battle between Michael and Israel's enemy. Likewise, the defeat of the dragon by Michael is not a separate event from Christ's defeat of Satan in his incarnation.

---

[7] Robbins, *The Revelation of Jesus Christ*, 150–51.

Michael's victory is the heavenly counterpart of the earthly reality of the incarnation. The outcome of the struggle between good and evil is not determined on earth. It has already been settled in heaven. Satan's defeat in heaven assures the victory of the church on earth. G. B. Caird wrote, "Michael's victory is simply the heavenly and symbolic counterpart of the earthly reality of the Cross."[8]

    The dragon and his angels are defeated in heavenly battle and cast down to the earth. "And the great dragon was thrown down, that ancient serpent, who is called the devil and Satan, the deceiver of the whole world—he was thrown down to the earth, and his angels were thrown down with him" (12:9). As Jesus faced the cross and anticipated his victory, he said, "Now is the judgment of this world; now will the ruler of this world be cast out" (John 12:31). When the seventy disciples reported the success of their mission, Jesus said, "I saw Satan fall like lightning from heaven" (Luke 10:18). In this same kind of language, John says that the incarnation dealt the staggering blow to Satan's kingdom. Six times in Revelation 12 John uses the expression "thrown down." The verb *ebleth* literally means "bounced." It is the beginning of the end. This casting down does not mean the devil's complete destruction. It means he finds a new stage on earth on which to carry on the conflict against God and all good. The suffering of God's people in the world is not a sign of Satan's victory. It is a sign of his realization of defeat. Since Satan could not destroy the child, he goes after the woman.

    John gives further identification to the dragon in verse 9. In addition to being the great dragon, he is "that ancient serpent" which brings recollection to Genesis 3. John also calls the dragon "the devil and Satan." The name *Satan* comes from a Hebrew word which means "adversary" or "accuser." The accuser takes the sins

---

[8] Caird, *The Revelation of St. John the Divine*, 154.

of people and throws them at God day and night (cf. 12:10). The dragon hassles God's people through the constant engendering of guilt. John also uses the title "devil" *(diabolos)* which means "the slander" to describe the evil one. The devil constantly tries to slander God's Word and character. The devil persistently says that God's people are not worthy of God's love because of their sin. The devil works havoc by accusing God and his people.

John also says that Satan is "the deceiver." Jesus calls him "the father of lies" (John 8:44). He experiences deceit about his place in the universe. He wants to control history and to be God. He deceives human beings to think they can become as God. He plays games with the truth.

John further says that the dragon seeks to kill. That accounts for the fact of his red color, the color of blood. He kills people's hopes, integrity, spirit, reputation, meaning, and compassion. Listening and yielding to the evil one runs the risk of death to abundant life in this age and the access to everlasting life in the age to come.

The Celebration of Victory

John hears another loud voice. Remember the expression "loud voice" does not necessarily communicate volume but value. It indicates the supreme importance of what is about to be said. "And I heard a loud voice in heaven, saying, 'Now the salvation and the power and the kingdom of our God and the authority of his Christ have come, for the accuser of our brothers has been thrown down, who accuses them day and night before our God" (12:10). This unidentified voice celebrates the victory of God over Satan in the earthly ministry of Christ. The heavenly inhabitants recognize the victory of God in the incarnation. Notice the time of victory—"now." This adverb points to the dividing line in human history, which is Christ's death and resurrection. Christ's work defeated the devil. This hymn of victory honors God. It ascribes to

God salvation of his people accomplished in Christ. It celebrates the power to overcome Satan. It heralded the kingdom which the Lord gave to Christ. God rules history through his Son.

The hymn celebrates Christ as the one who defeated the devil. The one who accuses God and his people "has been thrown down." The devil knows that he has been "thrown down" by Christ. But the devil knows that history is not over, so he seeks to get as much evil work done before history ends. In his death throes Satan unleashes all the evil he can. He could not defeat Christ, so he goes against the church in the time remaining before the Lord's return.

The battle with Satan has been won. But the enemy does not surrender, and the battle continues. John tells now how God's people can win over Satan. "And they have conquered him by the blood of the Lamb and by the word of their testimony, for they loved not their lives even unto death" (12:11). First, Christians win the war over Satan by what Christ did for them, not by what they do. The primary cause of the Christian's victory involves Christ's great redemptive act. Second, believers also win the battle against Satan because of "the word of their testimony." The way to counter Satan's deceit is with the truth about Jesus. If any word does not have consistency with Jesus, then it needs to be rejected. Third, believers win the struggle with Satan by dedicating themselves to Christ. They do not love their life even to death. Death does not involve the worst thing that can happen to a believer.

Because of what Christ has done and because Christ's victory extends to his followers, the voice from heaven calls for heaven to rejoice. "Therefore, rejoice then, O heaven and you that dwell in them! But woe to you, O earth and sea, for the devil has come down to you in great wrath, because he knows that his time is short!" (12:12). The defeat of Satan brings rejoicing in heaven. It refers to those who dwell permanently with God. While the defeat ("thrown down") of Satan brings rejoicing in heaven, it brings sadness on the earth and sea. The reason for the pronouncement of "woe" comes because of the relatively short time between Satan's defeat and his final destruction. The time will be before the final coming of Christ. Satan does all the harm he can during this time because he knows that his time is short. John takes a turn in the drama after verse 12 from the evil intruder's invasion of Christ to the evil intruder's invasion of Christ's followers.

The Evil Intruder Attacks Christ's Followers
12:13–17

The first part of John's vision in 12:1–6 gives a snapshot of Christ's earthly ministry where the evil intruder seeks to destroy Christ. Beginning in 12:7 and continuing through 12:12, John inserts an interlude or parenthesis to expand on Christ's defeat of the dragon. In the third part of the vision in 12:13–17, John depicts a mad devil frustrated over defeat. John picks up where he left off in 12:6, namely the description of the woman fleeing into the wilderness. This third part of the vision describes the evil intruder's attack on Christ's followers.

The Dragon Pursues the Woman

Satan recognizes that he cannot defeat Christ, so he turns his attention to the woman and the rest of her children. "And when the dragon saw that he had been thrown down to the earth, he pursued the woman who had given birth to the male child" (12:13). Interestingly, the dragon "saw" or realized that he has been cast down to earth. This hints of the supreme superiority of God. Previously, the dragon fought against Michael in heaven, but now he finds himself limited to fighting on earth. At this point he turns his anger against the woman.

The Exodus experience appears throughout this part of the

vision. The pursuit of the woman resembled Pharaoh's pursuit of the children of Israel as they fled from Egypt (Exod. 14:8). There is a double meaning in the verb pursue (*edioxen*), which means both pursued and persecuted.

In 12:6 John records the woman's fleeing into the wilderness to a place prepared for her by God. Now John expands on the woman's flight to the wilderness in 12:14. "But the woman was given the two wings of the great eagle so that she might fly from the serpent into the wilderness, to the place where she is to be nourished for a time, and times, and half a time" (12:14). There appears another reference to the Exodus experience alluding to Exodus 19:4, "I bore you on eagles' wings and brought you to myself." The picture of rescue on eagle's wings became a standard motif in Jewish thought. The closest parallel is Isaiah 40:31, where Israel is told that the faithful "shall mount up with wings like eagles," which means they will rise above their earthly trials through the great strength that God provides.[9]

Look back for a moment at Revelation 12:6. The woman flees into the wilderness where she has a place prepared by God. To the Hebrews escaping from Pharaoh, the wilderness represents a place of safety and liberation. It also depicts a place of divine nourishment and provision. The woman's stay in the wilderness lasts for 1,260 days. This term is an apocalyptic period for the domination of evil and persecution. Like Israel the church has been redeemed from bondage but has not yet arrived in the promised land. God's people are still on earth on the way to the promised land. During this time God's people are on earth suffering trials and persecution. God protects and provides for them during their pilgrimage on earth.

---

[9] Osborne, *Revelation*, 82.

The Dragon Tries to Destroy the Woman

The dragon adopts a more severe measure than mere pursuit. He tries to destroy the woman. "The serpent poured water like a river out of his mouth after the woman, to sweep her away with a flood" (12:15). The river of water which flowed from the dragon's mouth could have symbolized Pharaoh's charge to drown the male children of the Israelites in the Nile (Exod. 1:22). Or it could have been a symbol of the dragon of the sea when Israel escaped Egypt. In Scripture the onset of enemies is represented as a flood of waters (Ps. 124:4–5; Jer. 47:2). Whatever the pictures symbolize, the truth is evident that the dragon wanted to destroy God's people.

As the dragon seeks to drown the woman, a miracle occurs. "But the earth came to the help of the woman, and the earth opened its mouth and swallowed the river that the dragon had poured from his mouth" (12:16). The opening of the earth echoes the destruction of the men of Korah when in the wilderness they were swallowed by the earth and went down alive into Sheol (Num. 16:31–33). In times of difficulty, God delivers his people in one way or another.

The Dragon Continues to Vent His Rage

John writes a significant word in 12:17: "then." This dragon has failed to prevent the mission of the male child (Christ). He has failed to overwhelm Israel and the early church. Now he proceeds to attack the rest of the woman's offspring. "Then the dragon became furious with the woman and went off to make war on the rest of her offspring, on those who keep the commandments of God and hold to the testimony of Jesus. And he stood on the sand of the sea" (12:17). Once more (cf. 12:12) the dragon is angry. The dragon proceeds "to make war on the rest of her offspring." This expression refers to persecutions against all individuals of the church that are committed to Christ. The term "rest of her offspring" refers to the church down through the ages until the end of time.

We must never forget the original historical circumstances which prompted the writing of Revelation. The Romans persecuted believers who would not give allegiance to the emperor. They would not say, "Caesar is Lord." It violated their creed, "Jesus is Lord!"

John describes the faithful believers as ones who "keep the commandments of God and hold to the testimony of Jesus." These present-tense Greek participles stress the continuing perseverance of the church in loyalty to Christ. The phrase "keeping God's commandments" occurs again in 14:12 where it is linked to remaining faithful to Jesus. The commandments probably refer to all of the commands of Christ. The church remained faithful in their witness of Jesus. They would not yield to the pagan power.

Satan continues to be at war with all Christians. He could not defeat Christ, so he does what he can in opposing God's people. A strange line appears at the latter part of verse 17, "And he stood on the sand of the sea." This is John's method to introduce the methods the dragon uses to make war on the church. The dragon takes his position to summon and direct his subordinates. These are Satan's agents on earth to carry on the warfare against the church.

John records truth prevalent in the other books of the New Testament. The difference is in technique not in truth. John uses apocalyptic language to tell that an evil intruder has invaded history. This intruder tried to destroy Christ. He did not. Christ defeated the devil, and the devil became angry and proceeded to wage war against Christ's followers. John tells his readers that believers win the battle with Satan by Christ's action and power. The war continues. It will continue until God completely destroys the devil. If you cannot wait, turn to Revelation 20:10. You will seek what Richard Bewes says in the title of his book—*The Lamb Wins*.[10]

---

[10] Richard Bewes, *The Lamb Wins: A Guided Tour through the Book of Revelation*, new ed. (Ross-shire, GB: Christian Focus Publications, 2000).

Chapter 12
The Historical Manifestations of Evil

Revelation 13:1-18

SCHOLARS REPORT THAT A MAN named Stephen Langton divided the Bible into chapters in the thirteenth century. They also say that Robert Stevens divided the Bible into verses in the sixteenth century. Modern readers of Scripture profit greatly from these chapter and verse divisions. But at times a chapter or verse division interrupts the flow of the story or idea.

Having a chapter division between Revelation 12 and 13 interrupts the dramatic development of the story line. Revelation 12:1-13:18 belongs together as one complete story. The drama in the section begins with the vision of a woman clothed with luminaries. She was pregnant, and she cried out for the child to be delivered. Along with the sight of the woman, another sight appeared: a great red dragon. The dragon sought to destroy the male child, but the child escaped the dragon's fury. The woman fled into the wilderness where God nourished her for 1,260 days.

John gives a flashback in the drama to report the cosmic war with the dragon. The flashback pictured the effect of Christ's incarnation. Christ, the male child, defeats the devil, and heaven celebrates over this momentous victory. But the dragon did not accept defeat. He knows he has power to destroy until he will be ultimately destroyed. Therefore, the action continues in the story line of the dragon pursuing and persecuting Christ's followers. This action closes at the end of chapter 12, but the dramatic action continues.

Chapter 13 continues the dramatic action reported in chapter 12. At the end of chapter 12 (verse 18), the dragon stands on the sand of the sea, and beginning in 13:1, John sees a beast rise out of the sea (13:1-10). This drama is not told in the future tense as a prediction. It is a narrative of John's continuing vision told generally in the past (aorist) tense. The description of this beast from the sea clearly aligns itself with the dragon. The world worships this beast from the sea. John also sees a second beast from the earth that promotes the worship of the first beast (13:11-17). The events of chapter 13 follow the events in chapter 12. Actually, the events of chapter 13 represent the same struggle depicted in chapter 12. They are only seen from a different perspective. Chapter 12 presents the cosmic battle against evil, and chapter 13 presents the historical manifestations of evil.[1] The dragon carries out his work by two earthly entities, the beast from the sea and the beast from the earth.[2]

What is the message of these two beasts? Probably John pictures the power of imperial Rome and the cult of emperor worship. The beast from the sea seems to represent the Roman Empire. The beast from the earth probably refers to the Roman enforcement of emperor worship. The beast from the sea and the beast from the earth definitely symbolize earthly evils prevalent in John's day. The dragon is a pseudo-heavenly embodiment of evil, and the beasts are historical manifestations of evil. They portray Roman evil in the forms of a totalitarian state and a corrupt

---

[1] Trafton, *Reading Revelation*, 124.

[2] Reddish, *Revelation*, 249.

idolatrous practice.[3]

Studying Revelation 12:1–13:18 in light of what it meant to the first readers will help to see how meaningful it becomes to future readers. Rome was not the first world power to try to control the freedom, will, thought, and actions of God's people. Egypt, Assyria, Babylon, the Seleucid rulers, and others exercised power over God's people. John writes with the idea that the totalitarian effect will not end with Rome. The "last days," or the time between Christ's first coming and his final coming, will be filled with world powers opposing the cause of Christ. Until the end of time, Satan will have his helpers in the historical manifestations of evil. Problems arise for God's people when world powers seek ultimate loyalties. The church does render unto Caesar what belongs to Caesar, but the church remains faithful to Christ when presented with loyalty to Caesar or Christ.

These two beasts do not belong in just the memory of biblical antiquity. They have relevance throughout human history. The drama started in Revelation 12:1. The dragon continues to pressure and persecute God's people with malicious evil. History has numerous reports of how Satan has used world power and evil rulers to accomplish his malicious evil. George Lucas, creator of *Star Wars* and perhaps the greatest imaginator of our time, is right. There is a Force. There is a Force at work in the universe, and it is more evil and sinister than George Lucas ever imagined.[4] Students of the book of Revelation need to see what these two beasts meant to the original readers so they can see what they mean to modern readers.

---

[3] Ashcraft, "Revelation," 312.

[4] Johnson, *Discipleship on the Edge*, 240.

The Beast Out of the Sea
13:1–10

The dragon stands on the seashore awaiting the emergence of the first beast. The reason he stands on the sea is to call forth his agent to help him oppose the followers of Christ. Throughout the Revelation, "the sea" symbolizes the realm of evil. The scene is dramatic as the dragon stands on the shore and the beast arises from the sea. The appearance of this beast from the sea unfolds gradually: first the horns, then the heads with the crowns, and finally the body, with its resemblance to the animal kingdom. John then proceeds to give numerous characteristics of this beast from the sea.

The Description of the Beast

The appearance of the expression "I saw" leads to a vivid description of this beast from the sea. "And I saw a beast rising out of the sea, with ten horns and seven heads, with ten diadems on its horns and blasphemous names on its heads. And the beast that I saw was like a leopard; its feet were like a bear's, and its mouth was like a lion's mouth" (13:1–2). The ten horns and seven heads come from Daniel (Dan. 7:2–7). The dragon also had ten horns and seven heads (12:3), but the order in Revelation reverses the dragon's "seven heads and ten horns." The heads seem to be the main feature with the dragon while the horns are the main features with the beast. The imagery of the seven heads and ten horns parallel the description of the dragon. It shows the beast is united with the dragon but has a separate role. The dragon is the king of the evil empire, but the beast is the agent for the king. The ten diadems symbolize the rule of the beast over human affairs.

John also describes the beast from the sea as having "blasphemous names on its heads." The beast from the sea stands against Christ and seeks to usurp his power. In Daniel 7:25, the beast "speaks words against the Most High." This beast from the sea in Revelation does the same thing. Probably these "blasphemous names" allude to the titles of divinity attributed to the Roman emperor. Such terms as "savior," "lord," "god," or "son of God" were used. These titles and the allegiance they represent belong to God and to God alone. Any attribution of them to anyone else is blasphemy. Domitian demanded such titles for himself.

John describes the beast as a composite of three other animals. It corresponds closely with Daniel's account of four animals which also come up from the sea (Dan. 7:2-7). Daniel's beasts are in chronological, historical order: lion (Babylon), bear (Media), leopard (Persia), and a beast different from the other three (the Greek Seleucid rulers). Later, Jewish interpreters identified the fourth beast with Rome. John's description differs. "And the beast that I saw was like a leopard; its feet were like a bear's, and its mouth was like a lion's mouth" (13:2a). John reverses the order and describes Rome as a ferocious composite of the three kingdoms that immediately preceded it.

John does not identify the beast out of the sea. For hundreds of years, many interpretations have been given to the beast out of the sea. In light of John's apocalyptic method, the beast seems to represent Rome, the world power during John's time. This beast represents the aggregation of powers expressing themselves in opposition to Christ. It is sinful humanity, estranged from God, organized in hostility to God. When John writes, this beast is personified in the Roman Empire. But the idea is much larger. Rome was only one in the successive forms of the same God-denying world power.[5]

The Authority of the Beast

John says the beast from the sea receives his authority from

---

[5] Robbins, *The Revelation of Jesus Christ*, 156.

the dragon. "And to it the dragon gave his power and his throne and great authority" (13:2). The connection between the dragon and the beast from the sea is obvious. The dragon gives the beast three prominent attributes. First, the dragon gives him "power," which seems to mean the ability to perform mighty deeds in the eyes of the world. Second, the dragon gives the beast "his throne," which could mean "his dominion." The beast receives sovereignty over this world from the "god of this world." Finally, the dragon gives the beast "great authority." The beast with its evil deeds gets power and authority from the dragon. The totalitarian claims of the Roman Empire with its obsession with power appear to John to be an earthly counterpart to Satan's kingdom of evil.

John unmasks the Roman Empire and its pretensions to dominance and authority. Satan is the real power behind the empire. The emperors may claim to be divine, but their real power comes from Satan. They are demonic rather than divine. The empire over which they rule is an agent of Satan.

John wants his readers to know that the dragon's power is limited. Throughout verses 5–8, John describes the power and authority of the beast as that which "was given" or "was allowed" (13:5, 7). These passive verbs illustrate the use of the "divine passive," which is a way of referring to the activity of God. The works of Satan and his cohorts fall under God's control. Only God is absolutely sovereign. John does not speak of a theological dualism in which Satan is an equal adversary to God. For John the outcome has already been decided in Christ's earthly ministry. Satan continues his assault against God only because of the permissive will of God. But ultimately the activity of Satan will come to an end. He may battle with the saints during history, but at the end Satan loses completely. Therefore, the beast's power and authority are both temporal and limited.

The Resiliency of the Beast

John provides another detail about his beast from the sea. "One of its heads seemed to have a mortal wound, but its mortal wound was healed, and the whole earth marveled as they followed the beast" (13:3). Two interpretations exist about the beast's wound. Some think this reflects a parody of the death and resurrection of Christ. When Christ defeated death, he gives the signal of the defeat of the world power. But world power continues to exist in spite of its fatal wound. If its dominion dies, it rises again and lives under new forms and new names.

Others think John refers to a historical incident which prevailed in his day. He recalls the Nero *redivivus* rumor claiming that Nero would come back and reclaim his throne. Writers give two versions of this rumor. One reports that Nero committed suicide in 68 AD, but they think that did not really happen. So people feared Nero was in hiding, waiting to reclaim his rule. The other report claims that Nero had died but would come back from the dead to resume his reign. Whatever the case, John thinks Roman emperors would arise who possessed the spirit of Nero.[6]

Whatever interpretation one adopts, we need to see what John is telling us. He seems to be saying that the beast is resilient. Just when we think he has been destroyed, he rises again in another form. Egypt, Babylon, the Medes, the Persians, and the Seleucid kings fell, but evil world power appears again with Rome. The history of the world reflects the rise and fall of world power. Just when Nazism falls, communism appears. When communism falls, terrorism appears. The leopard, bear, and lion appear again and again during the course of history.

The Attraction of the Beast

The beast from the sea, or world power, has a bewitching

---

[6] Reddish, *Revelation*, 250.

power. It has a pseudo-divine power. The world is attracted to the beast from the sea. "And they worshiped the dragon, for he had given his authority to the beast, and they worshiped the beast, saying, 'Who is like the beast, and who can fight against it?'" (13:4). The world was astonished over the power of Rome. The politics and military attracted the people of Asia Minor. The power of Rome seemed so complete and so strong that people could not see any other way of life.

People turned from admiration to worship. The word "worship" appears two times in verse 4. People turned to worship the Roman emperor. They confessed, "Caesar is Lord!" To worship the beast (world power) involved the worship of the satanic power behind him. These idolatrous worshippers made two liturgical affirmations. First, they said, "Who is like the beast?" They felt that no world power compared to Rome. People actually sang praise to the beast. God alone is incomparable, and the beast once more usurps what belongs only to God. Second, the worshippers say, "Who can fight against it?" John answers that question when he writes that the dragon "conquered" the saints for a time. The dragon and the beast from the earth may oppose God for a time, but ultimately they will be completely destroyed.

The Limitation of the Beast

John wants his readers to understand that Satan is not sovereign, so he writes of Satan's limited power and time. "And the beast was given a mouth uttering haughty and blasphemous words, and it was allowed to exercise authority for forty-two months. It opened its mouth to utter blasphemies against God, blaspheming his name and his dwelling, that is, those who dwell in heaven. Also it was allowed to make war on the saints and to conquer them. And authority was given it over every tribe and people and language and nation, and all who dwell on earth will worship it, everyone whose name has not been written before the foundation of the world in the book of life of the Lamb who was slain" (13:5–8). John focuses on a key word "was given" (*edothe*), which has been seen in other parts of Revelation. It is a divine passive demonstrating God's control over all things. This verb appears three times in verses 5–8, which indicates three major activities God allows the beast to do.

God allows blasphemy and slander (12:5–6). The haughty and blasphemous words depict the beast's attempt to do or say things only God can do or say. There are three objects of blasphemy: the name of God, his dwelling, and those who dwell in heaven with God. Blaspheming the name of God means to speak evil of who he is and what he does. God's dwelling seems to be equated with God's people. John's words must have come home to his readers with full force, for to regard the emperor as divine was the supreme blasphemy.[7]

God allows the beast to make war with the saints and overcome them (13:7). John seems to echo Daniel 7:21 where the little horn wages war against the saints and conquers them until the Ancient of Days comes and pronounces judgment in favor of the saints of the Most High. John adopts the pattern here. The evil abuse against God's people comes under God's sovereign control. The people of God share in Christ's victory over Satan. Though Satan wages war during history, his end comes with Christ's return.

God also allows the beast to receive universal worship (13:7–8). The fourfold formula of tribe, people, language/tongue, and nation seems to refer to the unbelievers who follow the beast, oppose God, and persecute God's people. John divides humanity into two groups: those who worship the beast and those who worship Christ. Those who worship Christ have their names written in "the book of life of the Lamb who was slain" (v. 8). It is the register of those who have been saved by faith in the crucified Lamb of God. The fact that their names were "written before the

---

[7] Morris, *The Revelation of St. John*, 168.

foundation of the world" carries the assurance that even though they seem to be powerless before the attacks of the beast, they are in the keeping providence of God and have been since the foundation of the world.

John not only gives the limitations of the beast's power; he also gives the limitation of the beast's time to oppose God, to war with the saints, and to worship the beast. The beast is allowed his power for forty-two months. This represents the apocalyptic way of saying a limit of time represented the last days between Christ's two comings. There is to be an end to the power and influence of evil, and God has fixed the time for the end. God has fixed a specific time for the end of evil.

The Victory over the Beast

John calls for solemn attention to the character and works of the beast from the sea. "If anyone has an ear, let him hear" (13:9). This appeal appears frequently in Revelation (2:7, 11, 17, 29; 3:6, 13, 22). If God allows the beast to wage war on his people and to conquer them, what must God's people do?

Verse 10 contains both a statement of fact and an encouragement to faithfulness. Those faithful to Christ can expect persecution and suffering. In their persecution and suffering, they are not to defend themselves by the use of the sword. "If anyone is to be taken captive, to captivity he goes; if anyone is to be slain with the sword, with the sword must he be slain" (13:10). This appears to be a quote from Jeremiah 15:2. One may go into captivity, but the Christian must not resort to the use of the sword. John simply wants the readers to face the facts that suffering comes to those committed to Christ.[8]

But what is a Christian to do? Victory for believers rests on an encouragement or faithfulness to Christ. "Here is a call for the

---

[8] Caird, *The Revelation of St. John the Divine*, 169.

endurance and faith of the saints" (13:10). The resources Christians can use involve endurance and faith. The word for "endurance" (*hupomone*) does not mean passively bearing hardships. It means "courageously accepting the worst that life can do, and turning it into glory."[9] The word for "faith" means that loyalty which will never waiver in its utter devotion to Christ.

The church cannot defeat world powers with violence. The church is not to resist force with force. Suffering patterned after the example of Jesus constitutes the heart of Christian devotion. The church stakes its existence on the imitation of the Lamb. The course of action against world powers constitutes endurance and faith.

The Beast from the Earth
13:11–18

The beast from the sea is not alone. John sees a second beast coming from the earth. This second beast is a henchman of the first beast. The beast of the earth receives its authority from the first beast out of the sea. This second beast seems to be totally dedicated to promoting the beast from the sea.

Most interpreters conclude that this beast from the earth is the imperial religious establishment. A provincial council in Asia composed of representatives from various towns supervised emperor worship. The first beast symbolized the world power of the Roman Empire, and the second beast symbolized the subtle and deadly power of false religions or idol worship. John takes time to give insights about this beast from the earth.

---

[9] William Barclay, *The Revelation of John*, vol. 2 (Philadelphia: Westminster, 1959), 127.

The Description of the Beast

This second beast arises out of the earth. It seems to be less terrifying in its description than the beast out of the sea. It has only two horns, whereas the first beast has ten horns and seven heads. "Then I saw another beast rising out of the earth. It had two horns like a lamb and it spoke like a dragon" (13:11). To come out of the earth means this beast exists in a historical, settled human society. It symbolizes the deadly power of false religion.

This other beast parodies the description of Christ as the Lamb with seven horns (5:6). The horns of this false prophet depict the power of evil forces in defiance against God and his will. This beast from the earth "spoke like a dragon." Like the beast from the sea, the false prophet acts as the agent of the dragon and speaks with his voice. His words and his commands are satanic in their deception and cruelty. This beast appeared in John's day through the priesthood, which enforced the rites of emperor worship.

The Activities of the Beast

More important than the beast's appearance are the beast's activities. He has no independent role. Notice the chain of authority: the dragon gives his authority to the first beast (13:7). That beast gives his authority to the second. It exercises all the authority of the first beast in its presence" (13:12). The second beast's activities relate solely on the first beast.

Equipped with the authority of the dragon and the beast from the sea, the beast from the earth attempts his activities. John mentions five activities of the beast from the earth. First, the beast from the earth attempts to make the earth's inhabitants worship the first beast. "And makes the earth and its inhabitants worship the first beast, whose mortal wound was healed" (13:12). The beast from the earth persuades people to worship the first beast. There can be no doubt that the second beast identifies with the promoters of the cult of the emperor. No one exploited the worship of the emperor more than Domitian, who assigned himself the title *Dominus et Deus noster*, "Our Lord and God."[10]

Second, the second beast performs magic on behalf of the first beast. "It performs great signs, even making fire come down from heaven to earth in front of people, and by the signs that it is allowed to work in the presence of the beast it deceives those who dwell on earth" (13:13-14). The beast impresses and deceives gullible people like the magicians of Egypt who imitated the signs God gave through Moses (Exod. 7:8-19). In particular, the false prophet parodies Elijah, who called down fire from heaven at Mount Carmel (1 Kings 18:36-39). These counterfeit signs/miracles in Revelation 13:14 fall under divine control. The repetition of the divine passive, "was given," anchors the action in God's control.

Third, the beast from the earth orders the people to set up an image or statue in honor of the first beast. "Telling them to make an image for the beast that was wounded by the sword and yet lived" (13:14). As a result of the beast's orders, numerous idolatrous statues to the emperor appeared throughout Asia. Ephesus, for example, had temples dedicated to Julius Caesar, Augustus, and Domitian. Worship of the emperor prevailed throughout the Roman province of Asia.

Fourth, the beast from the earth gives power to make the first beast's image speak and to cause those who refused to worship the image to be killed. "And it was allowed to give breath to the image of the beast, so that the image of the beast might even speak and might cause those who would not worship the image of the beast to be slain" (13:15). Another example of the signs attributed to the beast involved the giving of life to the image of the first beast, enabling it to speak. The power to make statues speak through ventriloquism was widely known in the ancient world. Legends grew up around the person of Simon Magus (Acts 8:9ff).

---

[10] Beasley-Murray, *The Book of Revelation*, 216–17.

Early Christian literature relates how he brought statues to life. Of course John emphasizes that this power of the beast did not reside in it. It "was allowed" to do this. The apparent quickening of the beast imitates the divine claim to divine power. Only God creates life.[11]

The image not only spoke but also passed the sentence of death. Those who would not worship the image of the emperor had the death sentence. False religion seeks to convince people that they must conform to world power's wishes or suffer the consequences.

Fifth, the beast from the earth uses economic boycott to coerce emperor worship. "Also it causes all, both small and great, both rich and poor, both free and slave, to be marked on the right hand or the forehead, so that no one can buy or sell unless he has the mark, that is, the name of the beast or the number of its name" (13:16–17). What did John mean by the marks of the beast? Whatever the mark means, it affects every human being: the small and the great, the rich and the poor, the free and the slave. The mark given to those who refuse to worship the emperor seems to be a parody of the mark given to the servants of God (7:3). God's people are sealed with a mark to indicate they belong to God, and the worshippers of the emperors are marked to indicate where their loyalties belong. According to John, one either belongs to God, or one belongs to the beast. The meaning of the "mark" has various explanations. Some see a literal mark on a person's forehead or right hand. Others think John speaks symbolically. John seems to be saying that those who participate in emperor worship "mark" themselves with behavior resembling Satan's character.

Maybe the mark's identity lies in recognizing that once again the beast mimics Jesus Christ. Jesus puts his mark on his people. Is it a literal mark? No, it is more real. In Jesus' case the

---

[11] Ladd, *A Commentary on the Revelation of John*, 184.

mark or seal is his name. It does not mean that his literal name *Jesus* is written on his followers' foreheads. Instead, the "name" means his character. The mark of Jesus Christ is his character in believers. So, too, the mark of the beast is not a tattoo on the forehead or the right hand. It is the character of the beast implanted in the soul. G. K. Beale thinks the mark on the forehead represents ideological commitment, and the "hand" represents the practical outworking of that commitment.[12] These verses (16-17) teach the ostracisms and boycotts to which believers are subjected if they persist in refusing homage to the world power. John expects the beast, aided by the false prophet, to achieve a totalitarian rule in which he has control over people with the purpose of compelling all to worship.

The Name of the Beast

John pauses briefly to make an additional attempt to identify this beast out of the earth. "This calls for wisdom: let the one who has understanding calculate the number of the beast, for it is the number of a man, and his number is 666" (13:18). John's observation of the demand for wisdom does not need to be overlooked on the way to interpret the number 666. John calls for readers to exercise extreme care and to seek divine wisdom in interpreting the number of the beast.

Numerous interpretations exist about the number 666. Two positions seem to be the most prominent. The first is what we shall call the gematria position. Those who espouse this view think that the number represents a practice of gematria, in which words or names are coded as numbers. In the ancient world, letters of the alphabet functioned as numbers also. For example, in the English alphabet A = 1, B = 2, C = 3, etc. Therefore any word or name could have numerical value, based on the sum of the individual numbers in the word. Although it is easy to turn a name into a number, it

---

[12] Beale, *The Book of Revelation*, 708.

is not easy to turn a number into a name. This explains why so many names have been suggested for the 666 of the beast. The name suggested most often is Nero. His name in Greek is *Neron Kaiser*. If you transliterate his Greek name into Hebrew and do the gematria, his name, *nron gsr* comes out to 666. Other interpreters suggest a symbolic meaning for 666. Seven is the number of perfection or completeness. Six is the number for incompleteness, imperfection, and even evil since it is one less than seven. Accordingly, 666 would be a triple evil. Three is the number for God, thus 666 would be an appropriate number for evil people who try to be God. The counterfeit trinity—the dragon, the beast from the sea, and the beast from the earth—try to substitute emperor worship for worshiping God. But it always falls short—666. The beast from the earth persuades people to substitute allegiance and commitment from God to the world powers.

Satan's battle against humanity primarily involves a religious war. The beast from the earth in a sense is the high priest for the imperial cult. He persuades people to worship the beast from the sea or world power. The beast from the sea's ultimate motivation comes from the dragon or Satan. John's readers see the high council of the region and the priest of the imperial cult placing pressure on people to participate in emperor worship. Also, people are expected to participate in the trade guild feasts, which involved idolatry and sexual immorality. Refusing to worship the emperor and to participate in guild ceremonies cost people their status in the community, their jobs, and sometimes their life. Satan and evil were not just philosophical or theological discussions among Christians in Asia. Satan's using force to worship the emperor was a real historical manifestation of evil.

Satan or the dragon continues to enlist world power and false religion to oppose the people of God. The beast from the sea comes back after a mortal wound (13:3). World power continues to come back despite its fatal wound. If its dominion falls, it rises again. It lives under new forms and new names. Just when Rome falls, communism arises. Just when communism falls, nationalism appears. Just when nationalism becomes obsolete, terrorism arises. Evil world powers exist through the course of history until Jesus comes.

In light of the continuing power of Satan, many "antichrists" (1 John 2:18) have risen and fallen. This beast from the earth has its mortal wound healed and appears in another form with a new name (13:12). False teachers draw people away from Christ to worship false gods. Many "religions" exist today which depreciate Christ and persuade people to worship another god. Probably the most insidious religious movement of our time is not labeled a religion but secularism. People make humanism, materialism, hedonism, and other expressions their god. The beast from the sea operated in John's day seeking to turn people away from Christ to other loyalties. The beast from the earth has been healed or appears in another form today. John in Revelation calls each generation of Christians to be faithful to Christ.

Chapter 13
An Interlude about the End of History

Revelation 14:1–20

IN THE LATE 1800S AND EARLY 1900S, Edward Stratemeyer created a series of novels entitled "The Hardy Boys." Other writers continued the series after Stratemeyer's death.

Frank and Joe were the teenage sons of their detective father Fenten Hardy. Unbeknown to their father, the boys constantly sought to snoop in the action of their father's cases. The novels contained the Hardy boys' involvement in kidnaping, smuggling, robbery, missing persons, and haunted houses.

I remember reading one of the novels entitled *The Secret of the Old Mill*. The novel relates how Frank and Joe became involved in one of their father's cases. The villains in the story captured the boys and took them to an old mill. As I read, my anxiety level increased, wondering what would happen to these boys. I knew if they were killed, I would have no more Hardy boys books to read. I could not take the suspense, so I turned to the end of the book. I read where Frank and Joe enjoyed time with their parents. I went back to the suspense part and continued reading, knowing how the events would end.

John's vision of the dragon, the beast from the sea, and the beast from the earth creates suspense for the readers. The scenes do not comfort the readers. Admittingly, the dragon has been thrown down from heaven. But he still takes revenge on the offspring of the woman. What the dragon and its cohorts do to the Christians in 13:1–18 brings great fear. The vision of cruel persecution is suddenly interrupted by a message of comfort. It is appropriate, then, for John to stop in the dramatic action and once again offer an interlude of comfort. You will remember that an interlude appears between the action of the sixth and seventh seals (7:1–17) and the sixth and seventh trumpets (10:1–11:14). As with the other interludes, this interlude functions to offer reassurance to the faithful. It gives a picture of the end which follows suffering and persecution.

John pictures the course of history filled with much suffering and death as depicted in chapters 12 and 13. What comfort do the faithful have? If Satan and his cohorts wreak such havoc on God's people, is there any hope? Chapter 14 answers that question through visions of reward for God's people and punishment for the wicked.[1] In chapter 14, John gives the reader a brief look at the end before he writes extensively about the end. Chapter 14 contains three loosely connected scenes. Each begins with *kai eidon*, "then I looked" (v. 1), "then I saw" (v. 6), and "then I looked" (v. 14). John sees the Lamb and the 144,000 (14:1–5); he sees three flying angels with messages of judgment (14:6–13); and he sees two visions of harvest (14:14–20).[2] All of the visions have some insight about future hope in light of the present adversities.

A Picture of God's People at the End of History
14:1–5

John has written about the great powers of Satanic evil embodied in the two beasts as they have forced the world into idolatry. Now he abruptly turns to a vision of the Lamb and his

---

[1] Reddish, *Revelation*, 271.

[2] Trafton, *Reading Revelation*, 133.

army standing on Mount Zion. This turn in the drama gives welcome relief to the readers. The readers turn from the dragon and the beasts to the Lamb who stands on firm and holy ground. The readers turn from persecution and martyrdom to security on Mount Zion.

The Lamb and His Followers

In contrast to Satan's beast, who occupied the sea and land, the Lamb occupies the higher ground of Mount Zion. Probably John echoes Joel's prophecy that on Mount Zion God's people would escape the great and terrible day of the Lord (Joel 2:32). "Then I looked, and behold, on Mount Zion stood the Lamb, and with him 144,000 who had his name and his Father's name written on their foreheads" (14:1). Suddenly John sees the Lamb standing on Mount Zion accompanied by 144,000 who bear his name on their foreheads. Obviously John contrasts the beast of chapter 13, whose followers have his mark on their right hand or forehead. The Lamb is the same one John mentioned in 5:6, whom the second beast attempted to impersonate. He is the Lamb worthy to take the scroll, which is the meaning and course of history, and to open it (ch. 8). He is the Lamb who receives the adulation of the immeasurable multitude in heaven (ch. 7). Now he is the Lamb standing victorious with his followers on Mount Zion.

John sees the Lamb standing on Mount Zion. David took Jerusalem from the Jebusites by capturing the "stronghold of Zion," which he renamed the City of David. Solomon later built the temple on a hill north of the City of David. Hence, the site of the temple along with Jerusalem itself came to be known as "Mount Zion." Earthly Jerusalem was seen in the biblical tradition as a counterpart of the heavenly city and symbolized security, protection, and the presence of God.[3] The mountain in John's

---

[3] Reddish, *Revelation*, 273.

vision doesn't exist on earth. It is a heavenly Zion. The scene John sees seems to depict the Lamb in the throne room of heaven.

John's vision not only contains the sight of the Lamb, standing on Mount Zion, but it also contains the Lamb's followers standing with him. The Lamb's followers consist of 144,000, who represent all the followers of Christ. The 144,000 represent the same groups John described in 5:9-10 and 7:1-8. It stands in striking contrast to those who worship the beast (13:12). John sees all of the faithful Christians standing in the presence of Christ with the name of God inscribed on their foreheads in contrast to those who have the mark of the beast. Bearing the name of Christ means to share in his nature. Believers have allowed Christ to unite his life with their lives. This indwelling allows the possibility of being Christlike.

The New Song of the Redeemed

John hears music coming from the heavenly throne room. "And I heard a voice from heaven like the roar of many waters and like the sound of loud thunder. The voice I heard was like the sound of harpists playing on their harps, and they were singing a new song before the throne and before the four living creatures and before the elders. No one could learn that song except the 144,000 who had been redeemed from the earth" (14:2-3). John likens the marvelous music to a waterfall, a clap of thunder, and an orchestra of harpists. A choir sings a new song before the heavenly audience. This choir consists of the 144,000 standing with the Lamb on Mount Zion. The choir sings the song before the throne, before four living creatures, and before the elders.

John does not say why only the 144,000 could learn the song. But since John immediately refers to them as "redeemed from the earth," it is a legitimate inference that the song is connected to that experience. Without the experience of redemption, no one could sing the song. "Redeemed from the earth" means all who come from the earth, but they have been delivered from their "earth nature."[4]

The Characteristics of the Redeemed

The triple usage of "these" calls attention to the distinguishing marks of the redeemed. The first mark is faithfulness. "It is these who have not defiled themselves with women, for they are virgins" (14:4). Adultery and fornication are widely used in Scripture as a figure of idolatry. The statement that the redeemed are "virgins" is to be taken metaphorically as a symbol of the faithful Christians who have not participated in emperor worship or any other form of idolatry. They are pure in their relations with Christ.[5]

The second mark of the redeemed is dedication. "It is these who follow the Lamb wherever he goes" (14:4). The redeemed follow Christ, even if it means suffering or death. With the use of the present tense "follow," John stresses ongoing fidelity to the Lamb.

The third mark of the redeemed is their specialness. Christ ransomed them from slavery with is own blood. "These have been redeemed from mankind as firstfruits for God and the Lamb" (14:4). This means that the 144,000, in a special sense, belong to God. They are a holy offering to the Lord. Their specialness is also reflected in their speech. "And in their mouth no lie was found, for they are blameless" (14:5). By contrast the beast maintains his power by deception. The 144,000 represent people of special integrity, uncontaminated by falsehood or hypocrisy. They did not confess, "Caesar is Lord," to escape punishment by the Romans.

John describes the 144,000 as ones who remain faithful to

---

[4] Morris, 167.

[5] Robbins, *The Revelation of Jesus Christ*, 167.

Christ. They are so committed to Christ that they will follow him, even if it means suffering and death. They are different from the world. They are God's special possession consecrating themselves to the service of God.

John assures the readers of the security of God's redeemed people. John returns the readers to the 1444,000, the great multitude. Despite all that the dragon tries to do, the Lamb has a group faithful to him. They do not have the mark of the beast on their foreheads. They belong to God and to the Lamb, and they are protected forever by the Father and the Lamb.

The Three Angels with Messages of Judgment
14:6–12

The second vision of chapter 14 consists of messages from three different angels: "Then I saw." Each angel proclaims the coming judgment of God. By calling the angel of verse 6 "another angel," John makes a distinction from angels previously mentioned in the book. The vision of the three angels continues with insight about the end. A vivid contrast exists between the evil intruders and the followers of Christ. The followers of the Lamb stand with the Lamb victorious on Mount Zion. But the evil intruders suffer God's judgment at the end.

The First Angel

The first angel calls for people on the earth to decide for God. It is the time to decide for God. "Then I saw another angel flying directly overhead, with an eternal gospel to proclaim to those who dwell on earth, to every nation and tribe and language and people. And he said with a loud voice, 'Fear God and give him glory, because the hour of his judgment has come, and worship him who made heaven and earth, the sea and the springs of water'" (14:6–7). The angel flies in midheaven, which symbolizes that the message could be seen and heard by all the world. The fourfold enumeration of nation, tribe, language, and people emphasizes that the angel's message is for worldwide proclamation. The angel proclaims "the eternal gospel." It is the good news of God's redeeming grace in Christ. The angel makes an appeal for people to decide for Christ.

The angel's proclamation includes a summons to "those who dwell on earth" to respond, to fear and glorify God, and to worship the Creator. The angel's message has a sense of urgency for people to respond: "Because the hour of his judgment has come." The time to decide for God is always "now." The people are called to "fear God," which means to submit to God with reverence and obedience. To those who respond in repentance to the angel's message, this is indeed good news, for they will share in God's eternal kingdom.

The Second Angel

The second angel makes an advance announcement of the fall of Babylon. "Another angel, a second, followed, saying, 'Fallen, fallen is Babylon the great, she who made all nations drink the wine of the passion of her sexual immorality'" (14:8). The angel announces the fall of Babylon as if it has already occurred. The introduction of this symbolic reference to Babylon assumes the readers understand the allusion. Because ancient Babylon destroyed Jerusalem and the temple, the name came to be associated with any world power who opposed God. For the early church the Roman Empire became the contemporary Babylon. Leon Morris says, "Babylon is the great city, the symbol of man in community opposed to the things of God."[6] For John, Domitian is the new Nebuchadnezzar, demanding that the people worship the image he has constructed (Dan. 3). Rome has become the terrible persecutor

---

[6] Morris, *The Revelation of St. John*, 180.

of God's people, the new Babylon, that is, the enemy of God.[7]

John echoes Jeremiah when he states that Rome has made all nations drink the wine of her impure passion (see Jer. 51:7). Rome attracts people with her power and her riches. By her demands to worship the emperor, she makes God's people commit "fornication" or unfaithfulness to God. People in Asia become intoxicated with idolatry or emperor worship.

Not only does Rome entice people to drink of this cup of idolatry, but it is also the cup of wrath. Drinking from the cup of Rome brings terrible consequences. It brings people under divine judgment. Any city or system intoxicated with itself must drink inevitably of the wine of the wrath of God. This fall of Rome is described at greater length in a later vision (chapters 17–18).

The Third Angel

The third angel warns all the people not to identify themselves with world power and describes the retribution upon those who do. "And another angel, a third, followed them, saying with a loud voice, 'If anyone worships the beast and its image and receives a mark on his forehead or on his hand, he also will drink the wine of God's wrath, poured full strength into the cup of his anger, and he will be tormented with fire and sulfur in the presence of the holy angels and in the presence of the Lamb. And the smoke of their torment goes up forever and ever, and they have no rest, day or night, these worshipers of the beast and its image, and whoever receives the mark of its name'" (14:9–11). To "worship" the beast means submission to it, affirmation of its supremacy. The worshipers of God have his seal upon them (7:1–8), and they also have Christ's name and the Father's name imprinted on their foreheads (14:1). Likewise, the worshipers of world power and his image have his mark upon them (13:11–18). The object of a

---

[7] Reddish, *Revelation*, 277.

person's devotion changes him or her into its character. Therefore, one either has the seal of Christ or the mark of the beast.

John states the penalties for bearing the mark of the beast. They will be the objects of divine wrath. They will "drink the wine of God's wrath, poured full strength into the cup of his anger." Wine was often mixed with water to make it weaker. The punishment, however, of the followers of the beast will be full strength. John describes God's wrath with imagery from God's judgment upon Sodom and Gomorrah (Gen. 19:24). The worshipers of the beast will be tormented with fire and sulfur. John thinks the consequences of rebelling against God follow sinners in the life to come. In contrast to the rest of the saints (14:13), the worshipers of the beast have no rest day or night. Their state is one of continuous agony. It is a state of constant restlessness.

John follows the third angel's announcement with an exhortation. "Here is a call for the endurance of the saints, those who keep the commandments of God and their faith in Jesus" (14:12). In light of all the beast seeks to inflict upon the followers of Christ, John sees an opportunity for the church to show its loyalty and character. "Endurance" means steadfastness in tough circumstances. "Faith in Jesus" means the believers' relationship with Christ and their trust in him. Both reliance upon Christ and steadfastness are important in trying times.

This section of chapter 14 closes with a voice from heaven instructing John to write down a beatitude. "And I heard a voice from heaven saying, 'Write this: Blessed are the dead who die in the Lord from now on.' 'Blessed indeed,' says the Spirit, 'that they may rest from their labors, for their deeds follow them!'" (14:13). It is important that the readers heed these words, for they begin with a "voice from heaven" and end with a message from "the Spirit." This statement is one of seven beatitudes in Revelation for the people of God (1:3; 14:13; 16:15; 19:9; 20:6; 22:7, 14). The one in 14:13 seems to relate specifically for martyrs. The words "from now on" could indicate that John has in mind the faithful believers who died in the persecution by the beast. But all believers who die in the Lord are blessed. This blessedness involves "rest from their labors." This "rest" is the final rest in eternity for which the temporary rest of 6:11 prepared. They will no longer experience trials and persecution. This period of rest the believers enjoy differs drastically from the lack of rest imposed on those who worship the beast (14:11). This blessedness of the believers also involves reward because "their deeds follow them." This statement does not imply a works righteousness which could indicate that people have earned their way into God's favor. To say their deeds follow them is a way of saying that God recognizes their faithfulness. The works or "deeds" represent a manifestation of believers' close relationship with Jesus Christ. John assures believers that sacrifice and service for God will not go unnoticed. It will accompany them to the throne of God.

The Images of God's Judgment at the End
14:14-20

This third section begins with the same words as the two previous sections—*kai eidon*—"Then I looked." The section contains two scenes, both depicting the judgment of God at the end of history. One might wonder if the two scenes portray God's punishment against the wicked or if one is punishment on the wicked and the other depicts the ingathering of the righteous. John echoes Joel 3:13, which depicts images of punishment against the wicked. The first scene of the grain harvest seems to symbolize the gathering of the redeemed (14:14-16). The second scene of the grape harvest seems to symbolize the judgment of the unredeemed (14:17-20). Both the grain and the grape harvest picture judgment at the end of history.

The Grain Harvest

John sees an angel sitting on a cloud with a sickle. The harvest of the earth is ripe and is reaped. In the agriculture analogy, the harvest represents the end. Three angels have already announced judgment. Now the judgment takes place. "Then I looked, and behold, a white cloud, and seated on the cloud one like a son of man, with a golden crown on his head, and a sharp sickle in his hand" (14:14). The one who performs the harvesting is "one like a son of man." It is the same description of Christ used in 1:13. More than likely this figure is to be understood as Christ. The wearing of a golden crown and the fact that he sits on a cloud seem to identify him with Christ. The sickle symbolizes the reaping of a harvest. John uses the figure to symbolize Jesus Christ on his mission of ingathering the redeemed of the earth.

In this grape harvest scene, another angel acts as a messenger of the will of God to Christ in his capacity as Son of man. "And another angel came out of the temple, calling with a loud voice to him who sat on the cloud, 'Put in your sickle, and reap, for the hour to reap has come, for the harvest of the earth is fully ripe'" (14:15). Since the reaper takes orders from the angel, some think this son of man is an angel. However, this title, 'son of man," is used exclusively of Christ in the New Testament. The problem of Christ taking orders from an angel can be explained by pointing out that the angel bears the message of God. The fact that the angel comes out of the temple indicates that he comes from the presence of God and bears a message from God himself.

The angel announces, "The hour to reap has come." The time for the final harvest is the precise moment determined by God. The harvest of the earth is fully ripe. In God's hour the issue of history will be settled. The "harvest of the earth" is a frequent symbol for the final judgment of humanity. Usually the harvesting includes both the righteous and the unrighteous, as in Jesus' parable of the wheat and the tares (Matt. 13:24–30). But, in the context of the Revelation passage, the harvest of the grain seems to have special reference to the righteous. John simply states the result of the harvest. "So he who sat on the cloud swung his sickle across the earth, and the earth was reaped" (14:16). The One on the cloud casts his sickle on the earth, and the earth is reaped. The fuller description is described later in Revelation 19–20.

The Grape Harvest

In the second scene another angel appears from the temple with sickle in hand. John pictures in a dramatic way the overflowing wrath of God in store for those who deny his sovereignty and refuse his salvation. With a vivid figure of harvesting grapes, John stresses the ultimate results of those who rebel against God. "Then another angel came out of the temple in heaven, and he too had a sharp sickle" (14:17). If the grain harvest represents a gathering of the righteous, the vintage scene envisions nothing but unmitigated judgment. The sickle-bearing angel is also a messenger of God. The mission of this angel is to gather all the unredeemed as the Son of man gathers all the redeemed. Notice that the grape harvest is carried out by an angel.

Another angel enters John's vision of the grape harvest. "And another angel came out from the altar, the angel who has authority over the fire, and he called with a loud voice to the one who had the sharp sickle, 'Put in your sickle and gather the clusters from the vine of the earth, for its grapes are ripe'" (14:18). The angel comes from "the altar," which has been mentioned previously with the prayers of the saints (8:31). The prayers of God's people are now about to be answered. The angel is further identified as having power over fire. New Testament writers associated fire with judgment (Mark 18:8; Luke 9:54). The angel from the heavenly altar calls for the other angel to swing his sickle and gather in the grapes.

The idea of a harvest of grapes occurs elsewhere as a symbol of judgment. Joel prophecies, "Put in the sickle, for the harvest is ripe. Go in, tread, for the winepress is full. The vats overflow, for their evil is great" (Joel 3:13). Like the grain that has become ripe and must be harvested immediately, the grapes also are fully ripe and must be harvested. The crushing of the grapes represents God's wrath, which means God's punishment of the wicked.

Without hesitation the angel casts his sickle into the earth and gathers its vintage. "So the angel swung his sickle across the earth and gathered the grape harvest of the earth and threw it into the great winepress of the wrath of God" (14:19). The angel obeyed. He reaped the earth's vine and put what he gathered into the winepress. Grapes were usually pressed by being treaded by foot on a flat, hard surface in a vat. As the grapes were crushed, the juice ran into a reservoir from which it was collected and stored. John uses the imagery of the crushing of the grapes to depict God's punishment of the wicked.

Oddly enough, John places the location of the winepress outside the city. "And the winepress was trodden outside the city" (14:20). John does not specify what "city" meant. More than likely the reference places the activity of crushing grapes beyond the city walls. It seems to have no symbolic meaning.[8]

John's pictures of God's judgment overwhelm the readers. "And blood flowed from the winepress, as high as a horse's bridle, for 1,600 stadia" (14:20). Undoubtedly, this gruesome picture is not to be taken literally. One thousand six hundred stradia represented a distance of 184 miles. Numerous interpreters seek to report what this number means. Mitchell G. Reddish writes, "We should perhaps simply admit that we have no clue to the significance, if

---

[8] Ibid., 282.

any, that the number held for John."⁹ More than likely John uses the number as a hyperbole of the punishment and the great number judged. The forces of evil have seemingly achieved universal sway in John's day, but John gives them a "sneak peek" at the end where their overthrow is certain.

Suspense builds throughout the drama of Revelation. John describes various scenes of human history. In each scene he gives an element present in history from the time of Christ's first coming to his final coming. In many scenes John inserts brief descriptions about the end. He does not want the readers to have to roll the scroll ahead to see how things turn out. So he gives insights about the end.

Look at some examples about John's insight about the end. He writes about the opening of seven seals. The first four seals depict suffering as a part of human history. The fifth seal records how people prayed and asked how long the suffering will exist. John answers in the sixth seal with a vision of the end of history. Undoubtedly, readers wanted to know more about the end, but when the seventh seal opened, nothing happened but silence.

Next John hears the blowing of seven trumpets. He observes natural calamities occurring in the first four trumpets. He sees next in the fifth trumpet a vision of the onslaught of evil, and in the sixth trumpet he sees God's restraint lifted of ungodly nations. John thinks the "evilness" of evil and the instability of human kingdoms should drive people to repentance. But the trumpets, or the calls to repentance, become silent, and John sees the end of history in the seventh trumpet vision. The trumpets end with a picture of God's ultimate reign.

John moves from visions of the seals and trumpets to a vision of God's enemies, namely the dragon, world power, and

---

⁹ Ibid., 283.

false religion. These enemies oppose God and his people. John sees these enemies lasting only for a limited time. At the end of the vision of the enemies of God, John sees the Lamb standing on Mount Zion with his followers. He hears strong words about judgment from three angels. Then John sees a grain and grape harvest. The grain harvest represents the gathering of the righteous, and the grape harvest represents the punishment of the unrighteous. After the vision of the enemies and the end, John moves to another vision, where he gives another insight into history.

Each "sneak preview" about the end comforts the readers. Without a doubt they want more information about the end of history. But they either have to wait until Revelation 19:1–22:5 appears, or they can roll the scroll to read the last chapter to see a fuller picture about the end. Then the reader can return to the drama of the struggle of good and evil knowing that the Lamb wins.

Chapter 14
The Judgment of God Both During and Beyond History

Revelation 15:1–16:21

NO ONE CAN READ THE BOOK of Revelation without encountering the subject of God's judgment. On several occasions John has given insights into God's judgments, as in the vision of the seven seals and of the seven trumpets. In each vision he tells something that will happen at the end and something that is happening now in human history. The two harvests of 14:14–20, along with the reference to the "wrath" of God in 14:19, serve as an appropriate transition to the vision of the seven angels with the seven bowls, which complete the wrath of God (15:1).

Readers would seem to expect after the harvest scenes the picture of the new heaven and the new earth. But again John gives us a new insight about something taking place in history and something that will take place at the end of history. He gives a new series about God's judgment. He reviews, he recapitulates, he enlarges on the harvest scene. He shows in more graphic detail what the sixth seal has disclosed and what the seventh trumpet has announced. John presents the subject of God's judgment with the imagery of seven gold bowls full of the wrath of God. While these bowls refer especially to the end, they also allude to whenever in history the wicked fail to repent in answer to the initial and partial expression of God's anger in judgment. The final expression of wrath follows.

Before the dramatic action of pouring the bowls begins, John gives an introductory vision in chapter 15. He intends this vision to comfort and encourage God's people. They will be delivered from the wrath of God. Thus, before the scenes of judgment, there is a picture of God's people in glory. John evidently refers particularly to the blessedness of the martyrs who have died under the persecution of the beast. But in this picture John includes all the people of God who have struggled and conquered with evil and have entered into their heavenly blessedness.

God's judgment involves distinguishing between those who are his people and those who are not his people. The act of distinguishing is called "judgment." God makes a distinction between those who repent and those who do not repent. When time ends, judgment involves separating the redeemed from the unredeemed. God makes the judgment call. What causes this tragic separation? Separating the righteous from the unrighteous comes as a result of a human choice. Whenever people refuse to repent and continue to rebel, God gives them over to that choice. God's wrath in the New Testament does not mean capricious anger. Instead, God's wrath means God's settled disposition against those who rebel against him.

Frank Stagg writes that God's judgment "is present and future. . . . It has a future aspect as well as a present one."[1] God's judgment happens in time and at the end of time. The Bible does not depict God's judgment just at the end of history. God's judgment also takes place during the course of history. The subject

---

[1] Frank Stagg, *New Testament Theology* (Nashville: Broadman, 1962), 332.

History Under Control

of God's judgment is both retrospective and prospective. We can look back and learn of wicked persons and wicked world powers who have encountered the judgment of God. But we look ahead to a final judgment where God will ultimately separate the righteous from the unrighteous.

In the visions of the seven seals (6:1–8:5) and the seven trumpets (8:6–11:19), John presents images of God's judgment. After an interlude where John writes of the conflict between God's people and the power of evil, he comes to the vision of the seven bowls. He does not present a different judgment of God but the same judgment pictured in new images. After announcing the series of the seven bowls (15:1), John delays the beginning of the judgment scenes to offer a word of comfort of God's people.[2] This vision consists of a skillful preparation for the bowls (15:1–18) and a graphic pouring of the bowls (16:1–21).

The Preparation for the Bowls
15:1–8

John writes with comfort and encouragement in his mind. Before he describes the fierceness of finality of the seven bowls, John comforts the redeemed in chapter 15 as a prelude to the pouring of the bowls. He focuses first on the future of the redeemed before he writes of the fate of the unredeemed. John comforts the readers in three visions in chapter 15. Each vision begins with *kai eden*—"then I saw" (v. 1), "and I saw" (v. 2), and "after this I looked" (v. 5). John sees a vision of the seven angels with the seven bowls (15:1), the conquerors of the beast (15:2–4), and the seven angels coming from the heavenly temple (15:5–8).

---

[2] Reddish, *Revelation*, 289.

The Seven Angels with the Seven Bowls

John introduces not only the opening scene in chapter 15 but the entire bowl series in chapter 16. Verse 1 serves as a superscription over what follows in chapters 15–16. "Then I saw another sign in heaven, great and amazing, seven angels with seven plagues, which are the last, for with them the wrath of God is finished." This is the third sign John has seen, the first being the woman clothed in the sun (12:1) and the second being the great red dragon (12:3). This sign consists of seven angels holding the seven last plagues. The word "plague" literally means "a stroke or a blow."[3] The word had become proverbial since the visitations in Egypt, for God's punishment upon the deficient pride of godlessness. This third sign is described as "great" and "amazing," which distinguishes the sign as outstanding. Such a description is not given to the other two signs. This language appears in 15:3 as a description of the amazing deeds of God.

The mission of the "seven angels with seven plagues" provides a kind of summary of the implications of their coming actions. These plagues are the last the earth will know. In them God's wrath reaches its *telos*, or its end. These plagues come "last" because they culminate what has gone before and include all the expressions of divine indignation toward defiant pride and godlessness.[4] These bowls symbolize God's ultimate expression of his wrath against evil. God gives people time to repent. He bears long and warns often, but the last time finally comes. Robert Mounce says, "They are the last of the plagues in that they complete the warnings of God to an impenitent world."[5]

---

[3] Robbins, *The Revelation of Jesus Christ*, 177.

[4] Ibid.

[5] Mounce, *The Book of Revelation*, 285.

These plagues are "last" but not in the sense that they follow chronologically the other disasters. They are "last" because after them will come the final judgment and the consummation of God's kingdom. The next chapters, Revelation 17–18, give a picture of the destruction of Babylon. These chapters give details of what has been announced in the last bowl plague, namely the fall of Babylon. Chapters 17–18 offer elaborations and developments of the seventh plague.[6]

The Conquerors of the Beast

After John sees the seven angels with the seven plagues, he sees a vision of the conquerors of the beast in heaven. "And I saw what appeared to be a sea of glass mingled with fire—and also those who had conquered the beast and its image and the number of its name, standing beside the sea of glass with harps of God in their hands" (15:2). The scene resembles the one in 4:6 where John sees in front of the throne of God something like "a sea of glass." The scene in 15:2 has "a sea of glass mingled with fire." This combination of sea and fire seems to represent God's holiness and justice. John uses additional imagery to intensify the great majesty of God. His main purpose is to communicate that God's people reside in the presence of God after their death.

The saints in this vision stand beside the sea of glass as conquerors. They have emerged victorious out of conflict over three things: the beast, his image, and the number of his name. John pictures God's people as victors over the pressures of the world and the cosmic powers of evil. The three aspects of pagan world power over which the saints emerge victorious come from 13:1-2 (the beast), 13:14 (his image), and 13:17-18 (the number of his name). These aspects summarize how the beast forces people to worship him rather than God. The saints are victorious not because

---

[6] Reddish, *Revelation*, 290.

they survived but because they overcame through their suffering. They were probably put to death. But these martyrs had overcome by the power of Christ through their faithful commitment to Christ.

As soon as John sees the conquerors standing by the sea, he hears them singing accompanied by harps in their hands. The harps are appropriate instruments for praise. The song of the conquerors is a song of praise to God for his great and marvelous acts. "And they sing the song of Moses, the servant of God, and the song of the Lamb, saying, 'Great and amazing are your deeds, O Lord God the Almighty! Just and true are your ways, O King of the nations! Who will not fear, O Lord, and glorify your name? For you alone are holy. All nations will come and worship you, for your righteous acts have been revealed"(15:3-4). They celebrate the righteous and redemptive activity beginning with Moses and culminating with the Lamb. The Hebrews sang a song of thanksgiving after their deliverance from Egypt's bondage (Exod. 15:1-19). The redeemed celebrate a greater deliverance wrought by the Lamb.

This song consists of an initial statement of praise, consisting of two lines in synonymous parallelism (15:3) followed by a rhetorical question and three causal clauses (15:4). The song begins with praise for God's "deeds" and "ways." It characterizes God's work as "great" and "amazing." The saints address God's deeds with the title—"Lord God the Almighty." His power is incomparable. From God's deeds the song moves to God's ways. God's ways are just and true. God's judgments are seen to be both legally just and morally true. The conquerors praise God's ways with the title "King of the nations." These conquerors have God's universal sovereignty in mind.

After the statements of praise to God come, a rhetorical question is asked. "Who will not fear, O Lord, and glorify your name?" (15:4). To glorify the name of God means to praise him for who he is and what he has done. The rhetorical question expects the answer, "No one." The justice and majesty of God seem so compelling that John thinks everyone will bow in reverence and worship before God.[7]

The song ends with the reasons all should fear and glorify God. These affirmations begin with three uses of "for." In the Greek text, the word *hoti* appears three times. All should honor God, for he alone is holy. "For you alone are holy" (15:4*b*). The word for holy is *hosios*, which is used only here and in 16:5. The word conveys the idea of perfect purity. The second affirmation is "for all nations shall come and worship you."[8] The conquerors affirm the universal sovereignty of God. The Roman Empire claimed dominion over all other nations. John knows that only this king is the Lord God, the Almighty. Third, God's sentences on all people are clear: "for your righteous acts have been revealed." The judicial sentences of God relate to all nations either in the way of mercy or in the way of condemnation. In the end God's sentences will be plain to all.

Nothing in the song sung by the conquerors calls attention to them or the way they overcame. The victors fix their attention exclusively on the Lord. William Barclay says, "Heaven is heaven because in it at last all self and self importance are lost in the presence of the greatness and glory of God."[9]

The Seven Angels Emerge from the Holy Temple

A third introductory phrase—*kai meta tauta eidon*—("after this I looked") appears to prepare the readers for the vision of the

---

[7] Ibid., 292–93.

[8] The ESV does not translate the second use of *hoti* for "for." The *KJV* translates *hoti* three times.

[9] Barclay, *The Revelation of John, vol. 2*, 158.

bowls. "After this I looked, and the sanctuary of the tent of witness in heaven was opened, and out of the sanctuary came the seven angels with the seven plagues, clothed in pure, bright linen, with golden sashes around their chests" (15:5-6). When John sees this vision, he sees the temple open. The expression "the sanctuary of the tent of witness" seems to refer to "the tent of meeting" in the wilderness. The tabernacle symbolizes the presence of God (Exodus 38:21; 40:34). The terms should be in apposition—"the sanctuary—that is the tent of witness." John sees the sanctuary opened, and it gave him a clearer vision into the presence of God. The angels come from the presence of God to fulfill God's promises to bless his people and to judge their enemies. The plagues or bowls which follow have God's fullest sanction.

John describes the clothing of these seven angels. They wear pure, bright linen with golden sashes around their chests. This dress could designate the priestly function of these angels. The fabric of the priests' vestments came from linen. Golden sashes were also worn as a sign of priestly function. The garments of these seven angels coming out of the sanctuary identify them as priests/mediators of God's final judgments on the earth.

One of the four living creatures in the heavenly scene gives the seven angels seven golden bowls full of the wrath of God. "And one of the four living creatures gave to the seven angels seven golden bowls full of the wrath of God who lives forever and ever" (15:7). The "living creatures," which appear numerous times in Revelation, represent creation. Seemingly the forces of nature may be regarded as the agents of divine judgment. The wrath of God means the operation of God's righteous law against sin. His statutes are eternally righteous. G. K. Beale thinks John echoes Isaiah 51:17, 22 where Isaiah said twice that the bowl or the cup of (God's) wrath is poured out on sinful Israel. Now John thinks that God's wrath is to be poured on the believers' tormenters, namely

Babylon.[10] The bowls symbolize God's action to punish sinners.

John characterizes God as the one "who lives forever and ever." The eternality of God is part of his sovereign majesty. Many of the hymns in Revelation ascribe praise to God who is "forever and ever" (5:13; 7:12). In 15:8 John seems to refer to the eternity of God to remind readers that even though evil may seem to control human history, God is the eternal one, and his purposes cannot be defeated ever.

When the angels receive these bowls of wrath, the sanctuary is filled with smoke. "And the sanctuary was filled with smoke from the glory of God and from his power, and no one could enter the sanctuary until the seven plagues of the seven angels were finished" (15:8). In the Old Testament, God frequently made his presence known by a cloud or smoke. When God descended on Mount Sinai, smoke covered the place (Exod. 19:18). When the presence of God filled the tabernacle in the wilderness, a cloud rested on it (Exod. 40:34). The smoke in Revelation, which fills the heavenly sanctuary, symbolizes the presence of God in all his glory and power to execute his judgment upon evil. What did John mean by saying, "No one could enter the sanctuary until the seven plagues . . . were finished?" Perhaps it means that no one can understand God's judgments until they are finished and have achieved their ultimate purpose. Or the expression could mean that no one can stop God's appointed time of judgment.

The Pouring of the Seven Bowls
16:1–21

The readers have been prepared in chapter 15 for what comes in chapter 16. They have been introduced to the seven bowls of God's wrath. They have been comforted that they will be safe

---

[10] Beale, *The Book of Revelation*, 806.

by seeing the martyrs on the heavenly shore. The angels have received their bowls of wrath, and they stand ready to pour the contents of the bowls out on the earth.

John hears an unidentified voice from the heavenly sanctuary that issues the command for the bowl plagues to begin. The pouring of the seven bowls pictures the final judgment of God upon the enemies of Christ and his church. T. F. Torrance describes God's wrath, "The wrath which the angels are about to pour out upon the earth is a pure and sinless wrath, priestly in its function and golden in its integrity. No bestial passion, no spite, no hate, no anger of sin at all in it."[11] The bowls come as the natural, automatic reflex of God's holiness. They are the logical response of holiness to evil.

In chapter 16 John writes about the seven angels pouring out the contents of the bowls on the earth. Similarities exist between the seven trumpets and the seven bowls. Both the trumpets and the bowls draw heavily for their symbolism from the plagues on Egypt. The bowls are much more severe and intense than the trumpets. The first four trumpets affect the environment, but the first four bowls fall directly on humanity. The following bowls express God's wrath upon the beast who frustrated God's purpose in the world. Without a doubt the bowls have an immediate reference to the world power of Rome, but they apply to anyone who refused to acknowledge Christ as Lord. The seventh bowl pictures the overthrow of Babylon, the capital of the beast's empire. What is announced in the vision of the seventh bowl is described in detail in chapters 17 and 18. The seven bowls appear in rapid succession without the customary interlude appearing between the sixth and seventh visions.

---

[11] Torrance, *The Apocalypse Today*, 130.

The First Four Bowls

An order comes to pour out the bowls. "Then I heard a loud voice from the temple telling the seven angels, 'Go and pour out on the earth the seven bowls of the wrath of God'" (16:1). This voice comes from the temple, which indicates its origin is with God. This voice must be the voice of God. The voice commands the seven angels to pour out the seven bowls containing the wrath of God.

The first four bowls, like the first four trumpets (8:6–12), target the earth, sea, fresh water (rivers and springs), and the sun. The primary difference is that the trumpets affected one-third of each aspect of creation, but the bowls damaged each completely. The first bowl falls upon the earth. "So the first angel went and poured out his bowl on the earth, and harmful and painful sores came upon the people who bore the mark of the beast and worshiped its image" (16:2). This imagery comes from the sixth plague on Egypt, when the sores broke out on men and beasts. The earth, upon which the bowl is poured, is the place of the second beast. The people affected by this first bowl are those "who bore the mark of the beast and worshiped its image." This judgment is upon those who have chosen to side with the powers that oppose God.

The second angel pours his bowl into the sea and turns it to blood. "The second angel poured out his bowl into the sea, and it became like the blood of a corpse, and every living thing died that was in the sea" (16:3). The second bowl corresponds with the second trumpet (8:8), and both are influenced by the first Egyptian plague (Exod. 7:14ff). The sea becomes like the blood of a dead man. In such a state no life in the sea can be supported. All sea life dies. The second trumpet woe resulted in the death of one-third of life in the sea. The second bowl causes complete destruction. We need to remember that the sea is the origin and home of the dragon. Perhaps John intends to communicate the destruction of the beast's base, namely the sea.

The third angel pours his bowl upon the rivers and springs, then turns them to blood. "The third angel poured out his bowl into the rivers and the springs of water, and they became blood" (16:4). This bowl resembles the first Egyptian plague even more than the second bowl. In the corresponding trumpet plague, a third part of rivers and springs became bitter from a burning star (8:10-11). The third bowl becomes more intensive and extensive than the third trumpet. As the sea turned to blood, death was brought to every living thing, so the rivers and springs spread death when turned to blood. More than likely John thinks of the destruction of evil world power (Rome) in the third bowl poured on the sea. In the third bowl he could be thinking of the destruction of everything that supported world powers, as rivers and streams feed the sea.

As soon as the angel pours the third bowl, a heavenly commentary interrupts the flow of the narrative and explains the significance of the third bowl. "And I heard the angel in charge of the waters say, 'Just are you, O Holy One, who is and who was, for you brought these judgments. For they have shed the blood of saints and prophets, and you have given them blood to drink. It is what they deserve!' And I heard the altar saying, 'Yes, Lord God the Almighty, true and just are your judgments!'" (16:5-7). John hears "the angel in charge of the waters," a figure mentioned nowhere else in the book. In apocalyptic writings angels are assigned jurisdiction over certain areas of creation. This angel directs praise to God. He identifies God as the one who is and was, the holy one. He emphasizes both the eternity and holiness of God. The angel speaks of God as just and regards the action of turning water into blood as one of judging. This judgment may seem harsh, but the angel sees it as a righteous God bring retribution to the wicked. The angel also sees these judgments. These plagues represent God's means of bringing judgment against those who oppose God's plan and inflict suffering and death on his people. The primary point in this angel's song is that God is just in dealing with people. Those who are punished receive nothing less than they deserve. The ones who have killed the saints and prophets have been given blood to drink. Because they have shed the blood of God's people, now they are forced to drink blood when all supplies have been turned to blood.

After the angel's hymn of praise, the heavenly altar cries out, "Yes, Lord God the Almighty, true and just are your judgments." Who were these voices from the altar? More than likely these were the voices of the martyrs. The martyrs join the praise. They acknowledge that God's judgments are just. Those from the altar agree with the angel's song. They address God as "the Lord God the Almighty," and they affirm that God's judgments are "true and just."

The fourth angel pours his bowl on the sun. "The fourth angel poured out his bowl on the sun, and it was allowed to scorch people with fire. They were scorched by the fierce heat, and they cursed the name of God who had power over these plagues. They did not repent and give him glory" (16:8-9). The sun was darkened like the ninth Egyptian plague. This action parallels the fourth trumpet plague. In the fourth trumpet vision, a third of the sun, a third of the moon, and a third of the heavenly bodies were darkened (8:12). But here, the sun scorches people with a heat so fierce that it can be said to be with fire. The fourth bowl has the tone of finality.

John strongly emphasizes the effect of the sun by using the adjective "fierce." But sinners did not learn the lesson. They continued to curse the name of God. They did not repent. They did not give God glory. The sun, which is a blessing, became a curse. Like the sun, God's revelation of himself can be an instrument of a blessing or a curse. The one who accepts the light receives God's blessing. The one who refuses the light receives

God's judgment.

The first four bowls have ended. G. B. Caird thinks of these first four bowls as natural calamities and the last three bowls as political plagues. God uses nature to bring his judgment upon the ungodly. This appears to be the case in the first four bowls. The last three plagues give a picture of political disaster. Internal anarchy and external invasion lead to irreparable collapse. There is also a close parallel between the last three bowls and the three woes introduced by the eagles' screech and the last three trumpets. The fifth bowl looses smoke from the abyss and darkens the sun. The sixth bowl releases a demon from beyond the Euphrates, and the seventh bowl is accompanied by earthquake, thunder, and hail. The last three bowls have a fierceness and finality more than the last three trumpets.[12]

The Next Three Bowls

The fifth angel pours his bowl on the throne of the beast, and the beast's kingdom becomes darkened. "The fifth angel poured out his bowl on the throne of the beast, and its kingdom was plunged into darkness. People gnawed their tongues in anguish and cursed the God of heaven for their pain and sores. They did not repent of their deeds" (16:10-11). Until now the plagues have affected the followers of the beast, but now judgment falls on the beast himself. This fifth bowl resembles the ninth plague in Egypt (Exod. 10:21ff). In Jewish and Christian literature, darkness symbolizes strife, confusion, calamity, disorder, distress, and division. It is a condition of gloom where people are helpless.

The fifth bowl is no more effective than the fourth in bringing repentance. The people gnaw their tongues. This action symbolizes great spiritual pain, suffering, and torment. But in spite of the pain, people continue to curse God and to refuse to repent

---

[12] Caird, *The Revelation of St. John the Divine*, 204.

from their rebellion against God. Their hearts, like that of ancient Pharaoh, have been hardened. John probably alludes in this bowl to the waning of the beast, and he will emphasize this demise more in the remaining bowls.

The sixth angel pours his bowl on the great river Euphrates, causing the river to dry. "The sixth angel poured out his bowl on the great river Euphrates, and its water was dried up, to prepare the way for the kings from the east" (16:12). The sixth trumpet had a vision of the river where four are released to kill one-third of humankind (9:13-15). The sixth bowl results in the drying up of the Euphrates to make possible the crossing of the river by the kings from the earth. John's readers did know territory beyond the Roman Empire, the east of the Euphrates. Partheons lived in the area, and during the first century a persistent fear existed of an invasion from the land. The "kings of the east" probably refers to the Partheon rulers. The pouring of the sixth bowls removes the barrier and makes possible invasion from outsiders.

After John sees the restraint removed at the Euphrates, he sees demonic spirits coming out of the mouths of the dragon, the beasts, and the false prophets. "And I saw, coming out of the mouth of the dragon and out of the mouth of the beast and out of the mouth of the false prophet, three unclean spirits like frogs. For they are demonic spirits, performing signs, who go abroad to the kings of the whole world, to assemble them for battle on the great day of God the Almighty" (16:13-14). The readers know of the dragon and beast (chapters 12-13). But who is this "false prophet"? He has appeared as the beast from the earth in chapter 13, but he is not called by that name in chapter 16. He is a false prophet because he "deceives those who dwell on earth" (13:14). He leads people to worship the first beast.

John describes the unclean spirits coming from the mouths of this threesome with a symbol of frogs. John draws from the Egyptian plague where the second plague on Egypt was an infestation of frogs throughout the land (Exod. 8:1–15). John adapts that image and declares that demonic spirits infest the land like frogs did in Egypt. The fact that the unclean spirits come out of their mouths indicates that they give false teachings. They promote lies and propaganda. These demonic spirits reinforce their false words with the deceptive signs they perform.

These three unclean spirits have one main task to perform, namely of gathering people together for the final battle. This is not a war between nations but a war against God. The "kings of the whole world" (16:14) are not the same people as the "kings from the east" (16:12). John refers to the "kings from the east" as armies poised to invade and destroy Rome. These invading armies become agents of God's destruction and punishment on the evil Roman Empire. John gives a detailed description of the destruction of Rome in chapters 17 and 18. So the reference to the "kings of the east" refers primarily to the invasion of Rome.

John sees much more than his local life situation, namely the fall of Rome. He sees the ultimate destruction of all evil forces. He uses the expression, "kings of the whole world," to describe the universal influence of evil by the dragon, the beasts, and the false prophet. These evil ones will exert influences from the time of Christ's first coming to his final coming. But John tells of the "great day of God the Almighty." This day culminates God's purposes for his world and his people. The term "Almighty" reminds us that in the light of the might of the dragon, the beast, and the false prophet, God's power is greater.

In light of the continuous battle between God and the forces of evil, Jesus inserts a word to the church. "Behold, I am coming like a thief! Blessed is the one who stays awake, keeping his garments on, that he may not go about naked and be seen exposed" (16:15). Jesus likens his coming to a thief, which means it will be unannounced and unexpected. Then Jesus pronounces a blessing on those who are ready for his coming. The believers should not be caught unaware and unprepared. The church needs to maintain its watchfulness and personal holiness during the struggle with evil.

The three unclean and demonic spirits, like frogs, assemble the kings of the whole world at a place called Armageddon. "And they assembled them at the place that in Hebrew is called Armageddon" 16:16). The word *Armageddon* means literally "mountain (hill) of Megiddo." It probably refers to Mount Carmel, at the foot of which lies the plain of Megiddo in the valley of Esdraelon. This level piece of land was the scene of many battles. Deborah and Barak defeated the Canaanite kings at Megiddo. Also Ahaziah, king of Judah, was killed there. The place came to be associated where a decisive battle took place. John used Armageddon to describe the struggle of the forces of evil against good. It symbolizes the final battle between the Lamb and the dragon. It predicts the complete destruction of the demonic spirits. The Messiah will dispense the final judgment.

The seventh angel pours out his bowl into the air. The climax of judgment comes with the seventh bowl. This bowl pictures the complete destruction of evil. "The seventh angel poured out his bowl into the air, and a loud voice came out of the temple, from the throne, saying, 'It is done!'" (16:17). In apocalyptic literature the air was the abode of Satan who is "the prince of the power of the air" (Eph. 2:2). The loud voice which came out of the temple was the voice of God. The phrase "it is done" represents a single Greek word which indicates completed action.

The pronouncement of judgment of Satan's abode is followed by apocalyptic phenomena. "And there were flashes of lightning, rumblings, peals of thunder, and a great earthquake such as there had never been since man was on the earth, so great was that earthquake" (16:18). These convulsions and upheavals of nature usually accompany the special manifestation of God's presence in judgment.

As a consequence of God's judgment, the great city was divided into three parts. "The great city was split into three parts, and the cities of the nations fell, and God remembered Babylon the great, to make her drain the cup of the wine of the fury of his wrath" (16:19). This city, in view of the prophet, was probably Rome. John uses the name Babylon for Rome. It became the symbol of godless world power. Any nation or political power in history that sets itself against the kingdom of God is Babylon.

God makes Babylon, together with the nations who have followed her, to drink of the cup of his wrath. Babylon has given to the nations "the cup of the wine" of her impure passion and has led the kings of the earth to commit fornication with her. God remembers Babylon. The same judgment of God that is at work on a large scale in the history of the nations is at work on a smaller scale of individual life and experiences.[13]

John concludes the seventh bowl with an apocalyptic description of the consummation. "And every island fled away, and no mountains were to be found. And great hailstones, about one hundred pounds each, fell from heaven on people; and they cursed God for the plague of the hail, because the plague was so severe" (16:20-21). In a poetic way John depicts the magnitude of God's judgment upon mighty Rome and its cohorts. The islands and mountains flee before such terrible devastation. John refers to the seventh plague on Egypt in the conclusion of the seventh bowl vision. John describes with vividness the exaggerated weight of the hailstones in order to heighten the effect of the judgment and to give vividness to the imagery. Those struck by the hailstones have refused to acknowledge God. Even after this terrible hailstorm, they refuse to acknowledge the sovereignty of God.

John has "bifocal" spiritual vision. Out of one lens he sees the immediate situation in which he and his readers live. Out of the

---

[13] Robbins, *The Revelation of Jesus Christ*, 191.

other lens he sees the final judgment at the end of history. In his sight of the seals, trumpets, and bowls, he sees various situations taking place during history. He sees suffering, calls to repentance, and earthly judgments happening during earthly existence. But, in each one of these visions, he sees out of the other lens the end of suffering, the close of God's invitation to repent, and the judgment of all the earth.

John has also looked at the bowl visions with "bifocal" insight. He looked carefully at the inevitable fall of the Roman Empire. He saw the immediate situation. But through the bowls he glanced occasionally, as he did in the other three visions, at the ultimate end and outcome of history. In the bowl vision, John saw "bifocally." He looked primarily at the immediate situation of the fall of Rome, and he looked periodically at the ultimate situation of God's final judgment.

The closing of the bowl visions marks a transition. Beginning in 17:1 and continuing through 19:5, John looks exclusively at the immediate situation of the fall of Rome. Afterwards, he will look in 19:6–20:15 at the final judgment on all forms of evil. Since John saw bifocally, the readers of Revelation need to read bifocally. They need to see the immediate situation out of one lens and the ultimate situation out of the other lens.

Chapter 15
An Example of God's Judgment during History

Revelation 17:1–19:5

JOHN AND HIS READERS COULD not get their minds off the Romans. The presence of military and political personnel throughout Asia Minor constantly reminded the residents of the Romans. The Christians in Asia also saw majestic temples built in honor of various Roman emperors. Perhaps only a few believers had visited the majestic city of Rome, but they observed Rome's presence in the province of Asia. Most of the residents of Asia Minor heard of Rome's opulent wealth, booming businesses, and military might.

Rome also loomed large in the mind of John and his readers because of the Roman political practices. Asia Minor was a province of the Roman Empire, and the people had to live in submission to the Roman politics. In the last decade of the first century, the Roman emperor Domitian established the practice of emperor worship throughout the province of Asia. Domitian did this probably to solidify allegiance to Rome, and he was also infatuated with his self-importance. The government required all residents of Asia to acknowledge, "Caesar is lord." Most of the people had no problem with the political/religious confession. It was just another addition to the many gods and goddesses prevalent in the land.

A small segment of the population of Asia Minor had a large problem in acknowledging "Caesar is lord." This group followed Christ. Their creed was "Jesus is Lord." To acknowledge another as Lord meant a great act of unfaithfulness to Jesus. Therefore, many Christians refused to make this Roman confession. The Romans recognized this refusal as disloyalty to the Roman government. They instituted persecution against the Christians, which involved economic boycott, banishment to penal islands, beatings, and even death.

What was it like to be a Christian in Asia Minor? The believers existed in a political environment dominated by a pagan power. They lived subject to ridicule and slander from other religions. They lived in fear of persecution by the local Roman authorities. They could not get Rome off of their minds.

In light of the believer's life situation, the Spirit inspired John to address the immediate needs of the readers. Because of the persecuting practices of the Roman government, John writes a lengthy section which deals specifically with the doom of the Roman Empire. John's mind has been on Rome's fall before he gave it extensive treatment. In 14:8 he announced, "Fallen, fallen is Babylon the great." Of course, John did not mean the Mesopotamian city of that name. The name came to mean to the Jews any city, empire, or system opposed to the ways of God. John uses Babylon as a symbol of Rome. In 16:19 John writes, "God remembered Babylon the great, to make her drain the cup of the wine of the fury of his wrath." John makes an enlarged picture in 17:1-19:5 of God's judgment on Rome. John will write later of God's ultimate judgment on all forms of evil, but in this section he gives an example of God's judgment during history on the Romans. No judgment can be more expected from persecuted people than judgment on the present oppressors. They may believe in judgment at the end, but they want relief from their evil oppressor now. For that reason John turns to the immediate judgment on the Romans before he turns to God's final judgment on all forms of evil.

John writes in 17:1-19:5 to portray God's judgment on Rome. John seems to deal more specifically with the city of Rome rather than the Roman Empire, but actually they are one and the same. The words of this section related explicitly to the Romans, but they can apply to any godless world power in subsequent years. Robert Mounce writes, "John's images are timeless in that they portray the essential conflict of mankind from the beginning of time unto the end."[1] None of the words of Revelation, including 17:1-19:5, represent frozen fossils to be examined only for past remembrance. Furthermore, none of John's words present just speculative horoscopes predicting centuries ahead. He writes for the life situation of the first century, and these words also apply today. For John the defeat of Rome and the final overthrow of evil were closely related. The message of 17:1-19:5 is the inevitable fall of Rome, and the continuing message is that any leader of world power who opposes the cause of Christ is doomed. Our journey through 17:1-19:5 will first be to discover what John meant so we can see what it means to us. The journey through this section will take us to five obvious scenes.

Invitation
17:1-6

The drama of Rome's destruction begins with the appearance of an angel. The angel is one who has the seven bowls. The reference to "one of the seven angels" in 17:1 connects this vision with the previous vision of the bowls. The vision of God's judgment on Rome actually expands the previous vision of the seventh bowl. The angel invites the writer to view the judgment on

---

[1] Mounce, *The Book of Revelation*, 307-8.

Rome.

The Summons to View Judgment

The angel gives an invitation to John to show him the judgment of the great whore. "Then one of the seven angels who had the seven bowls came and said to me, 'Come, I will show you the judgment of the great prostitute who is seated on many waters'" (17:1). Actually, the judgment does not come until chapter 18, but John introduces the one who figures prominently in this section, namely "the great prostitute." Harlots possess a readiness to seduce men from their rightful allegiance. The prostitute represents Rome as a symbol of every city or system which is godless, cruel, idolatrous, and opposed to Christ. The word "Babylon" (v. 5) is significant. That ancient city on the Euphrates River was the historic and heartless enemy of Israel. Babylon embodied luxury and license of abominable idolatry and unbridled impurity. No name could capture more fully all the corrupting and seducing influence, all the false religion, and bloodshed, which John associates with the city of Caesars.[2]

John pictures the prostitute "seated on many waters." These waters represent peoples, multitudes, nations, and tongues. This description comes from Jeremiah 51:13, where Babylon is said to dwell "by many waters." The reference is to the numerous canals which distributed the waters of the Euphrates to the surrounding territory. John uses this as a symbol of the influence of Rome as it flows out throughout the entire world.[3]

The angel emphasizes the influence of the great prostitute on others. "With whom the kings of the earth have committed

---

[2] Charles R. Erdman, *The Revelation of St. John* (Philadelphia: Westminster Press, 1937), 128.

[3] Mounce, *The Book of Revelation*, 308.

sexual immorality, and with the wine of whose sexual immorality the dwellers on earth have become drunk" (17:2). Rome's wealth, power, and influence have allured many nations. These nations engaged in political and commercial alliance with Rome. They also participated in her idolatrous practices. The angel invites John to see Rome as a harlot seducing, alluring, tempting, and drawing people away from the true and living God. The people follow the great prostitute with such intensity that it is like intoxication. The angel shows John the reasons for judgment: committing sexual immorality with the kings of the earth and seducing the subjects of the kings by intoxicating them with the wine of her sexual immorality. The great city corrupted others by her idolatry and its materialistic seduction.

The Description of the Harlot

The angel carries John away in the Spirit into a wilderness. "And he carried me away in the Spirit into a wilderness, and I saw a woman sitting on a scarlet beast that was full of blasphemous names, and it had seven heads and ten horns" (17:3). Being carried away "in the Spirit" means a state of special, divine inspiration. John uses the term "wilderness" as a place to meet God. Moses met God in the wilderness. Elijah and John the Baptist met God in the wilderness. The angel takes John to the wilderness to see the description of the great prostitute. Morris Ashcraft writes, "Perhaps, it is in the wilderness that one can see the great city for what it is."[4]

John sees the great prostitute sitting on a scarlet beast. Scarlet is the color of the dragon. This beast on which the woman rides seems to be the beast that rose out of the sea (ch. 13). She is the persecuting power which rules by brute force and is the supreme enemy of Christ and his followers. Names of the

---

[4] Ashcraft, "Revelation," 330.

blasphemy covered the beast's body. This refers to the blasphemous claims to deity made by Roman emperors. They used such titles as *theios* (divine), *soter* (savior), and *kyrios* (lord). The beast, like the dragon (ch. 12), has seven heads and ten horns. The seven heads symbolize universal influence, and the ten horns symbolize complete human power.

John further describes the clothing of the woman sitting on the scarlet beast. "The woman was arrayed in purple and scarlet, and adorned with gold and jewels and pearls, holding in her hand a golden cup full of abominations and the impurities of her sexual immorality" (17:4). The prophet portrays the woman with luxuriant and ostentatious attire. Purple and scarlet indicate the color of royalty. Not only her clothing but also her accessories (gold, jewels, and pearls) picture wealth and extravagance. The woman has status, power, and affluence. The qualities enticed the world to follow her.[5]

The woman holds in her hand a cup "full of abominations and the impurities of her sexual immorality." The word *abomination* signifies anything detestable. In the Old Testament the word is associated with idolatry. The "impurities of her sexual immorality" describes how immoral and blasphemous her adultery is to God. The woman's attractive cup reflects the woman's enticement to join the great harlot in her evil ways. The "abominations and the impurities of her sexual immorality" describe the idolatrous beliefs and practices associated with emperor worship.

The Identity of the Woman

After describing the woman sitting on a scarlet beast, John sees her true identity. "And on her forehead was written a name of mystery: 'Babylon the great, mother of prostitutes and of earth's

---

[5] Reddish, *Revelation*, 325.

abominations'" (17:5). In 7:3; 9:4; 14:1; and 22:4, the people of God have God's name written on their foreheads. In 13:1, 16; 14:9; and 20:4, the worshippers of the world power have a blasphemous name written on their head or on their right hand. In 17:5 the woman, who represents the worshippers of world powers, has "Babylon the great, mother of prostitutes and of earth's abominations" written on her forehead. This inscription marks her nature as belonging to an evil world power. The title asserts that the great prostitute introduced in 17:1 is Babylon or world power opposed to God. Specifically, she is Rome, who, like Babylon of old, gained a reputation for luxury, corruption, and power. Babylon symbolizes all that allures, tempts, seduces, and draws people away from God. The word "mystery" means that only those to whom the meaning is revealed will grasp the significance of the title.

The latter part of verse 5 asserts that the great harlot (17:1) is Babylon, that is, world power which is openly opposed to God. John now combines the great prostitutes (worshippers of world power) and the beast or Babylon (world power), for in fact they are one. Babylon symbolizes all that allures, tempts, seduces, and draws people away from God. John further describes Babylon (Rome) as the "mother of prostitution and of earth's abominations." In the New Testament the phrase "son of" refers to a person's primary characteristic. Thus, to be called "mother of" means not only that it characterizes one but that that one has reproduced it in others. The unholy Roman Empire has seduced other nations into immorality and idolatry. William Barclay cites vivid statements made about Rome from Roman writers. Barclay writes that Tacitus called Rome "the place into which from all over the world all atrocious and shameful things flow."[6] Seneca called Rome "a filthy

---

[6] Barclay, *The Revelations of John*, vol .2, 188.

sewer."[7] Barclay writes, "John's picture of Rome is not in the least exaggerated; it is actually restrained in comparison with some of the pictures which the Romans themselves drew of their own civilization."[8]

In this identification vision of the great prostitute, John sees an additional sight. "And I saw the woman, drunk with the blood of the saints, the blood of the martyrs of Jesus. When I saw her, I marveled greatly" (17:6). This vision suggests not only the vast extent of Rome's slaughter but also the immeasurable effect that her murderous acts produced. In Revelation 17:4 the great harlot holds a gold cup that pictures her drunk with idolatry and immorality. Now John sees her "drunk with the blood of the saints, the blood of the martyrs of Jesus" (17:6). The metaphor suggests not only the vast extent of her slaughter but also the effect that her murderous acts produced. The woman is intoxicated with a fanatical zeal to destroy the Christians, and she enjoys that action. As a result of the vision of the great harlot, John is amazed. "When I saw her, I marveled greatly" (17:6). Literally, John's statement could be translated "amazed with great amazement." John has amazement over the seeming defeat of good and the seeming victory of evil. The angel has invited him to look at the judgment of the great harlot (17:1). Instead, he sees her destroying the people of God. Evidently, John needs more enlightenment.

Explanation
17:7–18

The angel responds to John's perplexity. "But the angel said to me, 'Why do you marvel? I will tell you the mystery of the

---

[7] Ibid.

[8] Ibid.

woman, and of the beast with seven heads and ten horns that carries her" (17:7). The angel promises to explain the details of the "mystery." The "mystery" means the truth of the woman and the beast can only be known by divine revelation. The angel interprets in light of God's revelation. Explanation comes only by divine enlightenment. Evidently the woman and the beast that carries her form one mystery. To know the one means to know the other. John uses *ho eides*, "that you saw," five times in the explanation. These expressions refer back to the vision in 17:1–6.

The Explanation of the Beast

John focuses attention primarily on the beast that carries the woman. "The beast that you saw was, and is not, and is about to rise from the bottomless pit and go to destruction. And the dwellers on earth whose names have not been written in the book of life from the foundation of the world will marvel to see the beast, because it was and is not and is to come" (17:8). Apparently a shift has taken place in the symbolism of verse 8. Earlier in chapter 17 the beast symbolizes the Roman Empire, but in verse 8 the beast represents a person, the emperor. The angel explains the beast as a parody of the title given to Christ in 1:4. The enigmatic phrase "was, and is not, and is about to rise" intentionally imitates God described as the one "who is and who was and who is to come" (1:4). The beast demands worship as "the god of this world" (2 Cor. 4:4). The "was and is not" parodies Jesus' death and resurrection. The beast imitates his return also (13:3, 12, 14). John refers to his "mortal wound that is healed." The angel contrasts the never-dying life of God with world power that constantly passes away to appear again in a new form. The angel gives the three stages of world power. It existed, it does not exist now, it comes back to go into destruction.

The beast ascends from the bottomless pit. This ascending

from the bottommost pit and going into destruction indicates permanent attributes of the beast rather than a single episode in his career. The beast's existence, nonexistence with existence, and subsequent reappearances describe the same truth as expressed by the "mortal wound was healed." Evil seems at times to disappear, but it only seems to do so. Repeated ascensions of anti-Christian despots rise down through history. The beast's ultimate destiny is settled, for it will "go to destruction." Here is the picture the angel paints. One anti-God world power arises and rules for a time. But after a while that power falls. For a time no anti-God power seems to be on the scene. But another one does arise and rules and then falls. This menacing monotony goes on throughout history until God declares, "That's enough!" He will then eliminate evil entirely. But, in the meantime, Christians must cope with anti-God powers like Rome and others.

The "dwellers on earth" marvel at the beast. These "dwellers on earth" represent the followers of the beast. Throughout Revelation this term means the unregenerate people. They are not listed in the book of life. The beast attracts them and awakens wonder in them. The dwellers on earth marvel because the beast was and is not and is to come. They wonder at the reappearance of the beast after his disappearance.

The Explanation of the Seven Heads

The angel moves further into the explanation of the beast. "This calls for a mind with wisdom: the seven heads are seven mountains on which the woman is seated; they are also seven kings, five of whom have fallen, one is, and the other has not yet come, and when he comes he must remain only a little while" (17:9–10). The angel first identifies the seven heads of the beast as seven mountains upon which the great harlot sits. First-century readers would probably understand "the seven mountains" as a reference to Rome.⁹ Rome began as a network of seven hill settlements on the banks of the Tiber River. Latin literature abounds with references to Rome as the city on seven hills. Some like Martin Kiddle take the number symbolically as "suggestion of the worldwide domination exerted by the Roman order of things."[10] More than likely, "seven hills" represents the city of Rome. This city antagonized and opposed the Christian faith. The beast comes from the abyss and becomes incarnate in the hostile world of which the city on seven hills is the governing center.[11]

The problem intensifies with the mention of seven kings, five of whom have fallen, one is, and one is yet to come. Many identify these "kings" with Roman emperors, but it is difficult. The problem comes on choosing which emperor with which to start. One could start with Augustus, whose reign is usually associated with the beginning of the empire. Or one could start with Julius Caesar as the first emperor. Some interpreters of this passage begin with Tiberius, who was emperor when Jesus was crucified. They think the death of Christ began a new era. Others start with Nero, the first emperor to persecute Christians. The problem intensifies more when questions arise about the three emperors whose reigns were 68–69 AD. Should these emperors be counted on the list? As one tries to calculate the seven kings as Roman emperors, difficulties arise which cause considerable doubt on interpreting the seven kings as emperors.

If the seven kings are not emperors, what do they represent? Henry Alford identifies the seven kings as empires not individual rulers. He lists Egypt, Ninevah, Babylon, Persia, and Greece as the

---

[9] Mounce, *The Book of Revelation*, 313–14.

[10] Martin Kiddle, *The Revelation of St. John* (London: Hodder and Stoughton, 1940), 348–49.

[11] Mounce, *The Book of Revelation*, 314.

five fallen ones. He thinks Rome is the present kingdom, and the one to come is the Christian empire.[12] William Hendriksen has a different listing and makes the "seventh" a "collective title for all antichristian governments between the fall of Rome and the final empire of antichrist that is going to oppress the church in the days preceding Christ's second coming."[13] One basic problem with interpreting the "kings" as empires is the Greek word for *king* is translated throughout the New Testament as "king," not kingdom.

Perhaps the most satisfying way is to interpret the numbers in verses 10–11 symbolically. The number seven means completeness, thus the seven kings could symbolize the power of the Roman Empire as a historic whole. Seven probably carries symbolic value rather than historic value in the enumeration of emperors or empires. The expression "five of whom have fallen" represents rulers who have died. The expression "one is" symbolizes the one who currently occupies the throne. Next, John writes of "the other has not yet come." After the current world power falls, another will arise and reign "only a little while." John wants to emphasize that the Roman rulers have only a short time to run their course before they are followed by another.

The symbolism of the number continues. "As for the beast that was and is not, it is an eighth but it belongs to the seven, and it goes to destruction" (17:11). John arrives at the heart of this numerical riddle. The seven kings symbolize all of the Roman rulers. The five fallen kings symbolize those rulers who have died. The one who is represents the current ruler, and the seventh ruler is the one who follows the current ruler. Now John inserts another number in the riddle, "the eighth." The "eighth" symbolizes the

---

[12] Henry Alford, "Apocalypse of John" in *The Greek Testament*, IV (Chicago: Moody Press, 1958), 710–11.

[13] Hendriksen, *More Than Conquerors*, 203–4.

beast himself. This beast stands apart from the seven. He is the power behind the entire history of Rome. John says, "Look back and you will see ungodly governments that have fallen!" He says, "Look around you and you will recognize a godless government in your time." He also says, "Think ahead! If history lingers, other godless rulers will come and remain a while." John says, "Look beyond these earthly rulers, and you will see a supernatural power motivating these godless earthly rulers! And along the way John says, "Look at the end of ungodly rulers. Look at the outcome of the one behind these rulers. They go to destruction."

The Explanation of the Ten Horns

Next the angel explains the ten horns. They are ten kings. "And the ten horns that you saw are ten kings who have not yet received royal power, but they are to receive authority as kings for one hour, together with the beast. These are of one mind, and they hand over their power and authority to the beast" (17:12-13). Horns in apocalyptic literature earthly power. Evidently these ten horns are other ruling powers associated with Rome.

The angel's identification of horns with kings draws from Daniel's vision of the fourth beast. "As for the ten horns, out of this kingdom ten kings shall arise" (Dan. 7:24). The number ten is symbolic and indicates completeness. It does not point to ten specific kings or to ten kingdoms of a revived Roman Empire. The angel observes that these kings "have not yet received royal power." Their activity lies in the future. These kings have a specified relationship with the beast. They receive authority as kings for one hour with the beast. The kings symbolize the completeness of all nations subservient to world power. What John says in this verse is that the completeness has not been reached. Coming powers will continue to be hostile to God.

All the forces which join the pagan world power of Rome or any subsequent evil world power will rule but a short period.

The text says "one hour," an apocalyptic image which indicates a short period of time. With one mind these forces turn over their power and authority to the beast. Leon Morris writes, "They are willing collaborators."[14] These kings are the beast's allies or helpers.

The angel tells about these kings making war on the Lamb. "They will make war on the Lamb, and the Lamb will conquer them, for he is Lord of lords and King of kings, and those with him are called and chosen and faithful" (17:14). John has spoken of a final battle between the allies of the beast and the forces of God in 16:14. He describes the assembling of the armies at Armageddon "for battle on the great day of God the Almighty." The beast and his allies will be overcome by the invincible Lamb. John does not give details of this final battle in 17:15. He will return to the theme in 19:11-21. In 17:14 he simply assures that Christ will be victorious: "The Lamb will conquer them." The power of God has already defeated evil by Christ's death. Therefore, evil is doomed because it is already defeated by God's act in Christ.[15]

The angel announces that the Lamb is "Lord of lords and King of kings." These titles are used in other references for God (Deut. 10:17; Ps. 136:3; Dan. 2:47). This usage fits consistently with John's exalted view of Christ. Christ is so identified with God that the same titles can be applied to both.

Not only will the Lamb war and overcome, but his followers share in the battles and the victory. The Lamb is accompanied by those who "are called and chosen and faithful." These are the faithful followers of the Lamb mentioned in 14:15

---

[14] Morris, *The Revelation of St. John*, 212.

[15] M. Eugene Boring, "Revelation" in *Interpretation: A Bible Commentary for Teaching and Preaching* (Louisville: John Knox, 1989), 84.

who conquered "by the blood of the Lamb and by the word of their testimony" (12:11). The terms "called and chosen and faithful" describe divine ownership and perseverance. These followers belong to God because of his choosing, and they responded by choosing him. They have remained faithful in the midst of persecution.

The Explanation of the Beast's Destruction

So far the angel has described the beast rather than the great prostitute. Now the angel explains by identifying and describing the fate of the great prostitute. Before telling of the great prostitute's (Rome) destruction, the angel speaks of her great influence. "And the angel said to me, 'The waters that you saw, where the prostitute is seated, are peoples and multitudes and nations and languages'" (17:15). The fourfold grouping symbolizes the universal influence of Rome.

The angel next describes the inevitable fate of the great prostitute. "And the ten horns that you saw, they and the beast will hate the prostitute. They will make her desolate and naked, and devour her flesh and burn her up with fire" (17:16). The woman of chapter 17 (Rome) has been the lover of the beast. She has derived her power for a time from him and his evil cohorts. Now the ten kings and the beast turn on the woman. A hatred exists between the ten horns and the great prostitute. False religion develops the elements of its own destruction. Allies turn on each other and become the enemies. The angel describes the fate of the great prostitute when her lovers are through with her. The angel uses three metaphors to speak of Rome's destruction: strip her naked, devour her flesh, and consume her with fire. These metaphors picture judgment. To be stripped naked means to be exposed of her evil deeds. To eat her flesh depicts that the prostitute's enemies will prey on her and consume her. To burn her with fire means she will be completely destroyed. These metaphors describe the self-destructive power of evil. The beast turned on Rome and destroyed her, but the beast, also, will come to judgment.

The basic reason for Rome's fall is God's judgment. "For God has put it into their hearts to carry out his purpose by being of one mind and handing over their royal power to the beast, until the words of God are fulfilled" (17:17). In the Old Testament God punished Israel by permitting her enemies (Assyria, Babylon, and others) to attack her. John follows the Old Testament interpretation. Even though Rome's fall results from the hatred of her kind, the beast and the ten kings, it could be called the judgment of God. In God's world evil may prevail for a while, but it perpetuates its own power of destruction. Humans reap what they sow.

For the fourth time in chapter 17 the angel identifies and interprets a figure in the vision (vv. 8, 12, 16, 18). "And the woman that you saw is the great city that has dominion over kings of the earth" (17:18). The woman is the great city which rules over the kings of the earth. The city is Rome. But Babylon the Great means more than first-century Rome. Every world power which parades its wealth and promotes its idolatry continues the spirit of ancient Babylon. The angel's words extend beyond the immediate setting in the first century and sketch the fate of any world power that rebels against God. Throughout Revelation, John sees the defeat of Rome and the final overthrow of evil as closely related.

Announcements
18:1-8

In chapter 17 John describes the great city "Babylon." He ends the chapter with a prediction of Babylon's destruction by the beast and his cohorts, namely the ten kings (17:16). John introduces a new vision in 18:1—"After this I saw"—which centers specifically on the fall of Babylon (Rome). The angel John sees in 18:1 is not the same as the interpreting angel of chapter 17, for this is "another angel." The angel in chapter 18 seems to be an announcing angel. John gives a vivid description of this angel. "After this I saw another angel coming down from heaven, having great authority, and the earth was made bright with his glory" (18:1). The angel comes from the presence of God, empowered with a message from God, and reflecting the glory of God. The angel makes two announcements prefaced by the words, "And he called out with a mighty voice" (18:2*a*), and, "Then I heard another voice" (18:4).

The Announcement of the Fall of Babylon

The angel's first announcement is the fall of Babylon. "And he called out with a mighty voice, 'Fallen, fallen is Babylon the great! She has become a dwelling place for demons, a haunt for every unclean spirit, a haunt for every unclean bird, a haunt for every unclean and detestable beast" (18:2). The angel's words resemble the prophetic taunt songs found in Isaiah 23-24; Jeremiah 50-51; and Ezekiel 26-27. These prophetic songs announce with mockery the downfall or death of an enemy. The announcement repeats 14:8, where Babylon is introduced for the first time. John's use of the tense of the verb differs in verses 2-3, where John speaks of the fall of Babylon in the past tense, but in verses 4-24, he speaks of the destruction of Babylon as future. Mitchell Reddish comments that John's concern is not with "measurable time but with the 'right time.'"[16] In God's time the fall of Babylon will take place.

John uses four phrases to describe fallen Babylon: a dwelling place for demons, a haunt for every unclean spirit, a haunt for every unclean bird, and a haunt for every unclean and detestable beast. Rome will become a desolate city inhabited only by wild animals. The word "haunt" means "a cage" or "a prison." In the

---

[16] Reddish, *Revelation*, 340.

ancient world people thought demons lived in uninhabited areas. These four phrases draw a picture of utter destruction, emptiness, and desolation.

John proceeds to give the reasons Rome goes to destruction. "For all nations have drunk the wine of the passion of her sexual immorality, and the kings of the earth have committed immorality with her, and the merchants of the earth have grown rich from the power of her luxurious living" (18:3). John singles out two glaring reasons for Rome's fall. First, Rome participated in idolatry and led others to join in her acts. Rome seduced peoples and nations to pay homage to false deities. Second, Rome engaged in extravagant wealth. The merchants of the earth profited from their economic alliances with Rome. John will elaborate more on Rome's wealth and greed in 18:9–19.

The Announcement to Leave the City

Another voice speaks in verses 4–8. The fact that the voice comes from heaven indicates that it is God's message. The unidentified voice from heaven calls the people of God to separate themselves from Babylon in order to escape her punishments. "Then I heard another voice from heaven saying, 'Come out of her, my people, lest you take part in her sins, lest you share in her plagues" (18:4). This call resembles Isaiah's call for the people to flee ancient Babylon because of God's coming judgment on that city (Isa. 48:20; 52:11). Probably the call to leave is more symbolic than literal.[17] The people of God are called to leave idolatry, indulgence, and greed. Eugene Boring says, "The call to 'come out' is not a matter of geographical relocation but of inner reorientation."[18]

---

[17] Ibid., 341.

[18] Boring, *Revelation*, 184.

John uses a vivid hyperbole to depict the accumulation of the sins of Babylon. "For her sins are heaped high as heaven, and God has remembered her iniquities" (18:5). As a result of Babylon's sins reaching to heaven, God remembers her iniquities and brings judgment to the city. For God to remember does not mean a mental lapse. It is a way of saying that God is aware of someone or something and acts accordingly.

A change occurs in the people addressed. In verses 4–5, the message is addressed to the people of God, but in verse 6 the message is addressed to God's agents of judgment. They are commanded to do to Rome what she has done to others. "Pay her back as she herself has paid back others, and repay her double for her deeds; mix a double portion for her in the cup she mixed" (18:6). "Pay her back" has to do with recompense. It denotes requital, not revenge. The judgment is double because the sin is double. Rome will have to drink a double dose of the pain she inflicted on others.

The voice from heaven describes Rome's self-glorification and luxurious lifestyle. She glorified herself rather than God and lived the life of luxury.

> *As she glorified herself and lived in luxury,*
> *so give her a like measure of torment and mourning,*
> *since in her heart she says,*
> *"I sit as a queen,*
> *I am no widow, and mourning I shall never see."*
> *For this reason her plagues will come in a single day,*
> *death and mourning and famine,*
> *and she will be burned up with fire;*
> *for mighty is the Lord God who has judged her (18:7–8).*

Rome envisions herself supreme over all, and she expects that same estate to continue. Rome brags that she has not experienced the effects of war and loss of life. Rome's fault is not mere arrogance but an unquestioning faith in her own inexhaustible resources. She had no sense of need.[19]

Because of Rome's pride, presumption, and power, her destruction will come suddenly. The plagues which come are death, mourning, famine, and fire. The plagues usually accompany warfare. Rome may think it is invincible and supreme, but it will soon learn that "mighty is the Lord God who has judged her."

The announcements of Babylon's fate and the reasons for it are over. John does not give any narrative of the actual destruction of Babylon, which seems to indicate that the passage is about something deeper than Rome. John thinks of ultimate destruction of any world power aligned against God.

Lamentation
18:9–24

Those who benefited most from relations with Rome—kings, merchants, seamen—mourned her fall. None of the groups who grieve appear to be mourning over their love for Rome but only over what Rome could give them. The laments of these three groups resemble Ezekiel's lament over the fall of Tyre (Ezek. 26-28). The laments include the grief of kings, merchants, and seamen. Each lament concludes with, "Alas! Alas! You great city" (vv 10, 16, 19).

The Lament of the Kings

The first lament represents the kings or the political connections with Rome. "And the kings of the earth, who committed sexual immorality and lived in luxury with her, will weep and wail over her when they see the smoke of her burning.

---

[19] Caird, *The Revelation of St. John the Divine*, 223.

They will stand far off, in fear of her torment, and say, 'Alas! Alas! You great city, you mighty city, Babylon! For in a single hour your judgment has come'" (18:9-10). These kings represent the ruling heads of nations who have engaged in relations with Rome. They have participated in Rome's idolatry. They have shared in her luxuriant living.

Now the fortunes of the kings have changed. These kings mourn more for themselves than the fallen city. These kings express pain and sorrow as they observe the rising smoke of Roman disaster. The kings stand at a distance. They do not rush to rescue Rome. They are amazed that judgment could come so quickly.

The onomatopoeic word, *ouai, ouai*, translated "alas" has a desolate and mournful sound of grief. The kings stand in amazement over a city so great and strong as Rome falling so suddenly. Those who admired her power look at Rome's moldering ashes of destruction.

The Lament of the Merchants

The merchants join the kings in the lament over Rome's fall. They weep and mourn, not for Rome, but because its collapse deprived them of financial gain. "And the merchants of the earth weep and mourn for her, since no one buys their cargo anymore" (18:11). The kings mourned because of a political reason, but the merchants mourn because of an economic reason. The self-interest of the merchants is evidenced in their lament, "For in a single hour all this wealth has been laid waste" (18:17). They mourn the loss of their profit, not the destruction of Rome.

John gives a list of imports brought from all over the world into Ostia, the port of Rome. "Cargo of gold, silver, jewels, pearls, fine linen, purple cloth, silk, scarlet cloth, all kinds of scented wood, all kinds of articles of ivory, all kinds of articles of costly wood, bronze, iron, and marble, cinnamon, spice, incense, myrrh, frankincense, wine, oil, fine flour, wheat, cattle and sheep, horses and chariots, and slaves, that is, human souls" (18:12–13). John lists twenty-eight separate items. Each item reflects the luxury of Rome. Morris Ashcraft divides these items into seven categories: precious metals and stones (gold, silver, jewels, and pearls); luxurious clothing (fine linen, purple, and silk); expensive furniture (scented wood, ivory, and costly wood); building materials (bronze, iron, and marble); costly aromatic substances (cinnamon, spice, incense, myrrh, and frankincense); expensive food stuff (wine, oil, fine flour, and wheat); and slaves (human souls).[20]

John pauses to characterize Roman society. "The fruit for which your soul longed has gone from you, and all your delicacies and your splendors are lost to you, never to be found again!" (18:14) The fruits for which Rome desired have been listed in verses 12–13. Rome has longed for "delicacies" and "splendor." "Delicacies" means costly items or luxuries. "Splendor" means that which glitters or shines. John pictures Roman society as mainly interested in attractive materialistic luxuries.

The merchants' lament resumes following the listing of imports to Rome. Like the kings of the earth, the merchants stand a safe distance to weep and mourn. "The merchants of these wares, who gained wealth from her, will stand far off, in fear of her torment, weeping and mourning aloud, 'Alas, alas, for the great city that was clothed in fine linen, in purple and scarlet, adorned with gold, with jewels, and with pearls!" (18:15–16). John describes the great city in terms which almost reproduce the description of the great prostitute (17:4). The merchants supply her items of clothing. The merchants mourn because suddenly ("in one hour") her great riches lay desolate.

The Lament of the Sailors

The lament continues with a third group, those connected

---

[20] Ashcraft, "Revelation," 337.

with the shipping industry. "And all shipmasters and seafaring men, sailors and all whose trade is on the sea, stood far off and cried out as they saw the smoke of her burning, 'What city was like the great city?'" (18:17-18). Interestingly, Rome was not a seaport. The city of Ostia, located twelve miles away near the mouth of the Tiber River, was Rome's port city. John makes four references to people who make their living by the sea. The group, like the kings and merchants, stands far off.

As the seafarers watch the smoke rise from burning ruins, they cry out in amazement, "What city was like the great city?" (18:18). The sailors carry their mourning further than the kings or merchants. "And they threw dust on their heads as they wept and mourned, crying out, 'Alas, alas, for the great city where all who had ships at sea grew rich by her wealth! For in a single hour she has been laid waste" (18:19). The sailors cried out. The mourners threw dust on their heads, which was a common sign of deep grief. They wept and mourned. They doubled the grief—"alas, alas." They, like the kings and merchants, express surprise over Rome's sudden fall. What has prompted the sailors' sadness is their loss of income as a result of Rome's fall.

The Destruction of the City

Three groups have seen the destruction of the city, and they lamented. Some unidentified voice calls for heaven and the people of God to rejoice. "Rejoice over her, O heaven, and you saints and apostles and prophets, for God has given judgment for you against her!" (18:20). The voice orders celebration because justice has been done, and the Christian faith has been vindicated. Wrongs have been done to the Christians, and these are now put right.

Following the abrupt shift from lament to rejoicing, John sees "a mighty angel" carry out a symbolic act. "Then a mighty angel took up a stone like a great millstone and threw it into the sea, saying, 'So will Babylon the great city be thrown down with violence, and will be found no more'" (18:21). This act recalls an event in the days of Jeremiah when Seraiah the quartermaster was to go to Babylon and read a prophetic oracle against the proud city, bind a stone to it, and cast it into the Euphrates saying, "Thus shall Babylon sink, to rise no more, because of the disaster that I am bringing upon her" (Jer. 51:64). The mighty angel takes a millstone and hurls it into the sea, declaring that Babylon will disappear forever.

A list follows of things that will be forever absent from the city in the aftermath of her destruction.

> *And the sound of harpists and musicians,*
> *of flute players and trumpeters,*
> *will be heard in you no more,*
> *and a craftsman of any craft*
> *will be found in you no more,*
> *and the sound of the mill*
> *will be heard in you no more,*
> *and the light of a lamp*
> *shall shine in you no more,*
> *and the voice of bridegroom and bride*
> *will be heard in you no more (18:22–23).*

The words "no more" reverberate throughout the angel's pronouncement. The expression emphasizes the finality of God's judgment against the once busy city. The mighty angel emphasizes the absence of familiar sights and sounds of the city. No music will be heard. No craftsman can be found. No mills will turn, which points to the cessation of the daily activities of the preparation of food. No bridal parties will be heard. No lights will shine in the city. The absence of these sights and sounds emphasizes the complete destruction of the city.

The angel ends the speech with three reasons for Rome's

destruction. "For your merchants were the great ones of the earth, and all nations were deceived by your sorcery. And in her was found the blood of prophets and of saints, and of all who have been slain on earth" (18:23–24). The first reason for Rome's punishment is her obsession with material possessions. Wealth had become Rome's obsession. Second, she deceived nations by her sorcery. The word "sorcery" means "an act of deception." More than likely this refers to the deception Rome uses to deceive the world about strength and supremacy. Third, Rome killed the prophets and saints. From the martyrdom by Nero in Rome to the death of Antipas in Pergamum, Rome had on its hands "the blood of prophets and of saints."

John extends Rome's guilt to include "all who have been slain on earth." Though Rome is uppermost in John's mind, his condemnation of evil goes beyond the Rome of his day. He uses Babylon as a symbol for Rome, and it also symbolizes all people, institutions, and systems that oppose God and oppress God's people.

Celebration
19:1–5

The great city has fallen. God's people have been summoned to leave. Laments have been sung by various groups of mourners who witnessed the fall of Babylon. Now the focus shifts ("after this") from earth to heaven. John hears the sound of a great multitude in heaven.

The first five verses of chapter 19 make a fitting climax for the length discussion of the fall of Rome (17:1–18:24). The great multitude breaks out in jubilant celebration. This celebration differs from the dirges of the kings, merchants, and seafarers. John follows the three laments with three celebrations by the heavenly multitude (vv. 1–3), the twenty-four elders and four living creatures

(v. 4), and a voice from the throne (v. 5).

The Celebration of the Great Multitude

The phrase "after this" has occurred five previous times in Revelation (4:1; 7:1, 9; 15:5; 18:1). The phrase indicates a new vision. John uses "after this" in 19:1 to shift the scene from the destruction of Babylon to the celebration of the heavenly multitude. "After this I heard what seemed to be the loud voice of a great multitude in heaven, crying out, 'Hallelujah! Salvation and glory and power belong to our God'" (19:1). The singers sing a song of praise, beginning with the word, "Hallelujah." This transliterates a Hebrew expression meaning, "Praise God." The word appears four times in verses 1–5. The song ascribes to God "salvation," "glory," and "power." These three words describe God's redemption on behalf of humanity. "Glory" and "power" refer to God's majesty and splendor.

The word "for" in verse 2 introduces specific reasons for praising God. "For his judgments are true and just; for he has judged the great prostitute who corrupted the earth with her immorality, and has avenged on her the blood of his servants" (19:2). The heavenly multitude praises God because of his justice, his judgment, and his avengement. The heavenly chorus praises God for the downfall of evil by his hand.

For the second time the heavenly multitude praises God. "Once more they cried out, 'Hallelujah! The smoke from her goes up for ever and ever'" (19:3). A. T. Robertson calls verse 3 "a heavenly encore."[21] In this second outburst of praise, the great multitude once again sings, "Hallelujah!" The expression that her smoke "goes up for ever and ever" indicates that her destruction is

---

[21] A. T. Robertson, "The Revelation of St. John," in *Word Pictures in the New Testament*, IV (New York: Harper and Brothers, 1933), 447–48.

final.

The Celebration of the Twenty-four Elders and the Four Living Creatures

Earlier in the drama of Revelation (5:6–10), the Lamb took the scroll from the right hand of God, and the four living creatures and the twenty-four elders fell before him and praised the Lamb's worthiness to open the seals. Once again the four creatures and the twenty-four elders join in worship. This time they honor God for his just judgment. "And the twenty-four elders and the four living creatures fell down and worshiped God who was seated on the throne, saying, 'Amen. Hallelujah!'" (19:4). All of the heavenly court celebrates and ratifies God's judgment upon the rebellious and wicked city.[22] The words of the heavenly host are simple, "Amen. Hallelujah!" The "amen" indicates their assent to what has been said, and the "hallelujah" gives a great word of praise.

The Celebration of the Voice from the Throne

For the third time John hears a speaker. This speaker is not identified, but since the voice came from the throne, it must be considered as originating with God. "And from the throne came a voice saying, 'Praise our God, all you his servants, you who fear him, small and great'" (19:5). The voice summons all of God's people to join in the worship and praise of God. The "servants" do not represent a limited and select group, but the "small and great" indicate the entire group of faithful believers. These believers come from every socioeconomic level, and they represent every stage of spiritual maturity.[23]

---

[22] Reddish, *Revelation*, 361.

[23] Mounce, *The Book of Revelation*, 338.

At the time John wrote, Rome looked solid and secure. She is the only superpower in the world at the time. But John knew that things were not as they seemed. For several hundred years something was eating away at the heart of Rome. Rome was slouching toward Sodom. Then in August of AD 410, Alaric and his hordes of Goths pillaged Rome and destroyed it.

John predicts the fall of Rome, but he looks beyond Rome. Whenever "Babyloness" gets a hold on a world power, the end begins. John did not live to see the fall of Rome before his death, but he writes as if it has already happened. John writes that the judgment of God would inevitably come upon any world power that rebels against God. Numerous examples of God's judgment existed in John's day—Egypt, Assyria, Babylon, and others. Rome will be just another example of God's judgment against a nation that engages in immorality and promotes idolatry.

Chapter 16
The Images about the End of History

Revelation 19:6–20:15

VARIOUS HAPPENINGS SHOCK the world: three groups of terrorists hijack three airplanes, fly two of the planes into populated buildings, and thousands of innocent men, women, and children die; a cruel leader orders troops to invade another country, and a bloody war begins; a student brings a gun to school and kills some of his fellow students and teachers; a person opens fire in a business on people he does not know and injures and kills many; a sex offender caught molesting a small child admits to dozens of similar offenses; and an assassin shoots and kills a national leader. These tragedies and many others like them appear on world news each day. People often ask, "What is this world coming to?"

Tragic situations happened to Christians living in Asia Minor at the end of the first century. The Roman rule over the province turned into a problem. The Roman emperor demanded emperor worship in the main cities of the province. His action brought extenuating circumstances to the Christians. When all citizens in the province were forced to confess "Caesar is lord," many believers had a problem. They felt that confessing Caesar as lord meant an act of unfaithfulness to Christ. The Christian confession was "Jesus is Lord!" Some believers compromised and confessed lordship both to Rome and to Christ. They confessed to both in order to escape persecution or to save their jobs. But others refused to confess, "Caesar is lord," and their living conditions worsened. Roman authorities seized the property of some who would not give allegiance to Rome. Others lost their jobs because they would not participate in the idol worship and the immorality of the trade guilds. One of the main leaders of Christianity, John, was banished to the penal island of Patmos. Believers lived in constant fear of the various ways the Romans used to persecute. Some of the believers' family and friends lost their lives because of their commitment to Christ. These happenings prompted Christ's followers to ask, "What is this world coming to?" They could see no future but the ruthless rule of the Romans.

Actually, the question, What is this world coming to? arises in every generation. Numerous attempts have been made to predict where the history of civilization is leading. The ancient Greeks thought history was on a cyclical course. They thought as the four seasons of spring, summer, autumn, and winter repeat each year, so history repeats. Thinkers through the years consider history only in a cynical concern. They see events happening one after the other without any significance. H. A. L. Fisher, in his book *History of Europe*, expresses the notion of the cynical view: "Men more wiser and more learned than I have discerned in history, a plot, a rhythm, a predetermined pattern. These harmonics are concealed from me. I can see only one emergency following upon another as wave follows wave."[1] This view of history has little hope for the future and mainly a meaningless existence for the present.

Others adopt a catastrophic view of history. They think civilization will be destroyed by a nuclear war, a collision of an asteroid with earth, or by an ecological occurrence such as global

---

[1] Quoted in Billy Graham, *World Aflame* (Garden City, NY: Doubleday, 1965), 196.

warming. Patrick Geryl, a resident of Belgium, predicts the world will end on December 21, 2012. He predicts unprecedented catastrophes, such as volcanic eruptions, earthquakes, and polar reverses near the end of time. Geryl bases his ideas on the ancient Maya culture of Central America.

The Bible's view of history is neither cyclic, cynical, nor catastrophic. The biblical writers have a Christian view of history. They believe Christ started history: "For by him all things were created" (Col. 1:16*a*). They think Christ sustains history from its beginning until its end: "In him all things hold together" (Col 1:17). They teach that Christ will one day stop history: "Then comes the end, when he delivers the kingdom to God the Father after destroying every rule and every authority and power" (1 Cor. 15:24). New Testament writers thought that the end (*eschaton*) has already entered in the line of history in the person of Jesus Christ. Christ entered history in his incarnation, and he will conclude history by his return. God directs history on a linear line until he stops time. No one can mark on that linear linen when Christ will return, but we do know that with the passing of each day, the end gets closer.[2]

The writer of Revelation shares the same view of history as other biblical writers. Throughout Revelation John writes about Jesus being the Lord of creation. He tells of Christ "walking" with his people throughout the course of history. John frequently mentions the end of history at the Lord's final return. In each one of the visions of the seals, the trumpets, the enemies of God, and the bowls, John mentions some distinct characteristic of history, but he closes each view with a statement about history's consummation with the Lord's return.

In Revelation 19:6 the drama of Revelation takes a

---

[2] Frank Stagg, *New Testament Theology* (Nashville: Broadman, 1962), 327–28.

suspenseful turn toward the end. Indications about the end have been skillfully inserted about the end of time. But now in 19:6–20:15, John gives an expanded elaboration about the end. He gives four graphic pictures depicting some angle about the end. These images do not seem to follow a chronological order. Instead John gives the images synchronously or events occurring at the same time and coinciding in time. These images—a wedding, a battle, a reign, and a courtroom—picture an end which is yet to come. Though this is a *not yet*, there is an element of *now* in the images. The bride, or the church, prepares herself during history for the coming of the Bridegroom. When the Bridegroom comes, the bride lives eternally with the Bridegroom. God struggles with Satan throughout their lifetime. They can live victorious over Satan because of Christ's death, resurrection, and presence. But they long for ultimate deliverance. The Conqueror comes at the end and throws Satan into the lake of fire, where he is completely annihilated. The church hears and sees now the evidences for evil. At the end in the courtroom, they hear the sentence read on Satan—doomed to destruction. These images communicate the *now* of history, but they also picture graphic images of the *not yet*.

A Wedding
19:6–10

The mood changes in 19:6. The previous songs of 19:1–5 offer praise for the judgment and destruction of Rome. Beginning in 19:6 the writer turns from Rome's destruction to Christ's return and the destruction of the devil. John's first image of the end involves a wedding. Courtship ends with a wedding. Christ, the Bridegroom in this image, comes for his bride, the church. The image portrays the union of the Bridegroom and the church for eternity.

The Wedding Announcement

Every earthly wedding needs an announcement. The heavenly multitude praises God that the marriage of the Lamb is forthcoming. The heavenly voices announce that the end has at last arrived with a wedding. "Then I heard what seemed to be the voice of a great multitude, like the roar of many waters, and like the sound of mighty peals of thunder, crying out, 'Hallelujah! For the Lord our God the Almighty reigns'" (19:6). The forthcoming wedding announcement is preceded by the sound of a large choir, the roar of a mighty river, and great peals of thunder. These images introduce and underscore the ultimate reign of God on earth. In the historical context of a proud and powerful Roman Empire, John confidently calls God, "the Almighty." The heavenly multitude announces God as the true God and more powerful than any earthly ruler. He is the Lord "our" God. The use of "our" suggests that the all-powerful God chooses to relate to people in a personal way.[3]

The heavenly multitude continues the praise with an exhortation and an announcement. The choir exhorts, "Let us rejoice and exult and give him the glory" (19:7). The two verbs "rejoice" and "exult" appear in Matthew 5:12, where the cause of rejoicing comes over the greatness of reward awaiting those persecuted for the cause of Christ. In Revelation 19:7, the choir wants the bride to rejoice over the coming wedding.[4] After the exhortation the heavenly multitude makes a wedding announcement. "For the marriage of the Lamb has come" (19:7). As a way of expressing God's relationship with Israel, the people of God were often pictured as the bride or wife of God in the Old Testament (Jer. 3:20; Ezek. 16:8-14; Hosea 1-3). The New

---

[3] Mounce, *The Book of Revelation*, 339.

[4] Ibid., 340.

Testament writers adopted this image to portray the church as the people of God (Eph. 5:25-32). The writer of Revelation pictures a wedding where the Bridegroom, Christ, unites in a wedding with his bride, the church.

John probably had on his mind the practice of a wedding in his time. Marriages in John's day began with a betrothal, an agreement to be married. The betrothal could be for an indefinite period of time. The wedding day came with the groom's procession with his attendants to the bride's house. The bride awaits the coming of the groom by getting ready for the wedding. When the groom arrives at the bride's house, he takes her to his house, where they celebrate their union in a wedding. John's picture is the bride, the church, preparing herself for the Bridegroom's coming. When he comes, he takes the bride with him and they live and celebrate together forever.

The Preparation of the Bride

In John's image he writes specifically about the bride's activities while waiting for the Bridegroom to come. She prepares for his coming. "And his Bride has made herself ready; it was granted her to clothe herself with fine linen, bright and pure—for the fine linen is the righteous deeds of the saints" (19:7-8). Leon Morris translates "righteous deeds of the saints" as a "sentence of justification."[5] He thinks this translation is warranted because of the verb "was granted." The clothing results as a gift of God to his people. It is not provided by them. The church thus demonstrates this gift by faithful living.

The bride's preparation represents two sides of righteousness. On one hand God's righteousness comes as a declaration of righteousness when the believer trusts Christ. On the other hand believers continue to have "faith" in Christ, and this

---

[5] Morris, *The Revelation of St. John*, 227.

openness results in demonstrated righteousness. Thus, deeds of righteousness occur because of initial regeneration and because of continuing sanctification by the Holy Spirit.

The Guests at the Wedding

Weddings have a guest list. The marriage of the Lamb has a guest list. These are the persons allowed to come to the wedding celebration. An angel speaks to John about the guest list for the marriage of the Lamb. "And the angel said to me, 'Write this: Blessed are those who are invited to the marriage supper of the Lamb'" (19:9). The angel gives the fourth of seven beatitudes in the Revelation. The angel pronounces a blessing on those invited to the marriage supper of the Lamb. The word "blessed" has the connotation of the ensuing results of sharing life with God. The word has more spiritual meaning than material meaning.

The verb "are invited" indicates that an invitation has been extended at some point in the past, and the guests have responded affirmatively. The Groom takes the initiative to invite, and those who receive the invitation have the option of saying yes or no."The "blessed" people represent those who have said yes. Notice that in verses 7-9, John pictures the church as both bride and wedding guests. Both images stress the intimate relations of Christ with his followers.

The angel ends the blessing of the guests with an additional emphasis. "And he said to me, 'These are the true words of God'" (19:9). The angel concludes with a solemn confirmation of the truth and the certainty of the message. We must never forget that the words of Revelation were directed to a persecuted people. Good news about ultimate union with Christ and about the overthrow of evil brought joy and hope.

John becomes overwhelmed with the angel's message. He prostrates himself to worship the speaker. "Then I fell down at his feet to worship him, but he said to me, 'You must not do that! I am a fellow servant with you and your brothers who hold the testimony of Jesus. Worship God.' For the testimony of Jesus is the spirit of prophecy" (19:10). The angel rebukes John for worshiping anyone other than God, and the angel connects himself with John and other believers. Important differences do exist between angels and humans, but one striking similarity is that both angels and believers worship and serve God.

Both angels and believers belong to those who "hold the testimony of Jesus." The grammatical construction of "the testimony of Jesus" could be understood as an objective or a subjective Greek genitive. If objective, the testimony is about Jesus. If subjective, the testimony refers to the testimony Jesus gave. Probably the objective genitive seems the most likely interpretation: "testimony borne to Jesus." To take this meaning conveys the idea that the true "spirit of prophecy" always manifests itself in bearing witness to Jesus. At any rate both interpretations are true, but the objective seems to be the one John means in this verse.[6]

A Battle
19:11–21

A new scene appears in 19:11–21. John introduces the scene with the words, "Then I saw" (19:11*a*). In the previous scene Christ appears as a Bridegroom coming for his bride, the church. In this second scene Christ comes as a Conquering Warrior with his armies to conquer the beast from the sea and the beast from the earth. These images do not follow a chronological order of final events. Instead these images give a picture of the end of history from different angles.

The struggle between God and evil lies at the heart of

---

[6] Reddish, *Revelation*, 365–66.

Revelation. The story line moves toward the goal of the final defeat of evil. John presents the final overthrow of evil in an interesting manner. Evil forces fall in Revelation in the reverse order in which they appear. The dragon first appears in Revelation 12, the two beasts in chapter 13, and Babylon/Rome in chapter 16. When the drama of the ultimate destruction of evil begins, it beings with Babylon/Rome (ch. 17-18), followed by the two beasts (19:11-21), and finally the dragon (ch. 20).

The new scene in 19:11-21 has the picture of a battle. The armies of heaven accompany the Conquering Warrior to wage war against the beast and the false prophet. The image of the battle contains two units: the description of the Conquering Warrior (vv. 11-16), and the defeat of the two beasts and their followers (vv. 17-21).

The Description of the Conquering Warrior

In this vision John sees heaven opened, and he sees a rider on a white horse. "Then I saw heaven opened, and behold, a white horse! The one sitting on it is called Faithful and True, and in righteousness he judges and makes war" (19:11). The color of the white horse symbolizes victory. This white horse of 19:11 differs from the rider of the white horse in 6:2. The rider of the one in 6:2 is military conquest, but the one in 19:11 appears to be an image of the Christ. John's description of the rider has parallels or near parallels to Christ in the Revelation. The one distinctive element is the white horse.

John gives a detailed description of the rider. He gives his name as "Faithful and True." The names express the character of the rider. These names appear for Jesus in words to the church at Laodicea. "The words of the Amen, the faithful and true witness" (3:14). Christ is faithful because he fulfills everything the Scriptures reveal about him, and he is true because he personifies truth.

John continues with the description of the rider on the

white horse. "His eyes are like a flame of fire, and on his head are many diadems, and he has a new name written that no one knows but himself. He is clothed in a robe dipped in blood, and the name by which he is called is the Word of God" (19:12). John gives five vivid descriptions, and each one gives an insight about the rider's character. First, John sees his eyes as a flame of fire. Nothing escapes the vision of Christ. He knows everyone's thoughts and actions. Second, John sees many diadems on the rider's head. The picture symbolizes Christ's absolute sovereignty in the universe.

Third, John surprises the reader by saying the rider "has a new name written that no one knows but himself." John communicates that in Christ's nature are hidden depths which the finite mind cannot comprehend.

Fourth, John describes the rider "clothed in a robe dipped in blood." This blood does not represent the blood of Christ's enemies, but it represents Christ's own blood shed on the cross. The conquering Christ is the suffering Christ. John repeatedly makes the point that in his role of the slain Lamb, he overcame. Christ the Conqueror wins not by shedding the blood of others but by shedding his own blood.

Fifth, John again refers to the name of the rider as "the Word of God." There seems to be a parallel of this title of Jesus with the famous *logos* (Word) of John 1:1–14, but this is the only place in the New Testament where Jesus is called "the Word of God." The title in 19:13 is not so much the revealer of God as the authoritative Word of God. Jesus proclaims the judgments of God and acts as the agent of God carrying out God's judgment on the earth. He defeats the enemies not by physical violence but by declaring God's judgment against them.

After describing the character of the rider on the white horse, John describes the action of the rider. The rider acts in accordance with his character. "He judges and makes war" (19:11). Christ acts as both Judge and Warrior, and he does both in righteousness.

John proceeds to depict the battle the Warrior Christ wages against the enemy. The leader brings troops with him. "And the armies of heaven, arrayed in fine linen, white and pure, were following him on white horses" (19:14). Although some interpreters understand Christ's armies to be angels, they perhaps symbolize the redeemed, the church. They wear clothing usually worn by the righteous, and they resemble the dress worn by the bride. Though John calls those who accompany Christ "armies," he mentions no weapons or hostile action. The victory against evil is won by the Leader alone.[7]

After looking at the Leader and his armies, John comes back to the actions of the Leader against evil. He uses three images to describe how Christ executes judgment against the enemy. First, Christ wields a sharp sword from his mouth. "From his mouth comes a sharp sword with which to strike down the nations" (19:15). This picture points to the power of his word. He does not smite the nations with his armies but with his word. John's image of a battle represents a spiritual conflict, not physical violence.

Second, Christ rules with a rod of iron, a symbol of destruction. "And he will rule them with a rod of iron" (19:15). In Psalm 2 the Lord tells his anointed, "I will make the nations your heritage. . . . You shall break them with a rod of iron" (vv. 8–9). The shepherd leads his flock and defends them from vicious beasts. Jesus rules with a rod of iron. He protects the world from evil and acts in judgment.

Third, Christ treads the winepress. "He will tread the winepress of the fury of the wrath of God the Almighty" (19:15). The two nouns "fury" and "wrath" appear thirteen times in Revelation 6–19. Robert Mounce writes, "Any view of God which eliminates judgment and his hatred of sin in the interest of an

---

[7] Morris, 231.

emasculated doctrine of sentimental affection finds no support in the strong and virile realism of the Apocalypse."[8] The figure of the winepress points to God's judgment on evil.

John returns to a fourth reference to Christ's name. "On his robe and on his thigh he has a name written, King of kings and Lord of lords" (19:16). This image reminds the readers that their conquering Christ exercises as God's agent supreme authority and power over the earth. John leaves no doubt who is the supreme Lord.

The Defeat of the Two Beasts and Their Followers

The heavenly commander appears with his armies. Now the heavens open, indicating that the Warrior Messiah and his armies are about to engage in the final conflict. Prior to the battle, an angel appears and calls for birds to gather for the great supper of God. "Then I saw an angel standing in the sun, and with a loud voice he called to all the birds that fly directly overhead, 'Come, gather for the great supper of God, to eat the flesh of kings, the flesh of captains, the flesh of mighty men, the flesh of horses and their riders, and the flesh of all men, both free and slave, both small and great" (19:17–18). The angel's position, "standing in the sun," symbolizes a place where his voice could be heard. The birds of prey assemble to feast on the carcasses of the slain (Ezek. 39:17–20). This feast is called "the great supper of God." Like the redeemed invited to the marriage supper of the Lamb, the wicked of the earth will also participate in a great feast. The feast starts with kings and goes to officers, to heroes, to horses and riders, and to all people, free and slave, small and great. John reports the overthrow of evil in apocalyptic imagery, communicating that God's judgment is both universal and final.

John next sees the beast and his armies arrayed against the

---

[8] Mounce, *The Book of Revelation*, 347.

Warrior Christ and his armies. "And I saw the beast and the kings of the earth with their armies gathered to make war against him who was sitting on the horse and against his army" (19:19). The vision contains no description of a battle but passes directly to the outcome. "And the beast was captured, and with it the false prophet who in its presence had done the signs by which he deceived those who had received the mark of the beast and those who worshiped its image. These two were thrown alive into the lake of fire that burns with sulfur" (19:20). The beast and the false prophet represent personifications of hostility to Christ. They lead the antichristian forces in the world.

Both the beast and the false prophet are thrown into "the lake of fire." Other Jewish writings mention the place of judgment as a "deep valley with burning fire" (1 Enoch 54:1). The "lake of fire" symbolizes complete destruction. Rebellion against God ends in death of the deepest kind.[9]

John completes the picture of the destruction of the armies opposed to Christ. "And the rest were slain by the sword that came from the mouth of him who was sitting on the horse, and all the birds were gouged with their flesh" (19:21). The "rest" includes all the antichristian forces who followed the beast and the false prophet. These are slain with the sword that comes from the mouth of the rider on the white horse. Christ's word is both decisive and effective. Christ does not engage in physical combat with the enemies. Instead, when Christ speaks, he both judges and pronounces judgment against the enemies.

Readers gain insight and comfort about the end with the image of a battle. Throughout the troublesome course of history, enemies oppose God's will and way. The struggle between God and evil, according to Revelation 19:11–21, compares to a battle. This

---

[9] Donald W. Richardson, *The Revelation of Jesus Christ: An Interpretation* (Richmond: John Knox Press, 1939), 112.

battle ends with Christ the winner and with evil completely annihilated. Now one enemy of God remains, namely the dragon, or Satan. In the next image John pictures Christ's return on earth in the midst of evil, and he portrays Christ's ultimate reign when Satan goes to utter destruction in the lake of fire.

A Reign
20:1-10

John uses the image of a reign for the third image about the end. In fact, John uses the word "reigned" and "reign" in this section. The word for "reign" is the verbal form of the word "kingdom" (*ebasileuson*). The image portrays Christ's rule over evil during history and his ultimate destruction of evil at the end of history.

John says the same thing in his image about a reign as Jesus said about the "kingdom of heaven." God's kingdom came with the coming of Christ to earth. Jesus said, "Repent, for the kingdom of heaven is at hand." The word *kingdom* means the rule or reign of God. According to Jesus, his kingdom is "at hand," or it is now. Christ ruled during his earthly life and ministry over evil, and he rules now through his followers.

Jesus did not convey the idea that his kingdom rule is altogether *now* in history. But in his teachings Jesus conveys that the future is *not yet*. Jesus' reign will come in absolute perfection in the future. Jesus promises that one day the kingdom of this world will become the perfect kingdom of our God and his Christ.

John's image of a reign agrees with Jesus' teachings about the kingdom of heaven. Readers of Revelation learn in chapter 20 both the *now* and *not yet* of Jesus' reign. Christ bound the devil in his death and resurrection, but Satan still continues to work until Christ finally destroys him. John's image of Jesus' reign does not just picture the end. His image pictures the restraint of Satan during history along with the continuing work. John closes his image with the final destruction of Satan.

The Reign of Christ during History

John continues the victory events he shared in chapter 19. In the previous section the beast and the false prophet have been defeated and hurled to destruction. Their followers have also been destroyed. Now the dragon remains. John resumes the drama by telling of the restraint of Satan's power during history. "Then I saw an angel coming down from heaven, holding in his hand the key to the bottomless pit and a great chain. And he seized the dragon, that ancient serpent, who is the devil and Satan, and bound him for a thousand years, and threw him into the pit, and shut it and sealed it over him, so that he might not deceive the nations any longer, until the thousand years were ended. After that he must be released for a little while" (20:1–3). John seems to portray spiritual truth in the symbolic style of apocalyptic writing. The fact that the angel comes "from heaven" indicates that the angel has authority from God. This angel restrains the dragon in four ways: a key to the bottomless pit, a great chain, a pit, and a seal on the door of the pit. The angel did not have a literal chain, for Satan could not be bound with a physical chain. What then does John mean by the symbols? The symbols communicate the restraint or defeat of Satan. Throughout history Satan comes under God's jurisdiction.

The angel seizes the dragon and binds him for a thousand years. John pauses to identify the dragon as "that ancient serpent, who is the devil and Satan." What did John mean by the phrase "a thousand years"? There have been many disputes about the expression, some of them quite bitter, over the way to interpret the thousand years. Three prominent interpretations of the term "a thousand years" exist. Premillenialists think that Christ will return and then establish a literal thousand-year reign on earth. Postmillennialists see the return of Christ taking place after a thousand-year reign on earth. Amillennialists hold that the expression "a thousand years" stands for the whole time between the life of Jesus on earth and his final return. Notice that all three of these views advocate a reign of Christ, but they differ in point of time.

The angel with the key and the great chain in his hand symbolizes Christ himself. When was Satan bound? Christ says, "But no one can enter a strong man's house and plunder his goods, unless he first binds the strong man" (Mark 3:27). Christ clearly alluded to the binding of Satan. Again, Christ said to his disciples, "I saw Satan fall like lightning from heaven" (Luke 10:18). On the night before his death, Jesus tells his disciples, "Now is the judgment of this world; now will the ruler of this world be cast out" (John 12:31). All of these words of Jesus have reference to what John speaks of as binding Satan. With the death of Christ, Satan received a blow from which he will never recover. But he is not destroyed. During the period from Christ's ascension to his return, Satan is bound. He is deprived of his power against the saints. He cannot prevent the heralding of the gospel to the nations.

John has the distinct ability of concentrating on one thing at a time. He does not try to reconcile one of his pictures with another. In the image of the reign, John specifically says that Satan was restrained "so that he might not deceive the nations any longer, until the thousand years were ended." Looking ahead to 20:8, we find that this means Satan cannot gather the nations for the final consummation. The end is in God's control, not Satan's. During the period when Satan is bound, he cannot prevent the establishment of God's kingdom among the nations of the world.

John does not write chronologically in this image of Jesus' reign. Thus, John's statement "after that" in 20:3 is literally "after these things." John writes concurrently. B. B. Warfield thinks "it is quite possible that the binding of Satan and his loosing are contemporaneous events."[10] If this is the case, the thousand years and the release of Satan for "a little time" are concurrent. Satan was bound at the beginning of the thousand years. Also, after the thousand years began, Satan is loosed. During the thousand years Satan is bound in regard to the redeemed, but he is loosed in regard to the unredeemed. The binding and loosing happen concurrently until Jesus returns.

The Reign of the Saints with Christ

The angel interrupts the binding and loosing of Satan with another vision. He resumes the activity of Satan in 20:7. "Then I saw thrones, and seated on them were those to whom the authority to judge was committed. Also I saw the souls of those who had been beheaded for the testimony of Jesus and for the word of God, and those who had not worshiped the beast or its image and had not received its mark on their foreheads or their hands. They came to life and reigned with Christ for a thousand years" (20:4). John does not tell where he saw the thrones. The context seems to suggest heaven, not earth. The vocabulary of thrones and souls describes a heavenly place. The term "throne" appears forty-seven times in Revelation, and apart from the reference to Satan's and the beast's throne, the term refers to heaven (2:13; 13:2; 16:10). John's style throughout Revelation has been to shift scenes from earth to heaven and from heaven to earth. In 20:1-3, John pictures Christ's rule on earth during the church age, and in 20:4-6 he pictures the reign of the saints with Christ in heaven. The millennium of Revelation is the blessedness of the saints who have gone away from earth to be at home with the Lord. The time for the reigning of God's people with him in glory is the entire church age. This period has covered many centuries, and it will come to a close with the return of Christ.

---

[10] Quoted in ibid., 127.

Leon Morris thinks John takes the readers behind the scenes for a pastoral purpose. Morris thinks John wants the readers to see what has happened to the martyrs who have died for the Lord. They live because of their first resurrection, and they reign with Christ in heaven. Their martyrdom brought fear, despair, and defeat to their fellow believers, but the sight of them now reigning with Christ in heaven brings comfort.[11]

The vision of the saints in heaven has three interesting insights: the thrones of judgment, the souls of martyrs, and a thousand years of living and reigning with Christ. Notice first these saints are given "authority to judge." The expression could mean that they were given authority to exercise judgment or that justice had been done to them—judgment was given for them. Both insights are correct. Perhaps John thinks about how God highly exalts the redeemed by giving them the privilege of judging human beings and angels. This judging alludes not to the final judgment but rather to the authority the saints receive to rule as the Old Testament judges did.

Next John speaks of the "souls of those who had been beheaded for the testimony of Jesus and for the word of God." John describes martyrs beheaded by Roman executioners. These people are killed for their courage in witnessing for Jesus and proclaiming the word of God. Did John refer to another group when he wrote, "And those who had not worshiped the beast or its image and had not received its mark on their foreheads or their hands"? Does it refer to one group who died as martyrs and another group who died a natural death? John seems to be addressing only one group. The context seems to indicate the

---

[11] Morris, *The Revelation of St. John*, 234–35.

inclusion of all believers who have been faithful to the Lord.[12]

The third insight is "they came to life and reigned with Christ for a thousand years." When the believer departs this earthly life, they enter into perfect communion with Christ.

John pauses to give a contrast. "The rest of the dead did not come to life until the thousand years were ended. This is the first resurrection" (20:5). John often made contrasts in Revelation between good and evil, holy and profane, life and death. Now he contrasts those who have eternal life and those who do not have eternal life. The Greek word "come to life" (*ezesan*) does not mean live again but come into life with Christ. This is not the usual word for resurrection. When anyone trusts Christ, that person "comes to life" or is "risen with Christ" from spiritual death. All the redeemed were once "dead in trespasses and sins," but in Christ they have "come to life." The phrase "rest of the dead" refers to the unredeemed who do not "come to life." The spiritually dead who are not spiritually resurrected do not live during the whole Christian age. They are dead in the deepest sense of the word, experiencing in this life a life apart from God, and awaiting in the end a second death.[13]

John writes the fifth beatitude in a series of seven (1:3; 14:13; 16:15; 19:9; 20:6; 22:7, 14). "Blessed and holy is the one who shares in the first resurrection! Over such the second death has no power, but they will be priests of God and of Christ, and they will reign with him for a thousand years" (20:6). The terms "first resurrection" and "second death" are spiritual operations. No one who shares in the first resurrection is subject to the second death.

---

[12] Simon J. Kistemaker, "Revelation" in *New Testament Commentary* (Grand Rapids: Baker Books, 2001), 537.

[13] Robbins, *The Revelation of Jesus Christ*, 226.

The second death describes an eternal separation from God.

Those who share in the first resurrection have one negative blessing and two positive ones. Negatively, the second death has no power over those who have come to life in Christ; they serve God as priests and reign with him during all the end-times.

The Ultimate Reign of Christ

John reverts to a theme he has mentioned several times. He tells about the gathering together of all the forces of evil at the end to do battle with God. He mentions it quickly. The triumph of God comes certain and quick. "And when the thousand years are ended, Satan will be released from his prison and will come out to deceive the nations that are at the four corners of the earth, Gog and Magog, to gather them for battle; their number is like the sand of the sea" (20:7-8). Satan has been defeated, but he is still permitted to wage war on the earth. Just when he appears to be restrained, he breaks out in a new effort. However, the concurrent binding and losing of Satan will not last forever. Satan's ultimate termination is certain. Whenever the church age has reached its completeness in the mind of God, there is a resurgence of Satan.

Gog is the name of a chief prince, and Magog is the name of the land over which he ruled (Gen. 10:2; Ezek. 38:17). In Ezekiel 38, the names symbolized all the foes of the people of God. In apocalyptic writings Gog and Magog symbolize the forces of evil. John uses these terms to depict the last great attack of evil on the things of God. Satan will gather the greatest possible number to oppose God. This is the final battle.

John next describes the invasion of the evil ones. "And they marched up over the broad plain of the earth and surrounded the camp of the saints and the beloved city, but fire came down from heaven and consumed them" (20:9). John pictures the forces of evil placing the people of God in an apparent helpless position. The verb "surrounded" suggests a desperate situation. The reader expects a big battle, but no battle occurs. John shows with graphic symbolism divine intervention and the destruction of evil.

At last John writes of the ultimate end of Satan. "And the devil who had deceived them was thrown into the lake of fire and sulfur where the beast and the false prophet were, and they will be tormented day and night forever and ever" (20:10). John pictures Satan's fate as utter hopelessness. Every vestige of evil will be destroyed, and every enemy of the church will be destroyed. The triumph of Christ's reign is complete. The *not yet* has become the *now*.

A Courtroom
20:11–15

One by one the enemies of Christ and his church have been destroyed. What's next? Only people remain to be judged, both redeemed and unredeemed. John gives a final image of the end with a picture of judgment. The image in 20:11–15 has all the trappings of a courtroom: a judge, the examination of evidence, and the pronouncement of verdicts. Every person who has ever lived will be summoned to the courtroom to be judged with divine justice. When the verdict comes, people will be separated into two groups, the godly and the ungodly.

The Judge

John sees in the courtroom a great white throne with an unidentified judge upon it. "Then I saw a great white throne and him who was seated on it. From his presence earth and sky fled away, and no place was found for them" (20:11). The scene is one of infinite majesty. The throne represents the focal point of the vision and represents the supreme authority for the judgment of all people. John describes the throne with two adjectives, "great" and "white." "Great" symbolizes something larger than life which human beings cannot fathom. "White" depicts purity, holiness, and victory.

John avoids referring to the occupant on the throne as God. In typical Jewish fashion he describes the occupant as "him who was seated." John thinks God is too awesome to be described or even named. The Father is the Judge, and he judges through the Son. "The Father judges no one, but has given all judgment to the Son" (John 5:22).

Something about the One on the throne causes earth and sky to flee from him. The old order disappears to give place to the new. John depicts that the holiness of the One on the throne is so great the old creation must flee. In this creation there is no place for evil in its varied forms.

The Judged

John moves from the Judge to the judged. "And I saw the dead, great and small, standing before the throne, and books were opened. Then another book was opened, which is the book of life. And the dead were judged by what was written in the books, according to what they had done. And the sea gave up the dead who were in it, Death and Hades gave up the dead who were in them, and they were judged, each one of them, according to what they had done" (20:12-13). John pictures the destinies of people with the image of a solemn judicial procedure. The scene depicts the fact that none escape the judgment of God. John mentions two sets of books—"books were opened" and "another book was opened." The latter book is the "book of life." The first books contain records of everyone's deeds, both good and bad. These people will be judged in accordance with their records, but this does not imply a doctrine of works of righteousness. A person is declared right on the basis of whether his or her name is recorded in the book of life. The issue is not initial salvation by works but works that follow faith provide evidence of real faith.

The book of life contains the names of the redeemed. If one's name is written in the book of life, this person has a guarantee of admission into heaven. The Christian chooses God and accepts identity with Christ. If a person's name is not in the book of life, this person receives the sentence of separation from God.

John's mention of the sea and death and Hades indicates that all of the dead are included. No one is overlooked. Whatever way a person dies means he or she will be included in judgment.

The Judgment

John continues the discussion with insight about the judgment itself. "Then Death and Hades were thrown into the lack of fire. This is the second death, the lake of fire. And if anyone's name was not found written in the book of life, he was thrown into the lake of fire" (20:14-15). John assures the readers of the certain judgment on all who are enemies of Christ. The beast, false prophet, and dragon have been destroyed. Now John speaks of death as the common foe of all people and Hades of the common destruction. People dreaded Death and Hades. But now Death and Hades are thrown in the same place as the dragon, the beast, and the false prophet. This signifies the complete victory over all agents of evil.

John says that being cast into the lake of fire is the "second death." John does not use the phrase "first death," but he has alluded to that fact. The "first death is physical death, and "second death" is the punishment of the unredeemed.

John closes the image of the courtroom with the judgment of the unredeemed. Anyone whose name did not appear in the book of life will be thrown into the lake of fire. In the end people will share in the blessing of heaven or find their place in the lake of fire.

John answers the question, "What is this world coming to?" He writes that God and evil will continue to struggle throughout history until he decides to conclude this world order. Opponents will continue to oppose God and his people influenced by the dragon, the ancient serpent, the devil, and Satan. One day God will declare that history is finished, and Christ will come, and John tells us what it will be like in the end. It will be like a bride living with a bridegroom; it will be like a battle won; it will be like the full actualization of Christ's reign; it will be like the Judge declaring the righteous his and sentencing the unrighteous to separation from God.

Chapter 17
The Scenes of Life beyond History

Revelation 21:1-22:5

THE BOOK OF REVELATION RESEMBLES a series of video clips (visions). Some of the videos have the labels of the exalted Christ, the seven churches, the Occupant on the throne, the Lamb and the scroll, the seals, the trumpets, the enemies of God, the bowls, and images about the end. Each vision shows some aspect of history and concludes with an announcement of the end of history as well as a glimpse beyond history. When one video (vision) ends, another one begins. These videos do not run sequentially but concurrently. Each video clip fits in the time frame from the incarnation of Christ to his final return. When each video ends with a sight about the future, the reader's interest increases. Without a doubt the original readers as well as modern readers want to know more about the end and the life beyond.

John sees his final vision in 21:1-22:5. This vision differs from the previous ones. The final vision does not go through the long, troublesome course of history to characterize some happening in history. Instead, John's final vision involves one beyond earthly existence. This vision describes the final destiny of the redeemed. Readers rejoice to read of the conditions beyond their time on earth.

The book of Revelation has been dramatically moving toward the grand finale that pictures God's ultimate plan for the world—a new creation in which evil and rebellion have no place.[1] The dissonant echoes of conflict and judgment give way in this final vision to a majestic chorus of concord and hope.[2] The writer moves from the Lord's return, the destruction of God's enemies, and the final judgment to creation redeemed, paradise restored. The "not yet" that has been desired during history has become the "now" in eternity.

The final vision begins with a panoramic view of the new heavens and the new earth. In this vision John sees the new Jerusalem coming down out of heaven, prepared like a bride for her husband. Next an angelic guide brings John closer to the holy city so that attention focuses on the city itself. John sees high walls and twelve gates, which are made of gemstones, pearls, and gold. Then the angel takes John into the city where he sees the water of life flow from the throne of God and the Lamb and the tree of life bearing fruit and producing leaves for the healing of the nations. The vision ends with God and the Lamb. The redeemed gather around the throne. At last they experience the perfect presence of God and reign in his light forever.[3] Four scenes make up the image of life beyond for believers.

A New Order
21:1–4

---

[1] Reddish, *Revelation*, 401.

[2] Craig R. Koester, *Revelation and the End of All Things* (Grand Rapids: Eerdmans, 2001), 191.

[3] Ibid.

John sees a new vision—"then I saw" (21:1). He has seen the vision of the doom of the wicked, and now he sees the bliss of the redeemed. An old order of rebellion and evil has passed away. A new order comes to view in this final vision. In this new order God's ultimate design for his people comes into being. This new order consists of God's presence with his people and the conspicuous absence of evil.

A New Heaven and a New Earth

From the fate of the evil, John turns to the blessedness of the good. "Then I saw a new heaven and a new earth, for the first heaven and the first earth had passed away, and the sea was no more" (21:1). The terms "heaven" and "earth" describe the comprehensiveness of God's creation. Isaiah spoke long before John about a new order: "For behold, I create new heavens and a new earth, and the former things shall not be remembered" (65:17). Isaiah visualized a time filled with joy and the removal of sorrow and suffering. The themes of joy and newness dominate the final vision in Revelation.

A major contrast exists between "new" (*kainos*) and "first" (*protos*). The "new" stresses the qualitative newness more than the temporal newness. There will be a whole new order, a new kind of existence where all the negatives of the "first" will be removed. All the discoloration carved by sin will be gone. Two ideas exist about the new order. One holds the view that there will be a total destruction of the present world and a new creation of heaven and earth. Others think John teaches a renovated or transformed earth. John R. W. Stott and many others follow the idea of a regenerated heaven and earth. Stott writes, "The new heaven and the new earth will not be a replacement universe (as if created *de novo*) but a regenerated universe, purged of all present imperfection, with no more pain, sin or death."[4]

Two expressions in the text could support the rejuvenated theory. First, the word "new" (*kainos*) designates something that already existed but now appears in a new or fresh way. This suggests that it is an existent heaven and earth that is completely transformed. Second, "passed way" does not have to mean annihilation or complete destruction. It could refer to the future renewal and the fulfillment of creation as God intended it. Revelation envisions not only the redemption of the individual person but the redemption of the whole of creation. Paul had this idea when he wrote "that the creation itself will be set free from its bondage to corruption and obtain the freedom of the glory of the children of God" (Rom. 8:21). God intends a new order for his world and his people, and Revelation has that picture of redemption.

In this new heaven and earth, there will be no more sea. The passing away of the sea seems out of place in light of heaven and earth passing away. The answer comes with the symbolic meaning of the sea in Revelation. The sea symbolizes evil. In the new order the old creation will be redeemed, and evil will be "no more." The dragon and all his allies that caused so much suffering will have been cast into the lake of fire, so rebellion and evil will be gone forever. The scene of the new heaven and the new earth has everything godly in it and nothing ungodly.

The New Jerusalem

John moves from the panoramic view of the new heaven and the new earth to a glimpse of the new Jerusalem. "And I saw the holy city, new Jerusalem, coming down out of heaven from God, prepared as a bride adorned for her husband" (21:2). The idea

---

[4] Stott, *The Incomparable Christ*, 224.

of a heavenly Jerusalem that becomes the ultimate home of God's people is not original with John. This idea was present in the various apocalyptic traditions (Isa. 54; 55, 60; Ezek. 40-48). John pictures the life beyond for believers as a city experiencing community or life together. Future existence is not necessarily individualistic but communal. The city symbolizes redeemed humanity, the church.

The expression, "coming down out of heaven," emphasizes the city's origin and source. Human effort did not bring the end or goal of history. It is the gift of God rather than the achievement of human beings. The new Jerusalem resembles "a bride adorned for her husband." The image stresses the sacred bond between God and his people. The church enjoys the most intimate relationships with God and finds their real blessedness in perfect union with him. Obviously, John does not depict the rebuilding of the earthly city of Jerusalem. This is a "new" Jerusalem that he sees. It differs qualitatively from the old Jerusalem. The Hebrews looked to Jerusalem as God's special city, the place where God dwells with his people. When John sees the new Jerusalem, he envisions a new community, a new way in which God dwells among his people.[5] Kiddle writes about the new Jerusalem, "It is a city which is a family. The ideal of perfect community, unrealizable on earth because of the curse of sin which vitiated the first creation, is now embodied in the redeemed of all nations."[6] A. M. Hunter writes, "The consummation of the Christian hope is supremely social. It is no 'flight of the alone to the Alone' but life in the redeemed community of heaven."[7]

---

[5] Reddish, *Revelation*, 402.

[6] Martin Kiddle, *The Revelation of St. John*, 415–16.

[7] A. M. Hunter, *Probing the New Testament* (Richmond: John Knox, 1971), 156.

The New Life

The unidentified voice from the heavenly throne declares in verses 3 and 4 the kind of life present in the city. The primary quality of the new order is relational. "And I heard a loud voice from the throne saying, 'Behold, the dwelling place of God is with man. He will dwell with them, and they will be his people, and God himself will be with them as their God'" (21:3). Motifs drawn from the Old Testament dominate the scenes of the new life. The covenant established at Sinai is now fulfilled. "I will make my dwelling among you. . . . I will walk among you and will be your God, and you shall be my people" (Lev. 26:11-12). God revealed himself in the tabernacle, and it symbolized his presence with the people. Jesus became Emmanuel or "God with us." He became flesh and dwelt (literally "tabernacled") among us (John 1:14). God dwells in his church during its time in history. After death the believer dwells with God in ultimate intimacy.

God will remove the sources of sorrow. "He will wipe away every tear from their eyes, and death shall be no more, neither shall there be mourning, nor crying, nor pain anymore, for the former things have passed away" (21:4). Life in the new Jerusalem will be everlasting joy and bliss. Sorrow, pain, and death will be eliminated. These things characterized the old order that has passed away. John lists some evils that do not exist in the new order—pain, sorrows, tears, and death. The new order reverses the curse of Genesis 3. Life as we know it is completely replaced by the new order. This describes the original creation fully restored in redemption, Paradise Regained.

The Divine Assurances
21:5-8

The drama in Revelation takes a dramatic turn at 21:5. The One who sits on the throne now speaks. This is noteworthy as one of the few occasions in Revelation where God himself speaks (1:8 and perhaps 16:1, 17). Usually an angel or an unidentified voice speaks. God speaks to assure the churches of John's days. Its persecuted and threatened members need to hear words of hope. God speaks directly affirming what the heavenly voice in 21:1–4 has spoken.

The Assurance of Change

In a lot of ways life was difficult for the readers of Revelation. It was hard to be a Christian in the environment where they lived. They longed for something different. God promises a change for these believers, "And he who was seated on the throne said, 'Write this down, for these words are trustworthy and true" (21:5). God's message begins with a call for serious attention—"behold." His first word summarizes what has been said in 21:1–4—"I am making all things new." Notice the present tense is used—"I am making." God continually makes all things new, here and now. "If anyone is in Christ, he is a new creation. The old has passed away; behold the new has come" (2 Cor. 5:17). The change has begun in Christ, but it awaits the complete change at the return of Christ. The process of change includes the physical world also. Change in the biblical sense involves not only the lives of people but also the change of the physical body and the physical environment.

God's message is so important that he commands John to write it. John can write God's message with complete assurance that what he says is "trustworthy and true." This is the second of three statements regarding the truthfulness of the prophecies (21:5; 22:6; 19:9). The other two are said by an angel, but the one in 21:5 is by God himself. These words can be trusted. The new order can be certain because the trustworthy and true God has promised it.

The Assurance of the Future

God continues to speak with words of assurance. The future seemed to be problematic to the first readers. The firm word of God helps them have certainty about the future. "And he said to me, 'It is done! I am the Alpha and the Omega, the beginning and the end'" (21:6a). God assures the readers that salvation history will come to a close and eternity will begin. God has the future of his people in his care.

The assurance of the future rests on the character of God as sovereign over history. God's title, "Alpha and Omega," is interpreted as "the beginning and the end." God was sovereign at the beginning of history or creation, and he will be in charge at the end as well. The title means that he not only controls the beginning and the end but also everything in between.

The Assurance of Satisfaction

God's making all things new includes the deepest satisfaction of human beings. "To the thirsty I will give from the spring of the water of life without payment" (21:6b). The figure of thirst symbolizes the sense of spiritual need. Augustine in his *Confessions* said, "You have made us for yourself, O Lord, and our hearts are restless until they find rest in you."[8]

A person's deepest satisfaction comes as a gift of God: "I will give." John pictures God as a spring of water. He assuages thirst. In the hot, dry climate of Palestine and Asia Minor, a spring of cool water would be a vivid symbol of satisfaction. Whatever the future will be like, it will hold the deepest satisfaction for God's people.

The Assurance of Inheritance

---

[8] Saint Augustine, *Saint Augustine Confessions* (Oxford, England: Oxford University Press, 1998), 1.

The section closes with the assurance of a distinct difference of those who are God's people and those who are not. "This one who conquers will have this heritage, and I will be his God, and he will be my son" (21:7). This inheritance for the believer comes because of a special relationship with God: "I will be his God, and he will be my son." This text contains a promise of inheritance. Followers of Christ inherit all the blessings of a new heaven and a new earth.

The reverse side to the believer's inheritance is the fate awaiting sinners. John lists a long catalog of those who are not part of God's kingdom. "But as for the cowardly, the faithless, the detestable, as for murderers, the sexually immoral, sorcerers, idolaters, and all liars, their portion will be in the lake that burns with fire and sulfur, which is the second death" (21:8). Eight epithets are used to describe those who preclude themselves from the kingdom of God. The "cowards" head the list. John speaks of a fear that in the last resort chooses safety before Christ. "Faithless" could mean those who lack faith or those who in testing time have been unfaithful to Christ. The "detestable" covers defilement of various kinds. More than likely the word refers to ideas and practices from pagan religions. The word "murderers" refers to the persecutors of the believers. The phrase "sexually immoral" refers to sexual sins in general. It relates to the sexually immorality practiced in the pagan trade guilds. "Sorcerers" or the practice of magic prevailed among the imperial cult to deceive people. "Idolatry" means to put anything in place of the one true God. The word "liars" perverts everything true and valid. This last summarizes the sinners who go to the lake of fire, the second death. The people of God live a different life from these eight vices. They also have a separate destiny and experience than the redeemed.

A Wonderful Environment
21:9-27

John continues with scenes of life beyond history. The original readers of Revelation lived in a hostile environment. The members of the seven churches belonged to a minority religion in an environment of conflicting religious pluralism. Being a Christian meant refusing to participate in pagan functions that would have severe social and economic consequences. Political pressure came upon the believers to divide lordship between Caesar and Christ. The believers lived in the environment of a "Secular City," where God was either ignored or opposed.

John turns to a comforting image of life beyond history for the believers. The scene is one of the new Jerusalem, the Holy City, the City of God, the Spiritual City. The scene portrays the idyllic environment that God's people enjoy when they die or when Christ comes. John sets up a deliberate contrast between "the bride, the holy city Jerusalem" and "the whore, Babylon, the mighty city." The introductory words of the scene closely parallel the opening words of the vision of Babylon (Cf. 17:1-3). John tells us that one of the seven angels who had the bowls of wrath spoke to him saying, "Come, I will show you the Bride, the wife of the Lamb" (21:9). The angel seems to be the one who, in chapter 17, summoned John to witness the judgment of the great whore (the wicked city of Babylon). At that time John was carried away in spirit into a wilderness. Now, by contrast, John is carried away in spirit to a great, high mountain to get a vision of "the holy city Jerusalem coming down out of heaven from God" (21:10). The saints living in the secular city get a glimpse of their life beyond the grave in the spiritual city.⁹

The Beauty of the City

Using the brilliance of precious stones, John attempts to describe the beauty of the holy city. "Having the glory of God, its radiance like a most rare jewel, like a jasper, clear as crystal" (21:11). The major characteristic of the holy city is that it contains "the glory of God." "The glory of God" means the abiding presence of God with all of his holiness and power.

When John tries to describe the beauty of the city, he could only do what he did when he attempted to describe the presence of God himself (4:3). He speaks of the city in terms of glittering gems. The word "radiance" describes the brilliance of light coming from the city. The city's brilliant beauty is then likened to "a most rare jewel." It is like "jasper, clear as crystal." The expression could mean shining like crystal or transparent like crystal. Jasper, as we know it, is an opaque stone. If it is crystal clear, it is not our jasper. Some think the diamond is meant. We cannot be certain about the identification of precious gems in antiquity. Whatever the view about the stone, whether jasper or diamond, the message is the same where John thinks the new Jerusalem is an absolutely beautiful place. The city's light comes not from the luminary bodies but from God. Believers have the assurance that their life beyond will be in a beautiful place.

The Wall, the Gates, and the Foundation of the City

After the initial awe from the glory of the city, John notes other factors in its eternal appearance. Any city in John's world would have walls, gates, and foundations. John seems to echo Ezekiel (48:30–35), who described a city that was named "The Lord Is There" (Ezek. 48:35–36). John first describes the walls of the holy

---

⁹ Reddish, *Revelation*, 405.

city. "It had a great, high wall, with twelve gates, and at the gates twelve angels, and on the gates the names of the twelve tribes of the sons of Israel were inscribed" (21:12). The walls of the city seem to describe its security. Leon Morris does not think the walls refer to security "for all enemies have been destroyed."[10] John mentions the wall first, but it is not described until 21:17-18. In 21:18 the wall is made of jasper, meaning its purpose is not for defense but for radiating the glory of God.

The walls contain twelve gates. On the gates the names of the twelve tribes of Israel appear. The twelve gates are distributed three on each side of the city. Over each gate an angel sits. More than likely, the angel controls who goes in and out of the city. With three gates on each side of the city, there is access from every direction: north, south, east, and west. The inscription of the names of the twelve tribes of Israel serves as a symbol to represent the church as the true Israel.

After describing the wall and the gates, John describes the city's foundation. "And the wall of the city had twelve foundations, and on them were the twelve names of the twelve apostles of the Lamb" (21:14). The combination of the twelve tribes in verse 12 and the twelve apostles is a way of describing Israel of old and the Christian church as united in God's final scheme of things. Paul thinks the household of God is built on the foundation of the apostles and prophets (Eph. 2:20). The holy city includes all the people of God from the old covenant and from the new covenant.

The Measurement of the City

John continues to focus on describing the holy city. He now talks about measuring the city. "And the one who spoke with me had a measuring rod of gold to measure the city and its gates

---

[10] Morris, *The Revelation of St. John*, 249.

and walls" (21:15). John was told to measure the temple (11:1). but only an angel is capable of measuring the holy city. The angel uses a measuring rod of gold. Perhaps the gold symbolizes the preciousness of the city's measurement.

The city that appears to John is foursquare. "The city lies foursquare, its length the same as its width. And he measured the city with his rod, 12,000 stadia. Its length and width and height are equal. He also measured its wall, 144 cubits by human measurement, which is also an angel's measurement" (21:16–17). How can a city be a cube? In ancient times the cube was held to be the most perfect of all geometric forms. By the use of the cube, John wants the readers to understand that the holy city, the new Jerusalem, is absolutely splendid with a harmony and symmetry of perfect proportion. The particular shape of the city resembles the inner sanctuary of the temple, the place of divine presence. A city foursquare would be the place where God resides with his people.

The Building Materials of the City

The building materials of the city are like no earthly city. "The wall was built of jasper, while the city was pure gold, clear as glass" (21:18). John describes the building materials in literal, earthly terms, but his words appear to mean that the city defies description. The wall did not have jasper built into it, but it was built with jasper. The One on the throne in 4:3 appears like jasper. In 21:11 the holy city, aglow with the glory of God, emits the radiance of precious jasper. Even the wall of the city speaks of the glorious presence of God.[11]

John adds the information that the city was pure gold. This gold is "clear as glass," unlike any earthly gold. Maybe John says the gold is so pure that it seems like transparent lass. Perhaps John accentuates a feature in the earthly Jerusalem. Herod's temple had

---

[11] Mounce, *The Book of Revelation*, 381.

a golden front that reflected the rays of the morning sun. It was so bright that those who looked upon it had to turn their eyes away from it. John could have seen in Herod's temple in Jerusalem a theme paralleled to the splendor of the holy city.[12]

John turns from the walls and the city itself to the foundation stones. "The foundations of the wall of the city were adorned with every kind of jewel. The first was jasper, the second sapphire, the third agate, the fourth emerald, the fifth onyx, the sixth carnelian, the seventh chrysolite, the eighth beryl, the ninth topaz, the tenth chrysoprase, the eleventh jacinth, the twelfth amethyst" (21:19–20). The precious stones seem to be reminiscent of those on the breastplate of the high priest and serve as a constant reminder that believers comprise a kingdom of priests. The communion that every believer has with God is so real that the whole city is a sanctuary.

The most amazing use of precious stones in this picture is the idea that the gates of the city of God each consist of one vast pearl. "And the twelve gates were twelve pearls, each of the gates made of a single pearl, and the street of the city was pure gold, transparent as glass" (21:21). In the ancient world pearls were of all stones most valued. The spectacle of a pearl large enough to serve as a city gate struck a sense of wonder. From the gate John moves to the street of pure gold. The gold is transparent, indicating that any flaw would show. If it were pure, it would really be pure. The gems, the pearls, and the gold communicate the wonder of all that God has prepared for his people after they die.

The Living Conditions in the City

John closes the image of the holy city by describing conditions that characterize the new Jerusalem. First, there is no temple in the city. "And I saw no temple in the city, for its temple

---

[12] Barclay, *The Revelation of John, vol. 2*, 272.

is the Lord God the Almighty and the Lamb" (21:22). The reason the city needs no temple is that the presence of God and of the Lamb is continually there.

Second, the city of God needs no created light. "And the city has no need of sun or moon to shine on it, for the glory of God gives it light, and its lamp is the Lamb. By its light will the nations walk, and the kings of the earth will bring their glory into it" (21:23-24). The glory of God provides the light. The city is flooded with light, and darkness of every kind is banished forever. John does not supply his readers with information about astrological changes. He gives theological truth about the splendor that radiates from the presence of God and the Lamb.

Isaiah predicted that the nations would be gathered together in Jerusalem under the banner of the Messiah (Isa. 60:3, 5, 11; 66:12). John says that Isaiah's prediction has been fulfilled in the gathering together of all nations into the holy city. The term "nations" refers to the Gentiles. The "kings of the earth," or human authority, find their true purpose in ministering to the needs of humanity. John has taken from the prophets' language and figures of speech which assert the participation of the Gentile people in the new order.

Third, the city of God has no need for closed gates. John continues his allusion to Isaiah 60:11, "Your gates shall be open continually; day and night they shall not be shut." The gates of a city were closed at night to keep out unwanted visitors. Yet in the holy city the gates will never be shut. "And its gates will never be shut by day—and there will be no night there. They will bring into it the glory and honor of the nations" (21:25-26). The "glory and honor of the nations" must mean they worship God in the eternal city. They will glorify and honor God for all eternity.

Fourth, the holy city has nothing unclean or shameful in it. "But nothing unclean will ever enter it, nor anyone who does what is detestable or false, but only those who are written in the Lamb's book of life" (21:27). The reference to "unclean" comes with qualities that characterize the empire of the beast. In Mark's Gospel, demons are called "unclean spirits," so the name became associated with the realm of evil. Anything unclean was antithetical to the sanctity of the temple or to the worship of God. In the holy city nothing "unclean" will be allowed.[13]

Also, no one who is "detestable" will have a part in the holy city. This is closely associated to the unclean. In Revelation 17:4–5, the great prostitute held up a cup in her hand, filled with abominations and impurities. These terms sum up the terrible sins of those who follow the great prostitute. They have no part in God's eternal city, for holiness is the chief characteristic.[14]

Anyone practicing falsehood will also have no part in the new Jerusalem. Beale thinks the reference to "false" refers especially to those who professed faith in Christ but contradicted it by their sinful lifestyle, which was the telling sign that they were false believers.[15]

The only ones permitted to enter the holy city are "those who are written in the Lamb's book of life." John uses the model of the roll of citizens in ancient cities and also the Old Testament register of the citizens of Israel. The book John cites is the Lamb's book, which communicates the thought that salvation depends on what Christ has done.

The Qualitative Life
22:1–5

---

[13] Osborne, *Revelation*, 765.

[14] Ibid.

[15] Beale, *The Book of Revelation*, 1,101

John has used various phrases about the living conditions in the holy city to prepare us for the blessedness of its inner life, 22:1-5. The word "life" (*zoe*) appears in these verses to depict the kind of existence God's people have in life beyond the grave. The readers have seen the glorious environment in the life beyond, and now they see the qualitative life experience of the life beyond. Eternal life does not just mean a quantitative existence but a qualitative existence that never ends. In this last section John gives us scenes of a qualitative life.

The Symbols of Eternal Life

John uses two symbols to describe the believers' existence in eternity: a river and a tree. "Then the angel showed me the river of the water of life, bright as crystal, flowing from the throne of God and of the Lamb through the middle of the street of the city; also, on either side of the river, the tree of life with its twelve kinds of fruit, yielding its fruit each month. The leaves of the tree were for the healing of the nations" (22:1-2). Both symbols of the river and the tree associate with life (*zoe*), which means "God's kind of life." John echoes Ezekiel 47 in the vision of the "river of the water of life." Ezekiel saw a river following beneath the temple in the restored Jerusalem. This river has life-giving qualities, nourishing the trees on its banks and turning the lifeless water of the Dead Sea into a water teeming with fish.

The image of the river source coming from the "throne of God" conveys the idea of eternal life coming from God. The term "river of life" indicates God's kind of life permeating existence beyond death for God's people. The "river of life" quenches every human thirst and provides lasting satisfaction.

The next symbol of eternal life is "the tree of life." On both sides of the river the tree of life grows. More than likely, the tree of life alludes to the tree of life from which Adam and Eve were excluded. At the end of the Bible's story, human beings return to enjoy the blessings which God originally intended. This tree bears fruit each month symbolizing the continuous blessings extended to God's people.

The leaves of the tree are used for "the healing of the nations." This provokes the question, From what do the nations need to be healed? The healing of the nations indicates that the population of the new Jerusalem will be made up of every kind of ethnic and national identity. More than likely John uses the term "healing of the nations" to describe God's surpassing and amazing grace.

The Blessing of Eternal Life

John again reassures the believers that the new Jerusalem will be free from all forms of evil. "No longer will there be anything accursed, but the throne of God and of the Lamb will be in it, and his servants will worship him" (22:3). Some interpreters think the allusion is to the "curses" pronounced on Adam, Eve, and the serpent in Genesis 3:14-19. The statement promises a reversal of the garden of Eden scenario.

The most important blessing of the life of the believer beyond death is the presence of God. "The throne of God and of the Lamb will be in it." John always returns to the theme that "heaven is where God is." Speaking of God means speaking also of the Lamb. All of the Christians' hope of eternal life can be summed up in the simple statement that we shall be with God.

Worship will be an important activity of life in the New Jerusalem. Believers will worship God and the Lamb. "They will see his face, and his name will be on their foreheads" (22:4). The God they worshipped from a distance can now be celebrated and praised face-to-face. The people of God will "see his face." To see God means to have the ultimate experience with him. John adds that the redeemed will have "his name on their foreheads." The name refers to God's character. God's people in the life beyond will reflect the likeness of God. The process of transformation begun in history will be brought to completion in the life to come.

Once again John returns to his vision that in the city of God there can never be any darkness, and there can never be any need of any other light, for the presence and the light of God are there. "And night will be no more. They will need no lamp or sun, for the Lord God will be their light, and they will reign forever and ever" (22:5). The believers' great privilege is not only to worship and serve God in a perfect environment but to reign with him forever.

Undoubtedly, the persecuted believers asked, "Is there life beyond this trouble?" People today want to know if there is life beyond death, and if there is one, what it is like. Don Piper's *90 Minutes in Heaven: A True Story of Death and Life* became a *New York Times* best seller in 2004. Piper writes about his tragic car accident, where he lay lifeless in the car. During that time he relates how he experienced the beauty, music, and glories of the afterlife. Later Piper returned miraculously to life on earth. He tells about ninety minutes he spent in heaven. Piper did a good job of describing the glories of the life beyond for believers.

But John does a better job of giving us insight about the believer's life beyond history. He gives us a scene of a new order, where the disorder in the moral sphere is removed and replaced by God's way. He describes the environment for believers beyond death as the new Jerusalem where beauty, security, inclusion, and perfect living conditions exist. John sees the life beyond characterized by a qualitative life that never ends. And most of all, the scene John gives of the life beyond involves an ultimate intimacy between God and his people that never ends. What a beautiful place and what a wonderful experience heaven must be!

Epilogue

Revelation 22:6–21

THE BOOK OF REVELATION ENDS in a practical manner. The epilogue reassures and confirms the visions that have been seen by John. The epilogue contains short sayings, practical exhortations, promises, assurances, blessings, and warnings. These last fifteen verses consist of short sentences, not closely related to one another. Each sentence repeats some previous phrase. Throughout the epilogue, the identity of the speakers is not clear. Christ seems to speak in verses 7, 12–13, 16, and 20*a*. In verse 9, the speaker identifies himself as an angel. John clearly is the speaker in verses 8 and 20*b*–21. The speaker in verses 6 and 10–11 could be Christ or an angel, and verses 14–15 and 18–19 may be from Christ or John.[1]

The epilogue does not need to be neglected. It reiterates some of the major emphases of the book. John writes in the style of the Semitic mind. His thoughts do not flow in sequential progress. Instead, his ideas come in a cyclic manner where he affirms one truth, moves to another truth, and returns to the previous truth. The epilogue will be studied around six indicative words.

---

[1] Reddish, *Revelation*, 423.

Verification
22:6–7

An angel seems to speak first. "And he said to me, 'These words are trustworthy and true. And the Lord, the God of the spirits of the prophets, has sent his angel to show his servants what must soon take place'" (22:6). The angel verifies to John that what he has heard and seen in the Revelation is "trustworthy and true." The expression "these words" seems to refer to the entire book of Revelation. The angel repeats 21:5 almost verbatim. This description of the prophet's message in the book parallels the character of Christ who is "faithful" in 3:14 and "true" in 3:7, 14; 19:11. Since God and Jesus revealed these visions through the angels, they are completely reliable and must be heeded.[2]

John repeats from 1:1 the process by which the visions have come. The description of God as "the God of the spirits of the prophets" verifies the source of John's visions. John connects with the line of Old Testament prophets. God through his angel makes known to John the message for the people. As in 1:1, 3 John seems to think the end is near, for he believes that the events he has described "must soon take place."

Christ speaks in verse 7 to verify the imminence of this return. "And behold, I am coming soon" (22:7). Christ wants his people to live with the expectancy of his coming. The early Christians lived in the expectancy of Christ's return happening soon. Every generation has a biblical right to believe that Christ will come in their lifetime. No one can set dates or calculate the time of his coming, but everyone can be prepared as if Christ is coming in the next minute.

Christ reminds both the writer of Revelation and its readers that hearing the message is not enough. One must be obedient to

---

[2] Osborne, *Revelation*, 780

the message. "Blessed is the one who keeps the words of the prophecy of this book" (22:7). This statement is the sixth beatitude of the book (1:3; 14:13; 16:15; 19:9; 20:6; 22:7, 14). John did not write to satisfy intellectual curiosities about the future but to encourage right, ethical, and spiritual living. The purpose of last things is to demand walking worthy of the Lord in light of his imminent return. Christ, therefore, pronounces a blessing on those who hear and obey his message.

John verifies that he has heard and seen all the things recorded in the book. "I, John, am the one who heard and saw these things" (22:8). His work does not represent an endeavor in human investigation or a flight into fanciful imagination. Interestingly, John falls before the angel to worship him for his role as revealer and interpreter.[3] "And when I heard and saw these things, I fell down to worship at the feet of the angel who showed them to me, but he said to me, 'You must not do that! I am a fellow servant with you and your brothers the prophets, and with those who keep the words of this book. Worship God'" (22:8-9). John has already been rebuked for another attempt to worship the angel in 19:10. The angel once more identifies himself as a "fellow servant" with John, the other prophets, and those who obey the words of the book. The angel gives John a command, "Worship God." There is only one worthy of worship—God alone.

Exhortation
22:10-11

The angel John tried to worship continues with two other exhortations. The angel commands John to make the message known. "And he said to me, 'Do not seal up the words of the prophecy of this book, for the time is near'" (22:10). Sometimes

---

[3] Mounce, *The Book of Revelation*, 391.

when the Old Testament prophets received revelations that did not relate to their immediate audience but to some future time, they were told to seal up the book of their prophecy. For example, Daniel was told to "shut up the words and seal the book, until the time of the end" (Dan. 12:4).

John's message was not designed for some future generation but for the entire Christian church, beginning in John's day and continuing to the current day. Since "the time is at hand," the message of judgment and hope need to be proclaimed.[4] The end is always near in the sense that each successive generation may be the last. Mounce writes, "The tension of imminence is endemic to that span of redemptive history lying between the cross and the parousia."[5] The imminence of the Lord's return appears several times in the epilogue. The emphasis in each reference seems to be on ethical responsibility.

In the second exhortation the angel pleads with the unsaved to think carefully about their choices in light of the imminent return of Christ. "Let the evildoer still do evil, and the filthy still be filthy, and the righteous still do right, and the holy still be holy" (22:11). If the unredeemed will not respond to the message of the end time, there is nothing more that can be done for them. The sinner becomes more habituated to sin and sees it as less serious. The righteous and holy person increases in the practice of holiness. Moral habits have become character for the redeemed and for the unredeemed. The time arrives when decisions for God are impossible because character has been developed by a lifetime of habitual action. The Lord's return will foreclose any possibility of

---

[4] Ibid, 392.

[5] Ibid.

change.⁶

The statement is not so deterministic when interpreted as an imperative. It functions as a warning and an exhortation. The angel exhorts the wicked to continue in their wickedness if that is what they choose. But they will pay the consequences. Also, the angel exhorts the righteous to continue to the right because that is what God demands.⁷

Announcements
22:12-15

The epilogue continues with Jesus speaking. He reiterates the imminence of his return. "Behold, I am coming soon, bringing my recompense with me, to repay everyone for what he has done" (22:12). One of the purposes of Christ's return is to fill the role of judge. The idea to "repay everyone for what he as done" occurs frequently in Revelation. The expression refers to both believers and unbelievers. Osborne writes "that this is not a 'justified by works' theology."⁸ The Scripture clearly teaches that a person is saved by grace, through faith, and not works (Eph. 2:8-10). But the Bible teaches both faith and works. People are saved by grace and judged by works. New Testament writers emphasize that authentic faith results in good works (James 2:14-26). The quality of a person's life provides the ultimate indication of what a person believes.

Christ then announces the ground of his authority to be the judge of all people. "I am the Alpha and the Omega, the first and

---

⁶ Ibid, p. 393.

⁷ Reddish, Revelation, 426.

⁸ Osborne, Revelation, 788.

the last, the beginning and the end" (22:13). These titles refer to the sovereignty of God and Christ. These titles set apart God and Christ from the entire created order. Christ can be the judge of people because he transcends all human experiences, sharing the eternal nature of God himself.

Now John adds an announcement about the blessing of the redeemed in contrast to the unredeemed. "Blessed are those who wash their robes, so that they may have the right to the tree of life and that they may enter the city by the gates" (22:14). John contrasts the destiny of those who decide for Christ with the fate of those who do not decide for Christ. Those who decide for Christ do not achieve their righteousness by human efforts but by Christ's work. The sins of the believer are forgiven by the accomplishment of the blood of Christ. God's people of faith have a right to the heavenly city and to the tree of life. Only those washed in the blood of the Lamb have access either to the tree or to the city. Eternal life and a blessed destiny come only by Christ's atoning work. John next describes those who do not have access to the heavenly Jerusalem and to the tree of life. "Outside are the dogs and sorcerers and the sexually immoral and murderers and idolaters, and everyone who loves and practices falsehood" (22:15). John describes six types of evildoers excluded from the heavenly city. Biblical writers used the term "dog" to describe impure persons (Matt. 15:22*ff*). Sorcerers, the sexually immoral, murderers, idolaters, and all who practice falsehood are excluded along with the dogs. John uses a picturesque way of contrasting the fate of the redeemed with the fate of the righteous. The unrighteous exist "outside" the heavenly city.

Confirmations
22:16

The entire book is "the revelation of Jesus Christ" (1:1).

Jesus now confirms himself as the One who sent the angel with the message. "I, Jesus, have sent my angel to testify to you about these things for the churches" (22:16). Jesus stresses that the revelation did not involve a private matter with John, but it was "for the churches."

Jesus next confirms his identity. "I am the root and descendent of David, the bright morning star" (22:16). The name "Jesus" identifies him as the one known historically by his disciples. But Jesus is more than a man who lived and died in Palestine. He is the Davidic Messiah—"the root and descendent of David." Jesus is also the "bright morning star" who heralds a new day of hope and promise.

Invitation
22:17

The narrative changes abruptly, and John becomes the speaker. He invites all the unredeemed to drink of the water of life. "The Spirit and the Bride say, 'Come.' And let the one who hears say, 'Come.' And let the one who is thirsty come; let the one who desires take the water of life without price" (22:17). The invitation comes through the Spirit-directed church, each redeemed person, and the inherent thirst of the human heart. The Spirit and the Bride utter the same voice, which indicates that the Spirit invites through the church. The members of the churches who listen to the reading of the book invite the unredeemed to come. The invitation is repeated to all those who have not yet drunk of the living water yet who thirst for it. The "water of life" is given freely, without money and without price. The invitation includes all the redeemed to come and receive God's mercy and drink of the water of life. The threefold use of the present imperative (come, let him come) means that the invitation to the unredeemed will be extended until history ends.

Admonitions
22:18-19

John now includes solemn admonitions against anyone offended by the message so much that they attempt to distort or misrepresent its teaching. "I warn everyone who hears the words of the prophecy of this book: if anyone adds to them, God will add to him the plagues described in this book" (22:18). John first admonishes readers not to add to the message. This warning goes to the seven churches where the message is to be read. If anyone adds to the book's teaching, that person will be afflicted with the plagues recorded in the book.

John's second warning admonishes readers not to subtract from the message. "And if anyone takes away from the words of the book of this prophecy, God will take away his share in the tree of life and in the holy city, which are described in this book" (22:19). Any person who takes from the book is among the enemies of Christ and the church. Rejecting the teaching of this book indicates the reader's lack of faith.

Conclusion
20:20-21

For the third time in chapter 22, Jesus gives his promise and assurance that he is going to return. "He who testifies to these things says, 'Surely I am coming soon. Amen'" (22:20). The answers to the problems of life do not rest in the human's ability to make a better world but in the return of the One who will ultimately redeem the world and the human race. Redemptive history remains incomplete until Christ returns. The church waits for this final act in the drama of redemption.

To Jesus' promise of his return, John replies with the Greek form of the Aramaic word *Maranatha*, "Come, Lord Jesus!" (22:20).

History Under Control

G. B. Caird writes, "Week after week that prayer was spoken and answered as the risen Christ made himself known in the breaking of bread."[9] The longing for the Lord's return stands at the heart of the Christian faith. His return means his redemptive work is complete.

Revelation ends with a benediction. Apocalyptic writings did not end with a benediction. But the presence of the benediction may be accounted for by the fact that Revelation began as an epistle, and it would be appropriate to close with a benediction. "The grace of the Lord Jesus be with all [God's people]. Amen" (22:21). John closes with the reminder that all believers depend on God's free grace.

In history we pass through sin, suffering and death. Moments of twilight and days of darkness happen to believers. Ultimately we will come at last to light for "there shall be no night there." To the church in the trying times, it seems like evening, but we look for the morning, the morning of the eternal day. Believers do not see yet all things put under the feet of Jesus, but we see Jesus, and our vision of Jesus is the promise and the prophecy of the coming victory. Christ is in control of history. That is the thought that confronts us again and again in the Revelation. James Russell Lowell expressed the thought poetically:

> History's pages but record
> One death grapple in the darkness
> Twixt old systems and the Word:
> Truth forever on the scafford,
> Wrong forever on the throne,—
> Yet that scaffold sways the future,
> And, behind the dim unknown,
> Standeth God, within the shadow,

---

[9] Caird, *The Revelation of St. John the Divine*, 288.

Keeping watch above His own.[10]

---

[10] James Russell Lowell, "Poems of James Russell Lowell—The Present Crisis," Great Literature Online, 1997, http://lowell.classicauthors.net/PoemsOfJamesRussellLowell/.

Selected Bibliography

Alford, Henry. "Apocalypse of John." *The Greek Testament*, IV, 544–750. Chicago: Moody Press, 1958.

Ashcraft, Morris. "Revelation." The Broadman Bible Commentary. Nashville: Broadman Press, 1972.

Augustine, Saint. *Saint Augustine Confessions*. Oxford, England: Oxford University Press. n. d.

Aune, David E. *Revelation 1–5*. Word Biblical Commentary. Dallas: Word Books, 1997.

_____. *Revelation 6–16*. Word Biblical Commentary. Dallas: Word Books, 1998.

_____. *Revelation 17–22*. Word Biblical Commentary. Nashville: Thomas Nelson, 1998.

Barclay, William. *Letter to Seven Churches*. Louisville: Westminster John Knox Press, 2001.

_____. *The Revelation of John*, 2nd ed. 2 vols. Philadelphia: Westminster Press, 1960.

Bauckham, Richard. *The Theology of the Book of Revelation*. New Testament Theology. Cambridge: Cambridge University Press, 1993.

Beale, G. K. *The Book of Revelation: A Commentary on the Greek Text*. New International Greek Testament Commentary. Grand Rapids: Eerdmans, 1998.

Beasley-Murray, G. R. *The Book of Revelation*. New Century Bible. London: Oliphants, 1974.

_____. *Highlights of the Book of Revelation*. Nashville: Broadman Press, 1972.

Beckwith, Isbon T. *The Apocalypse of John: Studies in Introduction with a Critical and Exegetical Commentary*. Eugene, Ore.: Wipf and Stock, 2001.

Bewes, Richard. *The Lamb Wins: A Guided Tour Through the Book of Revelation*. Fearn, Ross-shire: Christian Focus Publications, 2000.

Blevins, James L. *Revelation as Drama*. Nashville: Broadman Press: 1984.

Borchert, "Revelation." *New Living Translation Study Bible*. Carol Stream, Illinois: Tyndale House, 2008.

Boring, M. Eugene. *Revelation*. Interpretation: A Bible Commentary for Teaching and Preaching. Louisville: John Knox, 1989.

_____ and Fred B. Craddock. *The People's New Testament Commentary*. Louisville: Westminster John Knox Press, 2004.

Bowman, John Wick. *The Drama of the Book of Revelation*. Philadelphia: Westminster Press, 1955.

Brighton, Louis A. *Revelation*. Concordia Commentary. St. Louis: Concordia Publishing House, 1999.

Caird, G. B. *The Revelation of St. John the Divine*. Harper's New Testament Commentaries. New York: Harper and Row, 1966.

R. H. Charles, *A Critical and Exegetical Commentary on the Revelation of St. John*. The International Critical

Commentary. Edinburgh: T & T Clark, 1920.

Collins, John J. "Introduction: Toward the Morphology of a Genre." *Apocalypse: The Morphology of a Genre.* The Biblical Resource Series. London: Society of Biblical Literature, 1979.

Dana, H. E. *The Epistles and Apocalypse of John.* Dalllas: Baptist Book Store, 1937.

Dawn, Marva J. *Joy in Our Weakness: A Gift of Hope from the Book of Revelation.* Rev. Ed. Grand Rapids: Eerdmans, 2002.

Efird, James M. *Revelation for Today: An Apocalyptic Approach.* Nashville: Abingdon Press, 1989.

Ellul, Jacques. Apocalypse: *The Book of Revelation.* New York: Seabury, 1977.

Erdman, Charles R. *The Revelation of John.* Philadelphia: Westminster, 1936.

Ezell, Douglas. *Revelations on Revelation: New Sounds from Old Symbols.* Waco, Tex.: Word Books, 1977.

Faley, Roland J. *Apocalypse Then & Now: A Companion to the Book of Revelation.* New York: Paulist Press, 1999.

Ford, J. Massyngberde. *Revelation.* The Anchor Bible. Garden City, New York: Doubleday, 1975.

Graham, Billy. *World Aflame.* Garden City, New York: Doubleday, 1965.

Grant, Michael. *The World of Rome.* New York: The New American Library, 1960.

Gregg, Steve, ed. *Revelation Four Views: A Parallel Commentary.* Nashville: Thomas Nelson, 1997.

Guy, Laurie. *Making Sense of the Book of Revelation.* Regent Study Guides. Macon, Ga.: Smyth & Helwys, 2009.

Harrington, Wilfrid J. *Revelation.* Sacra Pagina. Collegeville, Minn.: The Liturgical Press, 1993.

Hendriksen, William. *More Than Conquerors.* Grand Rapids: Baker, 1944.

Hill, Craig C. *In God's Time: The Bible and the Future.* Grand Rapids: Eerdmans, 2002.

Hobbs, Hershel H. *The Cosmic Drama: An Exposition of the Book of Revelation.* Waco, Tex.: Word Books, 1971.

Hughes, Philip Edgcumbe. *The Book of the Revelation.* Grand Rapids: Eerdmans, 1990.

Hunter, A. M. *Probing the New Testament.* Richmond: John Knox, 1971.

Jeske, Richard. *Revelation for Today: Images of Hope.* Philadelphia: Fortress Press, 1983.

Johnson, Darrell W. *Discipleship on the Edge: An Expository Journey Through the Book of Revelation.* Vancouver, B.C.: Regent College Publishing, 2004.

Johnson, Dennis E. *Triumph of the Lamb: A Commentary on Revelation.* Phillipsburg, N.J.: P & R. Publishing, 2001.

Jones. Russell Bradley. *The Triumphant Christ. An Exposition of the Revelation.* Birmingham: Banner Press, 1971.

Keener, Craig S. *Revelation. The NIV Application Commentary*. Grand Rapids: Zondervan, 1960.

Kiddle, Martin. *The Revelation of St. John*. The Moffatt New Testament Commentary. London: Hodder and Stoughton, 1940.

Kistemaker, Simon J. *Revelation*. New Testament Commentary. Grand Rapids: Baker, 2001.

Koester, Craig, R. *Revelation and the End of All Things*. Grand Rapids: Erdmans, 2001.

Ladd, George E. *A Commentary on the Revelation of John*. Grand Rapids: Eerdmans, 1972.

Love, Julian Price. *The Revelation to John*. The Layman's Bible Commentary. Richmond, Va.: John Knox, 1960.

Lowell, James Russell. "Poems of James Russell Lowell—the Present Crisis." Great Literature Online, 1997. http://lowell.classicauthors.net/PoemsOfJamesRussellLowell/.

Maahs, Kenneth H. *Of Angels, Beasts, and Plagues: The Message of Revelation for a New Millennium*. Valley Forge: Judson Press, 1999.

Mangina, Joseph. *Revelation*. Brazos Theological Commentary on the Bible. Grand Rapids: Brazos Press, 2010.

McDowell, Edward A. *The Meaning and Message of the Book of Revelation*. Nashville: Broadman Press, 1951.

Metzger, Bruce. *Breaking the Code: Understanding the Book of Revelation*. Nashville: Abingdon Press, 1993.

Michaels, J. Ramsey. *Revelation*. The IVP New Testament Commentary Series. Downers Grove, Ill.: InterVarsity, 1997.

Moffatt, James. "The Revelation of St. John the Divine." *The Expositor's Greek Testament*, Vol 5, 279–494. Grand Rapids: Eerdmans, 1951.

Morris, Leon. *Apocalyptic*. Grand Rapids: Eerdmans, 1972.

Morris, Leon. *The Revelation of St. John*. The Tyndale New Testament Commentaries. Grand Rapids: Eerdmans, 1969.

Mounce, Robert H. *The Book of Revelation*. The New International Commentary on the New Testament. Grand Rapids: Eerdmans, 1977.

Newport, John P. *The Lion and the Lamb: A Commentary on the Book of Revelation for Today*. Nashville: Broadman Press, 1986.

Osborne, Grant R. *Revelation*. Baker Exegetical Commentary on the New Testament. Grand Rapids: Baker Academic, 2002.

Palmer, Earl F. *1, 2, 3, John, Revelation*. The Communicator's Commentary. Waco, Tex.: Word Books, 1982.

Peterson, Eugene H. *Reversed Thunder: The Revelation of John & the Praying Imagination*. San Francisco: Harper, 1988.

Polythress, Vern S. *The Returning King: A Guide to the Book of Revelation*. Phillipsburg, N.J.: P & R Publishing Company, 2000.

Ramsay, William H. *The Letters to the Seven Churches*. London:

Hodder and Stoughton, 1904.

Reddish, Mitchell G. *Revelation.* Smyth & Helwys Bible Commentary. Macon, Ga.: Smyth & Helwys, 2001.

Ressequie, James L. *The Revelation of John: A Narrative Commentary.* Grand Rapids: Baker Academic, 2009.

Richardson, Donald W. *The Revelation of Jesus Christ.* Richmond, Va.: John Knox, 1964.

Robbins, Ray Frank. *The Revelation of Jesus Christ.* Nashville: Broadman Press, 1975.

Robertson, A. T. "The Revelation of St. John." *Word Pictures in the New Testament,* vol. 4 New York: Harper and Brothers.

Rowley, H. H. *The Relevance of Apocalyptic: A Study of Jewish and Christian Apocalypses from Daniel to the Revelation.* London: Lutterworth Press, 1944.

Scott, E. F. *The Book of Revelation.* New York: Scribner, 1940.

Smalley, Stephen S. *The Revelation to John: A Commentary on the Greek Text of the Apocalypse.* Downers Grove, Ill.: InterVarsity, 2005.

Smith, Scotty, and Michael Card. *Unveiled Hope: Eternal Encouragement from the Book of Revelation.* Nashville: Thomas Nelson, 1997.

Smith, T. C. *Reading the Signs: A Sensible Approach to Revelation and Other Apocalyptic Writings.* Macon, Ga.: Smyth & Helwys, 1997.

Spilsbury, Paul. *The Throne, The Lamb & The Dragon: A Reader's Guide to the Book of Revelation.* Downers Grove, Ill., 2002.

Stagg, Frank. *New Testament Theology.* Nashville: Broadman Press, 1962.

Stott, John R. W. *The Incomparable Christ.* Downers Grove, Ill.: Inter-Varsity, 2001.

_____. *What Christ Thinks of the Church.* Wheaton, Ill.: Harold Shaw Publishers, 1990.

Summers, R. *Worthy Is the Lamb: An Interpretation of Revelation.* Nashville: Broadman Press, 1951.

Swete, Henry B. *The Apocalypse of St. John.* Grand Rapids: Erdmans, 1951.

Talbert, Charles H. *The Apocalypse: A Reading of the Revelation of John.* Louisville: Westminster John Knox Press, 1994.

Thomas, Derek. *Let's Study Revelation.* Edinburgh: Banner of Truth, 2003.

Torrance, Thomas F. *The Apocalypse Today.* Grand Rapids: Eerdmans, 1959.

Trafton, Joseph L. *Reading Revelation: A Literary and Theological Commentary.* Macon, Ga.: Smyth & Helwys, 2005.

Turner, William L. *Making Sense of the Revelation: A Clear Message of Hope.* Macon, Ga.: Smyth & Helwys, 2000.

Walhout, *Revelation Down to Earth: Making Sense of the Apocalypse of John.* Grand Rapids: Eerdmans, 2000.

Wilcock, Michael. *I Saw Heaven Opened.* Downers Grove, Ill.: InterVarssity, 1975.

Witherington III, Ben. *Revelation*. The New Cambridge Bible Commentary. Cambridge: Cambridge University Press, 2003.

www.ingramcontent.com/pod-product-compliance
Lightning Source LLC
Chambersburg PA
CBHW020348170426
43200CB00005B/97